Jalisco Condo Manual

A step-by-step GUIDE and REFERENCE MANUAL for Mexican condominiums

by Garry Musgrave

JALISCOCONDOS.ORG
HOW TO RUN A CONDO IN JALISCO

Jalisco Condo Manual
a step-by-step guide and reference manual for Mexican condominiums
by Garry Musgrave

Copyright © 2011 by JaliscoCondos.org. All rights reserved world-wide.

No part of this publication is allowed to be reproduced or transmitted in any form or by any electronic or mechanical means without written permission from the Author or Publisher (except by a reviewer, who is allowed to use brief excerpts in a review). Buyers of this book are given a license to use any sample forms or templates contained in the book for their own personal use. Any unauthorised use, sharing, reproduction, or distribution is strictly prohibited.

Disclaimer: Although the sources of information used for this book, as well as the information contained in it, are considered reliable, there is no warranty or guarantee of such. Neither the Author nor the Publisher makes any representations or warranties about the accuracy or completeness of the contents of this book, and specifically disclaim all warranties, including, without limitation, warranties of fitness for a particular purpose. No warranty is created or extended by sales or promotional materials.

This book is sold with the understanding that neither the Publisher nor the Author is engaged in legal, accounting, or other professional services. The buyer or reader of this book assumes all responsibility for the use of the information contained in the book. Each buyer or reader must carry out their own due diligence for issues of importance to themselves. Before making any decisions or commitments, carrying out any acts, or signing any documents, the buyer or reader should always get specific advice and help from professionals specialising in the issues in question. If legal advice or other expert help is needed, the services of a professional should be sought.

Neither the Publisher nor the Author is liable for damages arising from the use or application of the information in this book.

ISBN 978-0-9813533-1-9

Published by:
  JaliscoCondos.org
  #194 – 2416 Main Street
  Vancouver, BC
  Canada V5T 3E2

Toll free fax: 800-685-3847
Email: books@jaliscocondos.org

First published March 2011

    Front cover design by Rusdi Saleh
    Front cover photo by Jennifer Williams
    Indexed by Garry Musgrave

FREE BONUS PACK!

Receive a FREE pack of sample documents & templates for your use – just by registering your book online!

Register your book purchase to claim your **FREE** collection of <u>over 50</u> sample documents & Word and Excel templates **worth $29.95** – more than 140 jam-packed pages – useful documents that you can adapt for use in your condominium.

Your instant download will contain the following proven sample documents and templates:

- assembly call notice samples & templates
- sample assembly materials
- proxy form sample & template
- voting spreadsheet & scrutineer instructions
- guide: *"Owner's Guide to Condo Assemblies"*
- guide: *"How to Chair a Condo Assembly"*
- sample assembly scripts
- assembly minutes samples & templates
- council & committee meeting notice, agenda, & minutes
- annual condo budget
- monthly Administrator's report
- notice of by-law violation
- collection letters with templates
- request for construction/ renovation
- FAQ sheet for new residents
- and more …

Simply go to
registermybook.jaliscocondos.org
and fill in your book registration details –
your **FREE BONUS PACK** will then
be available as an **instant download**!

Table of Contents

Introduction.. xv
PART 1 – The Basics
What is a condo? 3
Definition of 'Condominium'..3
Pros and Cons of Condominium Ownership 4
Mexican Condos and the Homeowners Association 4
Associations in México...5
The Condo Law Eliminates Owners Associations 6
The Condominium Regime – A Legal Entity 7
The Concept of a 'Legal Entity' 8
General Laws Governing Legal Entities 9
Differences Between a Condo and a Fraccionamiento 11
Summary of Differences 11
Condo Buying Tips 15
Do an Inspection...15
Look at the Operating Budget..16
Look at the Reserves..17
Talk to the Administrator 18
Look at the By-laws..18
Look at the Minutes 19
What if You Can't Get Any of These? 19
Understand What You Own 19
The Jalisco Condo Law... 23
Basic Definitions...23
How is a Condominium Created? 24
Classification of Condominiums 26
1. Unique or Shared Common Property..................................26
2. Relationship Between Private and Common Property 26
3. Residential and Nonresidential 27
4. Municipal Services Condominiums 28
5. Duplexes 28
6. Public vs. Private...28
The Most Common Types...29
What is Common Property?...29
What is Co-owned Property?...30
PART 2 – Unit Owner's Rights and Obligations
What Are the Rights of Each Unit Owner?.................................. 35
Definition of an 'Owner' 35
Use of Common Property 36
Quiet Enjoyment 36
Proportional Ownership..36

"I Don't Use Some of the Common Property" 37
Participation in the Condo Administration 37
Equal and Fair Treatment 38
More Rights May be Given in the By-laws 38

What Are the Obligations of Each Unit Owner? 41
Comply With Condo Legislation and the By-laws 41
Pay Condo Fees 41
Hold an Annual Owners Meeting 41
Maintain Their Condo Units 42
Restricted Activities 42
Changes and Renovations to Condo Units 43
Changes to Common Property 44

PART 3 – The Condo Administration
Makeup of Your Condo Administration 49
A Four-Part Structure 49
Relationship Between Administrator and Council (Board) 50
Administration Salaries 51
Foreigners Need a Work Permit 51

Legal Responsibility of Your Administration 53
Fiduciary Duty 53
No Excuses! 54
Common Failures of 'Duty of Care' 54
Consequences of Not Following the Condo Law 55
Your Assemblies and By-laws May Have No Legal Validity 57
"Can't We Avoid the Law If We All Agree?" 58
Following the Law is Actually Easier 60
Get a Quality Translation of the Condo Law 61

PART 4 – The Condo Administrator
How is the Administrator Appointed? 65
The Condo's First Administrator 65
Appointing the Next Administrators 65
Resignation of the Administrator 67
Removal of the Administrator 67

What Are the Duties of the Administrator? 69
Act for Your Condominium 69
Be Responsible to Owners and Council (Board) 69
Administer Your condo Finances 70
Maintain the Common Property 71
Sue an Owner or Tenant 72
Other Duties 72
Administrator Can Delegate Duties – Not Responsibility 73
Who Should be Your Administrator? 73

Paying an Owner-Administrator	*74*
Hiring an Outside Administrator	*75*

Administrator Maintains Your Official Condo Records **77**
   Required Record Books 77
   Recommended Optional Records..77
   Attachments to Minutes 78
   Computer Records vs. Bound Record Books 78
   How Long Should We Keep Our Records? 79

Lessening the Burden on a Volunteer Administrator **81**
   Appoint an Assistant Administrator..81
   Appoint a Maintenance Manager or Committee..............................82
   Split the Work With a Management Company 82

PART 5 – The Administrative Council (Board)

What's in a Name: Council vs. Board? **87**
   Differences Between a Council and a Board.....................................87
   The Intent of the Condo Legislation 88
   Setting Up a Community-Oriented Mindset....................................88

How is the Council Appointed? **91**
   Council is Appointed at an Ordinary Assembly 91
   Resignation of a Councillor 92
   Removal of a Councillor 93
   Impeachment of the Entire Council (or Administrator) 95

What Are the Duties of the Council? **97**
   Act for the Owners 97
   Work With the Administrator 98
   Maintain the Common Property 100
   Other Duties...100
   Overstepping Its Authority 101
   Who Should Be on Your Council? 102

Makeup of the Council **105**
   Council President/Chair and Vice-President 105
   Why You Should Not Have a 'Treasurer'..106
   The Administrator Cannot Be on the Council 107
   Council Secretary 107
   Recommended Council Makeup 108

Your Council Must Always be Open and Transparent **111**
   Let Owners Know About Council and Committee Meetings 112
   Never Hold Closed Meetings...112
   Carry Out an Open Bidding Process 113
   Communicate, Communicate, Communicate 114
   Do You Need to Provide Condo Documents in Spanish? 115

PART 6 – Committees
Types of Committees 121
Standing Committees 121
Special Committees 122
Why Do You Need Committees? 125
Typical Committee Makeup 125
A Bridge Between the Owners and the Administration 125
More Advantages of Committees 125
Committees and the Administration 126
Councillors Shouldn't Be on Committees 127
Common Committees 129
Maintenance Committee (or Manager) 129
Construction Committee 131
Rules and By-laws Committee 132
Security Committee 133
Financial Audit Committee 134
Communications Committee 134
Welcoming Committee 135
Events Committee 136
Nominating Committee 137
Special Committees 137
Recommended Practices for Committees 139
Set Out a Clear Mandate 139
Special (Ad-hoc) Committee Creation 141
Committee Chairs 142
Quorum and Voting 143
Meeting Minutes and Committee Reports 143
Ex Officio Members 144

PART 7 – Overview of Condo Meetings
The Condo Assembly 149
The Ultimate Authority in a Condo 149
Terminology: 'Assembly' vs. 'Meeting' 149
Types of Assemblies 150
The Call Notice for the Assembly 150
Advance Notice 153
Terminology: 'Order of the Day' vs. 'Agenda' 153
The Order of the Day Must Be Followed 154
Resolutions Passed by an Assembly 155
Voiding the Resolutions of an Assembly for Lack of Notice 156
Granting of Powers 156
Reading and Approval of the Minutes at the Assembly 157
Protocolising and Registering the Assembly Minutes 158

Table of Contents

Holding A 'Notario-Friendly' Assembly 159
Chairing an Assembly 160
Request to Record the Assembly 161
Holding an Efficient Assembly 162

Council Meetings 163
Public Meetings With Advance Notice 163
Minimum Frequency of Meetings 164
Don't Hold In Camera Meetings or Executive Sessions 165
Meeting Agenda 166
Quorum 169
Voting on Motions 170
When Decisions Must Be Made Outside of a Council Meeting 170
Conflicts of Interest 171
Rules of Order 172
Meeting Minutes 172

Committee Meetings 173
Public Meetings With Advance Notice 173
No Minimum Frequency of Meetings 173
Meeting Minutes 174

Working and Information Sessions 175
Working Sessions 175
Information Sessions 176
Town Hall Meetings 176

PART 8 – Condo Assemblies

The Ordinary Assembly 181
Advance Notice 181
Minimum Frequency 181
Subjects That Can Be Dealt With at the Assembly 181
Quorum for the First Call 183
The Second Call 185
Turn Lemons Into Lemonade 185
Passing Resolutions 186
Meeting Plan for a Typical Ordinary Assembly 187
Assembly Minutes 191

The Extraordinary Assembly 195
Advance Notice 195
No Minimum Frequency 195
Subjects That Can Be Dealt With at the Assembly 195
Improvements to Your Common Property 196
Forcing an Owner to Sell 197
Dissolving Your Condominium 197
There's No Quorum and No Second Call 198

Passing Resolutions *198*
Meeting Plan for a Typical Extraordinary Assembly *200*
Assembly Minutes *205*

PART 9 – Rules of Order

Introduction to Rules of Order 209
Do We Really Need Rules of Order? *209*
What is a Deliberative Assembly? *209*
Parliamentary Procedure *210*
Basics of Parliamentary Procedure *211*
How Do These Rules Apply in a Condo? *212*
What Do the Rules of Order Consist of? *214*
Recommended Authority – Robert's Rules *214*
Adopting an Authority *215*
Condos Should Adopt a Scaled-Down Version *215*

Rules of Order Explained 217
Robert's Rules Citation Conventions Used in This Book *218*
Overview of Motions and Resolutions *218*
Wording of Motions *219*
Discussion Before Making a Motion *220*
Debating a Motion (Discussion) *220*
Mover Can't Oppose Their Own Motion *221*
Handling Problem Speakers *222*
Amending a Motion *222*
Voting on a Motion *223*
Voting Rights of the Chair *223*
Resolutions Passed by General Consent *224*
Secondary Motions *224*
Privileged Motions *226*
Subsidiary Motions *228*
Incidental Motions *233*
Appealing Rulings Made by the Chair *239*
Summary of Rules *240*
Communicating Your Rules *240*
Specific Recommendations *240*

Rules of Order for Assemblies 241
Recommended Changes to Rules of Order for Assemblies *241*
Explanations for Excluded Motions *242*
Preventing Nominations From the Floor *244*
Dealing With Secondary Motions at Assemblies *245*
Discussion on Motions *245*
Time-Limiting of Speakers *246*

Rules of Order for Council & Committee Meetings 247
   Relaxed Rules of Order for Council & Committee Meetings 247
   Abstaining From Voting 248
Chairing an Assembly or Council/Committee Meeting 249
   Goal of the Chair 249
   Skills Needed to Chair 250
   Things to Avoid 254
   Tips for Effective Chairing 254
   Other Responsibilities 257

PART 10 – Proxies
The Problem With Proxies 261
   What is a Proxy? 261
   What Does the Condo Law Say About Proxies? 261
   Disadvantages of Proxies 262
   Problem #1 – Voting Blocks 262
   Problem #2 – Uninformed Voting 262
   Robert's Rules' Position on Proxies 263
The Use of Proxies at an Assembly 265
   Proxies at an Extraordinary Assembly 265
   Proxies at an Ordinary Assembly 266
   Adopting the Use of Proxies in Your Condo 268
Legal Requirements for Proxies 269
   Minimum Legal Requirements 269
   Proxies Must Be From the Title Holder of the Property 270
   Proxies Should Be Submitted to an Authority 271
   General vs. Limited Powers 271
   Proxies Can be Dealt With by Email and Fax 272
   "I Changed My Mind!" 272
   Adoption of a Proxy Policy 273
Recommended Proxy Policies 275
   Avoid General Proxies (…again!) 275
   Validating Proxies at an Assembly 275
   Dealing With Changed Proxies at an Assembly 276
   Dealing With Proxies for Quorum at an Ordinary Assembly 276
   Recording a Proxy Vote 276
   Destruction of Proxy Forms – Don't! 277
   Sample Proxy By-law Article 277

PART 11 – Voting
Voting at an Assembly 281
   What are Condo Rights? 281
   Scrutineers: Their Duties and Functions 282
   Determining Quorum at an Ordinary Assembly 283

Proportional (Roll-Call) Voting Must Be Used For Resolutions 284
One Vote Per Condo Unit 285
You Need to Know Who Actually Owns Each Unit 285
If Someone Votes Illegally 287
Have a Registration Procedure 287
Passing a Resolution 289
Exceptions to Proportional Voting 290
Items Having No Motion or Vote 292
Motions That Can Be Passed by General Consent 292
Items That Always Need a Motion and Roll-Call Vote 294
Absentee Votes After an Extraordinary Assembly 295
Be Proactive: Get Support BEFORE Your Assembly 299

PART 12 – Elections

Legal Requirements for an Election at an Assembly 303
The Condo Law Has No Procedure for Election Voting 303
Coming Up With a List of Candidates 303
Adoption of an Election Policy 303
Possible Elections at an Ordinary Assembly 304
Possible Elections at an Extraordinary Assembly 304
Appointments at an Assembly – These Are Not an Election 304

Recommended Election Procedures 307
#1 Tip: Try to Avoid an Election! 307
Disallow Nominations From the Floor 312
Use of Ballots for Elections 313
Avoid a Show-of-Hands Election Vote 314
Avoid Partial Voting 314
Validation of Election Ballots 315
Keeping Election Ballots 316
Who Wins an Election? 317
Recommendation: Plurality Voting 320

PART 13 – Minutes of Assemblies & Meetings

Condo Assembly Minutes 323
Assembly Minutes Are Always Adopted at the Assembly 323
Public Registration of Assembly Minutes 323
Minutes Must Be in Spanish 324
Physical Format of the Assembly Minutes 324
What You Need to Register Your Minutes 326
What Should Be In Your Assembly Minutes? 327
Distribution of Assembly Minutes to the Owners 328

Council Meeting Minutes 329
No Public Registration of Council Minutes Is Needed 329
Physical Format of Council Minutes 329

What Should Be In Council Meeting Minutes?	331
Council Minutes Typical Outline	332
Misc. Practices	338
Distribution of Council Minutes to the Owners	340
Committee Meeting Minutes	**341**
No Public Registration of Committee Minutes Is Needed	341
Physical Format of Committee Minutes	341
Distribution of Committee Minutes to the Owners	341

PART 14 – Practical Matters

Your Condo Bank Account	**345**
Using A Commercial Bank Account	345
Using a Property Management Company's Account	346
Contract Workers vs. Employees	**349**
Mexican Labour and Social Security Laws	350
Types of Employment	350
Payroll Deductions	351
Standard Employment Expenses	352
General Employment Rules	353
Termination and Severance Pay	359
The Cost of Employee Benefits	360
Do We Really Need to Comply With All These Rules?	361

PART 15 – Condo Finances

Your Condo Budget	**365**
Your Condo's Fiscal Year	365
What Is a Budget?	366
The Structure of a Condo Budget	366
Part I: Operating and Maintenance Expenses	367
You Need to Allow for Inflation	371
Improvements Are Not Included	372
Part II: Operating Contingency	373
Part III: Reserves	375
Part IV: Income	378
Carry-Forwards: Surpluses and Shortfalls	378
Cash Flow Analysis	379
Getting Community Support for Your Budget	380
Approval of the Budget and Fees	383
How Detailed Should Your Budget Be?	384
Financial Reports	**385**
Monthly Financial Report	385
Monthly Reports Include Approved Improvements	388
Quarterly Financial Report	388
Report to the Annual Ordinary Assembly	388

Year-End Report *389*
Starting a New Fiscal Year With a Shortfall *390*

PART 16 – Fees and Assessments

All About Condo Fees 393
Code Article 1026 – The Key to Condo Fees *393*
The Legal Requirement to Pay *393*
Purpose of Condo Fees *395*
Fees Are Not for the Use of Facilities *396*
Terminology: 'Fees' vs. 'Dues' *396*
Requirement for a Reserve Fund *397*
Fees Must Be Paid Proportionally *397*
Due Date and Late Interest *401*
Tenants Also Have a Responsibility *403*
Owner's Right to a Statement of Account *403*
Declaration of No Fees Owed Letter on Sale of Unit *404*
Special Assessments *405*
Administration Members Must Be Up-to-Date *406*
Administrator Collects Fees and Reports on Delinquencies *406*

Collecting Overdue Fees 409
Ability to Force an Owner to Sell *409*
This Is An Expensive Proposition *410*
Have A Collection Policy *411*
Outline of a Typical Collection Policy *411*
Make Sure You Know Who Owns the Unit *414*
Don't Underestimate the Personal Touch *415*
Dealing With Mexican Owners on a Personal Level *416*
Keep a File on Each Overdue Owner *416*
Follow-up on Their Promises to Pay *417*
When the Delinquent Owner is a Mortgagee *418*
Applying Partial Payments *418*
Consider a Collection Agency *418*
Time to Turn Things Over to a Lawyer (**Abogado**) *419*
No More Threats – Time for Action *421*
What You Need to Go Ahead With Your Lawsuit *422*
Your Suit Might Not Finish *424*
Publicising Your Debtors *424*
Do Not Withhold Services or Restrict Access to Property *426*
Restricting Access to Water *427*

PART 17 – By-laws and Regulations

Overview of Condo By-laws 431
Quick Facts About By-laws *431*
Ranking of Regulations *431*

Minimum By-law Requirements *432*
Suggestions for More By-law Items *432*
Changing Your By-laws *434*
Getting Community Support for By-law Changes *435*
Republish the Full By-laws *436*
Don't Forget to Publicly Register Your By-laws *436*
Pay Attention to the Order of Your Assemblies *437*
By-law Language Must Not Be Vague *437*
When By-laws Aren't Authored in Spanish *438*
Terms Must Agree With the Condo Legislation *439*
Be Reasonable *442*
Enforcement of By-laws *442*
Problems With Non-Owner Tenants *444*
Financial Penalties and Sanctions *444*

Special Considerations for By-laws 449
Paint Colours and Architectural Standards *449*
No Pets or Kids *453*
Don't Get in a Flap Over Flags *454*
Noise Problems *454*
Avoid Unnecessary Restrictions *455*

PART 18 – The Transfer From the Developer

Overview of the Transfer 465
Developers – Law vs. Reality *465*
What is the Transfer? *465*
When Does the Transfer Take Place? *466*
Getting Ready for the Transfer *468*
What Does the Transition Team Do? *469*
Meetings With The Developer *470*

Preparing for the Transfer 471
Get a Copy of the **Escritura Constitutiva** *471*
Plans and Drawings Are Important *474*
Try to Get the Minimum Condo Records *475*
Make an Inventory of Assets *478*
Your Condo By-laws *479*
Fix Construction Issues Before the Transfer *480*
Inspect the Common Property Buildings and Structures *481*
Construction Problems: Gated Community Perimeter Wall *481*
Construction Problems: **Salitre** *482*
Dealing With **Salitre** *485*
Construction Problems: Drainage *486*
Construction Problems: Mould *487*
Construction Problems: Wood Rot *487*

Construction Problems: Termites *488*
Construction Problems: Septic Systems *491*
Your Goal is a Zero-Sum Transfer *492*
Continuity of Common Property Services *492*
Make Sure Utilities Are Paid Up *495*
Make Sure There Are Reserve Funds *499*
Your First Owner-Administration *500*

PART 19 – Effective Communications

Communications from Owners 503
   Written Communications *503*
   Verbal Communications *504*

Internal Communications 507

Tips for Effective Communications 509
   Send Out Council Meeting Minutes *509*
   Send Out Council Decisions and Condo Policies *509*
   Send Out Quarterly Financial Reports *509*
   Send Out Committee Status Reports *510*
   Publish a Condo Directory (Contact Sheet) *510*
   Consider a Condo Newsletter *511*
   Have a Condo Web Site *511*
   Create a Welcome Pack *512*

PART 20 – Resolving Disputes and Conflicts

Dealing With Complaints 517
   Complaints About Your Condo's Administration *517*
   Complaints About an Owner *520*

Dispute Resolution 525
   Mediation Is Better Than Court *525*
   Your Council Must Arbitrate Owner Disputes *525*
   Four-Stage Resolution Process *525*
   Council-Led Mediation (Internal Resolution) *526*
   Internal Resolution: Overview *527*
   Internal Resolution: Step 1 – Gather Information *527*
   Internal Resolution: Step 2 – Get Specific Suggestions *532*
   Internal Resolution: Step 3 – Get an Agreement *534*
   Internal Resolution: Step 4 – Follow-Up *534*
   Lawyer-Led Mediation (External Resolution) *535*

Dealing With People 537
   It's All About Attitude *537*
   What Are Difficult People? *537*
   The Administration's Perceptions of Owners *538*
   The Owners' Perceptions of the Administration *540*
   Character Assassination *541*

Don't Wash Your Dirty Linen in Public 544
PART 21 – Dissolution of the Condo
Dissolving a Condo Regime 549
FREE BONUS PACK!
Appendix A – More Resources
JaliscoCondos.org Web Site 553
Other Available Books 554
Jalisco Condo Law In English 554
Practical Guide to Buying Property in México 556
Upcoming Books from JaliscoCondos.org 558
How to Prepare & Track a Condo Budget – a step-by-step tutorial 558
How to Carry Out Your Own Condo Reserve Study 558
How To Write Effective Condo By-Laws 559
Appendix B – Language Conventions
Spanish Terms 561
Gender Neutral Terms 561
Language and Spelling Used in this Book 561
Index

Introduction

*A*re there correct and legal procedures that all condos in the state of Jalisco must follow? YES! YES! ... and ABSOLUTELY YES!

- *If you're part of a condo administration, or thinking of volunteering, don't you think you should know what the condo law says?*

- *If you own a condo, or are considering buying into one, wouldn't it help to have a resource with the information you need to discover whether your condo is following the correct procedures?*

You might find this strange, but when my wife and I bought a home in a Mexican condo several years ago, we didn't realise that it was a condo. Where we came from north of the border, condos were only ever apartments or townhouses – we had never seen individual lots or homes in a condo before. This is common in México.

This book resulted from my own frustration with trying to find accurate information about how a Mexican condo is supposed to work.

I discovered that there was no single source for this information, and that there were many misconceptions and inconsistencies. Not surprisingly, there are significant differences between Mexican condo law and condo laws north of the border.

I was amazed to discover that some condo owners (including those involved in the administration of their condos) were unaware that state condo legislation even exists. Many were either just applying their "knowledge" about condos from up north, or flying by the seats of their pants.

The Jalisco condo law clearly defines the administrative structure and operation of a condo. Amazingly, many of those I met who were aware of the law, weren't following it.

Standard practice seems to be based more on local "tradition" and opinion, than on any legal procedures.

Unfortunately, the consequences of not following proper procedures in your condo can range from disorganisation and conflict, all the way to reduced property values and legal problems.

Do you want to know more about what you bought, what you're considering buying, or how a condo is supposed to be run?

Look no further. This is the single most complete resource available for condominium operation in the state of Jalisco – PERIOD.

At first, you'll find my book to be a learning tool – in fact, it can be used as a training manual for members of your condo administration. After you've learned the material, however, I believe you'll continue to refer to it often as situations come up in your condo ... and they will. A lot of effort was put into both the Table of Contents and the Index to make it a usable reference work.

I sincerely hope you'll find my book to be a valuable guide and resource. I hope it'll help you to not only resolve issues within your condo, but also avoid future problems by doing things the correct way.

Even if the final answer to your condo problem isn't here, my book will point you in the right direction to find a solution, and give you enough information to know if this solution makes sense.

Along with detailed explanations of the Jalisco condo law, I've also given you advice and tips based on my own personal experience with most of the issues that affect condos.

I believe you'll find many valuable and helpful insights that you can put into practice right away in your condo, and avoid many common problems.

Garry Musgrave

About Condominio Vista del Basurero:

For the purposes of various examples in this book, I've created a fictitious gated condo called "**Vista del Basurero**" – with 22 lots and houses, located in Puerto Vallarta.

This condominium, the names of the owners, the property management company, and all other names are fictitious. Any resemblance to a real condominium, real owners, or any real companies is purely coincidental and unintentional.

About JaliscoCondos.org:

JaliscoCondos.org is a web site committed to giving you the most comprehensive and accurate information available about owning and running a condo in the state of Jalisco.

PART 1 – The Basics

What is a condo?

Chapter
1

I highly recommend that before you buy into a condo, or become a part of a condo administration, you understand what a condominium is (and what it's not), and how its legal structure differs from condos north of the border.

Definition of 'Condominium'

It may be easier for you to understand the concept of a condo if you know what it's *not*: it's not a type of building or structure (such as an apartment); but a type of **property ownership**.

It's a form of ownership that dates back to Roman times – and was part of the 1804 Napoleonic Code on which Mexican civil law is based.

> The term "*condominium*" is widely used around the world – especially in civil law countries such as México.
>
> It's used in Canada and the U.S. with the exception of the Canadian provinces of British Columbia (where it's called a "*strata title*") and Québec (where it's formally known as "*co-propriété divisée*" – and informally known as a "*condominium*").
>
> Australia also uses the term "*strata title*", while most of the UK uses the term "*commonhold*".

The main feature that separates condominium ownership from all other types of property ownership is that, as well as the private property of each owner, there are common facilities that are co-owned by all the property owners as a group.

In addition, these common assets are legally required to be managed by an administrative body consisting of unit owners.

In México, co-ownership of the common property is legally attached to the ownership of the private property.

This share of ownership in the common property is spelled out in the title to the private property, and can never be changed, sold, or separated from the private property.

The structure and methods of administration of a Mexican condo are clearly set out in the state condominium legislation.

Pros and Cons of Condominium Ownership

The benefits of condo ownership are:

- security;
- a feeling of community;
- shared maintenance and operation expenses that should result in high-quality community facilities; and
- a central responsibility for maintenance and management of the common property, relieving individual owners of this burden.

In exchange for these benefits, you give up a few personal freedoms – you can't always do as you please.

The foundation of condominium ownership is that a condo is managed according to the majority will of all owners – if you happen to be in the minority on an issue, you won't get your way.

The common property is owned by everyone, and its use and enjoyment are to be shared among all owners.

Mexican Condos and the Homeowners Association

Condos in the U.S. or Canada are generally run by an *"owners association,"* or some similar administrative structure. The state or provincial condo legislation defines this association, and makes membership in it compulsory for all condo unit owners.

México is significantly different in this regard, and this is one of the biggest stumbling blocks for foreigners – and the issue that causes the most confusion.

Associations in México

In México there are *Asociaciones de Colonos* (homeowners associations) to administer *fraccionamientos* (housing developments) as well as some older condominiums – generally, these are condos created before 1995.

Other areas in a municipality that are neither fraccionamientos nor condominiums may also have *Asociaciones de Vecinos* (neighbourhood associations). These associations are created to represent the community before the municipal government, run community centres and clubs, and plan and carry out community events.

Each of these is, in legal terms, an *asociación civil* (civil association) or *A.C.* that must be specifically created and registered. These associations are legal bodies, and must conform to the state's *Ley Orgánica Municipal* (Municipal Bodies Law).

> There are no circumstances under which an association magically springs into existence.
>
> An association doesn't exist just because a group of people decide to call themselves an *"association"*.
>
> The term *"association"* has a specific legal meaning in México, there must be an application made to the government, permission must be received to form the association, and the association must be registered in a public document.

The Condo Law Eliminates Owners Associations

Homeowners associations don't exist for condos that were developed after 1995 in Jalisco, and any newer condo created under this legislation is **not** a "**condo association.**" A homeowners association isn't needed to manage a condo.

The Civil Code rules that govern condominiums give you all the functions and benefits of an owners association, without the need to form a legal association.

The condo law also eliminates two major problems with running condominiums by an association in México:

- membership in an association can never be compulsory under Mexican law – this allows unit owners to opt-out; and

- the way the older condo associations were regulated was inconsistent, causing many problems.

The reason for this last problem is that the legislation covering associations in México is brief, and lacking in depth. This is deliberate, because associations vary so widely in their purposes that a "one size fits all" legislation is just not practical.

Instead, the legislation relies on statutes (by-laws) to regulate each association. This is to allow a tremendous amount of latitude for a different types of associations with varying goals. For example, the needs of an association of fans supporting a local soccer club will be quite different from those of an association to aid poor rural communities by setting up entrepreneurial projects.

From this you can see that association statutes can vary from simple to extremely complex – the last was the case for condominiums before 1995, and still is the case for fraccionamientos.

What is a condo? **7**

Apart from the opting-out problem, regulation by individual sets of statutes caused problems for condos.

Because association statutes varied so drastically from condo to condo, some owners weren't adequately protected, while others were over-regulated. The government felt that consistent rules were needed, so specific legislation governing condominiums was created.

The Condominium Regime - A Legal Entity

As a result of this decision, developments created under condo legislation from 1995 onward are set up as a *régimen del condominio* (condominium regime). This regime embodies all the features of an association, but **there is no association**.

It's important for you to know that the terms *"asociación"* (association) or *"A.C."* have a specific legal meaning under Jalisco State Law – they're **a distinct and different legal entity from a condominium regime**.

The use of these terms must be avoided when referring to a condominium in Jalisco **unless** your condo was developed before 1995, and is registered as an association rather than a condominium regime.

To know whether your condominium is incorporated into a condo regime or governed by an association, you must look at the *escritura constitutiva* (publicly registered document creating your condominium). This will clearly show whether your condominium is a condo regime or not.

If your condo was built after 1995, it will almost certainly be a condo regime, and an association must not be created.

> For the rest of this book, I'll assume that your condo has been incorporated into a condo regime, and that the condominium law applies to you.

The Concept of a 'Legal Entity'

As we have seen, the Civil Code now includes specific legislation for condos that creates a special legal entity called the "condominium regime" – all condo property is permanently bundled into this regime, and no owner can ever opt-out.

So, what is a **legal entity**?

The constitutions and laws of most countries were intended to give rights to (and control the behaviour of) people. As societies became more complex, it became necessary for laws to govern more than just individuals.

Modern laws define administrative structures such as corporations, associations, or societies. These defined structures are known as **legal entities** or **legal persons**. There are then specific laws to govern each of these just as if they were a special type of individual. Therefore, a company, an association, or a condo regime becomes a form of person, with special laws that apply only to it.

This technique allows laws to be more easily applied to nonpersons and, generally, in a different way than to an individual.

Mexican law is no different.

It recognizes two classes of legal persons: *personas físicas* (people, individuals) and *personas jurídicas* or *personas morales* (legal persons or entities such as companies and condo regimes).

What is a condo?

A *condominio* (condominium) is only one of about 14 *personas jurídicas* (legal persons) recognised by the Civil Code of the State of Jalisco in **Book One, Title Three – *"About Legal Persons"* –** specifically, **Civil Code Article 161.**

> As a matter of interest, other types of legal entities defined in the Civil Code include: federal and municipal governments; political parties; labour unions and employers; the various forms of Mexican corporations (such as an S.A. de C.V.); associations, societies, and foundations; condominiums; and foreigners.
>
> Each of these is a separate legal entity, and **is governed by a separate and specific section of the Jalisco Civil Code.**

General Laws Governing Legal Entities

Civil Code Articles 162 and **163** say that each of these listed legal entities can exercise all rights that don't conflict with their legal purpose, or that are prohibited by law – criminal acts, for example.

Further, these legal entities will be governed by: relevant laws, their *escritura constitutiva* (the publicly-registered document that set them up), and their statutes (in the case of condominiums, these would be its by-laws).

These laws and regulations are to be enforced by bodies that legitimately act for the legal entity. In the case of individuals, these would be governments and police. In the case of condominiums, this would also include the condo administration. This general rule **obligates your condo's administration to uphold the condo legislation** – this is also explicitly stated in the condo legislation itself.

The Code then goes on to define the specific rights, obligations, and limits of each legal entity separately.

The section of the Code that deals with the legal entity known as the *régimen del condominio* (condominium regime) is what forms the state condo law.

> Throughout this book I'll refer to specific articles from the **Civil Code of the State of Jalisco** ("*Civil Code*" or "*the Code*" for short) that make up the condo legislation that must be followed by all condominiums in the state.
>
> If you want to know exactly what the Code says (and you should!), get a copy of our companion publication, "***Jalisco Condo Law in English***". This is a translation of the portions of the Code that affect condominiums, and is an excellent reference for condo owners and members of a condo administration.
>
> If you want a better understanding of Mexican law in general, get a copy of my other book, "***Practical Guide to Buying Property in México***".

Differences Between a Condo and a Fraccionamiento

Chapter **2**

If you spend any length of time looking at property in México, you're bound to come across the term *fraccionamiento* or *fracc*. This is often a source of confusion for foreigners, with many believing that these are the same as condominiums.

This is not the case!

A *fraccionamiento* is a subdivision of a municipality (normally a housing development or industrial park) that has **not** been incorporated into a condominium regime.

Summary of Differences

This chapter is not a detailed discussion of fraccs (that would be another book), but a summary of the major differences between fraccs and condos.

As with a condominium, the developer of a fracc must get a permit from the local municipality. A typical application includes:

- a location plan of the overall property;
- a plan of the proposed development;
- deeds for each lot in the development; and
- an environmental impact study.

The municipality may also assist with hooking up basic utilities to the site, but the developer must install the infrastructure.

Many **fraccs** have their own water supply, along with a concession to distribute this water from CONAGUA (the National Water Commission). The federal government owns all sources of water.

There's an ongoing cost associated with this water that must be paid to the commission, and this is normally recovered by charging houses for water provision and distribution. This also applies to some condos who have their own water source (such as a well).

To qualify as a fraccionamiento, a portion of the housing development (a minimum of 15%) must be set aside for communal areas such as parks and playgrounds (and, in some cases, schools).

Optionally, there can also be communal facilities such as a pool, tennis courts, or a golf course. Existing streams and ponds must be protected.

In a fracc, the road system is almost always owned by the municipality. Often the fracc is responsible for maintenance. Other services and utilities may also be provided by the municipality. Although the municipality is responsible for supplying public services, it can allow the fracc to provide "municipal" services to the homes.

In a condo, however, all property within the boundaries of the condominium is private property belonging to the unit owners – including the road system, street lights, sewers, or other infrastructure. Extra services such as garbage collection are paid for by the condo, and funded by fees.

In a fracc, the communal areas are normally administered by the owners, and an *asociación civil* (civil association) or **A.C.** will have been legally set up for this purpose. Some fraccs are administered by the municipality or another public body – often because the owners association has failed.

This *Asociación de Colonos* (homeowners association) will administer the fracc, and provide various services such as repair and maintenance to common assets, water, or garbage collection.

Differences Between a Condo and a Fraccionamiento

> While *fraccionamientos* are similar in concept to a planned community in the US that is run by an HOA (homeowners association), there are some important differences:
>
> HOA's in the US have mandatory membership that's attached to the purchase of the home or lot. It's set out by the Articles of Incorporation, and imposes covenants and restrictions on the private property as well as any community property. The HOA is governed by its by-laws and ancillary rules and regulations.
>
> *Fraccionamientos* are almost identical **except** (and this is a **huge** exception) that there's no mandatory association membership, nor can there be under current Mexican law. This is arguably the biggest problem for fraccs – there is nothing to legally require compliance with its by-laws, or even payment of fees for owners who opt-out of the association. The statutes (by-laws) have no authority over nonmembers.
>
> **Article 184** of the Civil Code allows any member to leave an association after giving two months notice.

In a condo, the common property is always jointly administered by an Administrator and an Administrative Council (Board) – **there is no homeowners association.**

Fraccionamientos are governed first by the section of the Jalisco Civil Code that applies to associations (**Articles 172 to 189**), then applicable state and municipal laws, and finally by the statutes of the owners association. They're **not**, however, subject to the specific part of the Civil Code that applies to condominiums (**Articles 1001 to 1038**).

Fraccs suffer from two main problems (I've already touched on them) resulting from running a housing development by an association in México:

- membership in the association isn't compulsory under Mexican law – allowing owners to opt-out; and

- the statutes (by-laws) of the various fraccs vary enormously, creating many inconsistencies in important areas.

In a condo, "membership" is forced by legislation – all condo units are part of the condo regime, and this can never change.

Condos have by-laws, but these are generally not as complex as the statutes of a fracc. This is because many of the rules in a typical fracc association's statutes are already in the condo law. This means that all major governing regulations for a condo are backed by state law, and are consistent from condo to condo. A condo's by-laws only supplement the condo law by adding lower-level rules and regulations that are specific to a given condominium.

The condo law gives a condo administration specific legal powers to go after delinquent and troublesome unit owners. The association law that governs Fraccs has no legal remedies in this regard.

A fracc's only leverage against delinquent or problem owners is often provision of water, other services, or maintenance that they're only obligated to give to association members.

That said, there are federal regulations preventing cutting off total access to water, or access to an owner's property. The last is not normally possible anyway, since most fraccs don't own their roads – they shouldn't block access to anyone.

Condo Buying Tips

Chapter
3

While this book is mainly concerned with the mechanics, legalities, and practicalities of how a condo in the state of Jalisco should be run, there are some tips I can give you if you aren't yet a condo owner.

This chapter addresses a few specific issues you should be concerned with **before** you buy into a condo.

Do an Inspection

While I doubt that anyone would consider buying a home north of the border without a home inspection, people who are normally more sensible seem to throw caution to the wind when they cross the border into México.

In Jalisco, there's no law forcing either a seller or a real estate agent to tell you about problems or issues that a property may have – it's strictly *caveat emptor* (let the buyer beware).

Hire a home inspector, an engineer, or even a good contractor to look over your prospective purchase. Have them tell you what repairs are needed, along with a cost estimate. The cost of such an inspection is small compared to what not doing this might cost you in the long run.

As with up north, don't hire an inspector who's associated with the seller or their real estate agent – in particular, don't use their "free" inspector or engineer.

As well as the unit you're looking at, you should also have your inspector look at the major elements of the common property. If you're considering buying a condo apartment, you may need to arrange access for your inspector to some of the common areas (such as mechanical or elevator rooms).

You should tour the common property with your inspector. Check out the common gardens, pool, patio furniture, clubhouse, and other facilities. Look closely at the streets, street lighting, gardens, pools, or guard houses. Try to get a feel for the level of maintenance being done on the property. Are things looking shabby and falling apart (a danger sign!), or are they all in reasonably good repair?

Look at the Operating Budget

Ask for a copy of the current operating budget, and check it for reasonableness.

If possible, also get a copy of one of the Administrator's quarterly reports to see what sort of issues this condo is having financially – delinquencies and whether expenses track the budget, are examples.

The quarterly report must, by law, list all debtors and explain the debt. This will give you a sense of what level of delinquencies exist in this condo, and what impact this is having on the condo's finances.

You also want to get a sense of how well the administration is maintaining the condo property – this will directly affect future property values.

If this condo is still being run by the developer, and financial statements don't seem to be available, it's possible that the developer may be subsidising the condo expenses to keep the fees artificially low while condo units are being marketed.

This isn't unusual, nor is it a practice that's confined to México. It's important to know this. If this is the case, you need to be prepared for a spike in fees once the transition from the developer to an owner administration takes place. Many buyers are caught off guard by this.

Look at the Reserves

Ask about the reserve levels, the reserve funding plan, and the basis on which the reserve contributions and levels have been worked out.

If this condo has little or no reserves (without just having had a large unexpected or emergency repair), run, don't walk, to the next property on your list.

While better than nothing, reserve funding based on some arbitrary percentage of expenses or fees is just not adequate – I call this the "dart board" approach to reserve funding.

For a properly run condo, the basis of reserve funding must be a reserve study, and there must be a reserve plan in place.

Reserves are not just a lump of money that a condo accumulates and keeps in the bank "for a rainy day" – a financially healthy and well-managed condo will have planned maintenance and refurbishment expenses from the reserves almost every year.

Proper reserve funding is vital to the health, security, and preservation of the property values of a condo. A proper reserve plan makes sure that:

- ongoing long-term maintenance is being looked after on an ongoing basis so that the property isn't deteriorating; and

- condo owners are paying as they go, rather than relying on huge special assessments for big-ticket maintenance and refurbishment expenses (including emergency repairs).

Talk to the Administrator

Contact the Administrator, and ask pertinent questions about the condo budget, delinquencies, the reserves, and the level of ongoing maintenance.

The financial well-being of this condo is arguably your most important buying consideration.

Buying into a condo that isn't properly funded to operate and maintain the common property is a risky proposition.

Low condo fees may make one condo appear more appealing than another, but it can also be a sign that the administration is ill-prepared to fund ongoing maintenance, major repairs, or emergencies. As a result, the condition of the condo property can deteriorate (lowering property values), or you can be faced with significant special assessments to cover major costs as they occur.

Remember that two essential (and often overlooked) parts of a condo operating budget are the contingency and the reserve fund.

Look at the By-laws

My book will give you an excellent insight into how a condo in Jalisco is run and administered – the most important rules and regulations are in the condo legislation.

By-laws, however, are unique to each condo, and have extra rules and regulations to add to the state condo law.

You need to get a copy of these by-laws to get an idea as to how reasonable this condo is. By-laws need to strike a balance between making sure the condo runs smoothly and not being overly restrictive and controlling.

Look at the Minutes

Every condo is required by state law to hold one owners assembly each year in the first three months of the year (like an annual general meeting). This assembly appoints a new Administrator and Administrative Council (Board) for the coming year, and approves the operating budget and fees for the coming year.

As well as this annual assembly, there can be extraordinary assemblies that are held either at the same time or other times during the year to deal with other issues. These issues can include: approval of improvements to the condo property and their method of funding, changes to the by-laws, or suing an owner. It can be instructive to read these – they're generally publicly registered documents.

Often even more revealing, if you can get copies, are council (board) meeting minutes. These should give you an idea of the day-to-day issues that are occurring in this condo, as well as giving you insight into the management philosophy of the administration.

What if You Can't Get Any of These?

If you are buying a brand new unit from the developer, this is not uncommon. Ask pointed questions, and try to get answers (remember, they want to sell the unit).

If you are buying from an existing owner, and they do not have these, this condo may be poorly run. At a minimum, this shows very poor communication with the unit owners.

Understand What You Own

The boundaries of each private unit vary from condominium to condominium, depending on how they're set out in the establishing documents.

For a horizontal condo consisting of lots and houses, this is simple – the lot boundaries are clearly shown on a lot plan. Before you buy, you might consider hiring a surveyor to confirm the boundaries of your unit. This isn't normally needed unless you suspect something isn't right.

For a vertical condo with apartments, these boundaries can vary.

> Sometimes, the unit boundary is the unfinished interior walls – you own the paint or other finish applied to the walls, but not the walls themselves. The unit boundary could also be the centre line of the unit's walls (this is the most common in México).

> Hallways, elevators, stairs, laundry rooms, the building's exterior finish, or roofs are almost always considered common property.

If you plan to renovate your unit, the boundaries of your unit could be an important consideration when buying.

Your unit typically includes ownership of any appliances, fixtures, equipment, systems, or finishes that are entirely contained within your unit.

There could also be some parts of this condo (especially with a vertical condo consisting of apartments) that are called "exclusive-use common property." These are outside the boundaries of any private unit, but are reserved for the exclusive use of a particular unit.

Balconies, driveways, storage lockers, parking spaces, and front or rear lawn areas and patios for ground floor units, are some typical examples.

Therefore, the right to use one or more parking stalls or storage units may be included with your unit, but, while you might have exclusive access to them, you likely don't own these.

If your unit has any of these exclusive-use common facilities associated with it, it's important to be aware of any limits on when and how you're allowed to use them. For example, you might not be able to park an RV or boat in your parking spot, or there could be restrictions on what you can have visible on your balcony.

The Jalisco Condo Law

Chapter **4**

The condo law is in one section of the Jalisco Civil Code – **Book Three, Title Six –** *"About The Condominium"*. It's made up of **Articles 1001 through 1038.**

It's important that you know where the condo law is found, and have at least a basic understanding of its rules.

Basic Definitions

Civil Code Article 1001 defines the *régimen del condominio* (condominium regime) as a legal regime that combines:

1. methods of control over land or a building, along with the limitations of this control;

2. rules for a condominium's use and for determining its future; and

3. the right to joint and simultaneous use of common areas by all condo unit owners.

The private property of an owner in a condo consists of either an apartment or a house and lot (depending on the type of condo). This is called an *unidad privativa* (private unit).

As well as their private property, unit owners also hold a further exclusive ownership in a percentage of the common property.

> As a condo owner, you own a percentage of the common areas **as well as** your apartment or house – this is set out in your title document.
>
> This percentage can't be changed or disposed of, and if you sell your apartment or house, this percentage ownership in the common property is automatically sold with it.

The legal entity that regulates a condominium property is called a *régimen del condominio*. The property itself, consisting of all the private units plus the common property, is called the *unidad condominal* (condominium unit). More commonly, it's known as the *condominio* (condominium).

The registered title holders (owners) of the apartments or houses in a condominium are called *condóminos*.

How is a Condominium Created?

Civil Code Article 1006 outlines the creation of a condo regime.

A condominium regime is normally created by the developer, and whoever makes the application must have free title to the parcel of land that's to be incorporated into a condo regime.

The applicant must first ask for (and receive) permission to set up a condominium regime from the local municipality. This application process typically requires submitting various planning documents that might include site plans or environmental impact assessments.

Once this permission has been received, the applicant must use a *notario* (a lawyer with special training who is authorised by the state to create and file public documents) to formalise the creation of a condo in a publicly-registered document called the *escritura constitutiva* (establishing document – sometimes called the establishing deed). Once registered, this document legally establishes a condominium regime for this property.

At a minimum, this establishing document must contain the following:

- a legal description of the property including its location, dimensions, and boundaries;

- a history of the property, along with the clear title;

- proof of required concessions for water, and other similar rights;

- a general description of the buildings, infrastructure, and municipal services, along with a statement about the quality of materials to be used in the construction;

- separate descriptions of each private unit including its house or unit number, location, dimensions, boundaries, and its percentage ownership in the common property;

- a description of the common areas showing their locations, dimensions, and boundaries; also listed must be any common infrastructure, equipment, or furnishings;

- the classification of the condominium – for example, "simple horizontal residential;"

- proof of having gotten authorisation from the municipal authorities to set up a condominium regime, including any opinions, licenses, or reports that the town-planning authorities may have provided;

- details of the licenses and permits for construction;

- proof of having given a bond to the municipal authorities to guarantee both the quality of the construction and the completion of the work;

- the condominium's by-laws;

- the way the condo owners will pay the fees (as set out in **Civil Code Article 1026**);

- the plans of the condominium, the general plans of construction of the common property, and the construction plans of each of the private units.

Classification of Condominiums

There are several types of condominiums, and these are defined in **Civil Code Articles 1002 to 1005**.

Condos are classified according to their relationship to the common property, and the relationship between the private and common property.

There are classifications that apply to specific purposes:

1. Unique or Shared Common Property

When referring to the location and use of the common property, condominiums can be either **simple** or **compound**:

- A **simple condominium** is by far the most common type. This is where the condo units, common areas, infrastructure, and equipment are all contained **within a single condominium unit**.

- There are situations, however, where part of the common areas, infrastructure, or equipment is common to two or more separate condominiums that coexist on the same parcel of land – this is called a **compound condominium**.

2. Relationship Between Private and Common Property

When it comes to the allocation of the common and the private property, condominiums can be either **horizontal**, **vertical**, or **mixed**:

- A condominium is classified as **horizontal** when each owner owns a lot as their private unit. The private unit also includes the house and any other buildings and facilities that are built on the lot.

  The common property is separate from all private units.

  An example would be separate houses in a development such as a gated community that have been incorporated into a condominium regime.

- A condominium is **vertical** when the entire estate is common property, and one or more buildings are divided into private units.

  For example, a block of condo apartments.

- As you may have guessed, a condominium is **mixed** when it has both individual lots with houses, plus condo apartment buildings.

3. Residential and Nonresidential

- **Residential** condominiums are limited in physical size and population, and commercial activities are prohibited.

- **Nonresidential** condominiums are controlled by applicable town-planning and zoning regulations.

> This **residential/nonresidential** classification is partly decided by the town-planning zoning rules in effect where the property is located, and by the establishing document of the condominium.
>
> **Nonresidential** uses can range from office and business space, to warehousing, to manufacturing, and more.

4. Municipal Services Condominiums

There's also a special category of condominium called a *condominio de servicios municipales* (municipal services condominium).

These are publicly administered – generally by the local municipality.

Municipal services condominiums are a special type that you aren't likely to come across in a residential real estate purchase. They're publicly-owned, and used for urbanisation purposes in a community – subsidised housing or cemeteries are examples.

5. Duplexes

The last special case is the *condominio habitacional duplex* (residential duplex condominium).

This classification can only be applied to a duplex housing unit built on a single piece of property. Each of the two housing units is given half of the common property rights, the condo fees are equal, and the two owners jointly administer the condominium.

6. Public vs. Private

A **common misconception** is that condominiums can be further classified as either **public** or **private**.

There's no such distinction in the condo legislation.

It might be argued that the special case of the **municipal services condominium** can be considered as **public**. Therefore, all other condominiums (whether **residential** or **nonresidential**) would have to be considered as **private**. These terms have no legal meaning in the context of the governing section of the Jalisco Civil Code.

The point is likely moot since, even under this argument, any condo that you'd buy to live in would be private – therefore, the distinction is pointless.

The Most Common Types

While there will be exceptions, the majority of condominiums that you'll be living in or buying are classified as either a **simple vertical residential condominium** (such as condo apartments), or a **simple horizontal residential condominium** (such as a gated community of individual houses).

What is Common Property?

Civil Code Article 1007 defines common property as consisting of any of the following items **when intended for general use by all unit owners**:

- foundations, infrastructure, and municipal services; in a horizontal condominium (houses and lots) this doesn't include foundations of the individual houses, but would include foundations for such things as a guard house, an administration office, or a rec centre; in a vertical condominium (apartment blocks) this would be all foundations;

- ditches, wells, common-use water containers (*tinacos*), cisterns, and common-use water ducts and pipes for rain water and drainage;

- water treatment plants, septic systems, and absorption wells;

- common-use ducts for heating; likely only found in a vertical condominium, and rare in México (it's warm and sunny most of the time!);

- common-use ducts and connection posts for services such as gas and electrical power;

- wiring for telephone, cable television, and communal antennas for radio or television; generally these enter a condominium property underground, are buried below the common property, and end in one or more centrally-located junction boxes; the portion of this wiring inside an owner's private unit may or may not be common property – generally, it is common property for apartments, but is not common property for houses;
- administration offices, storage areas for condominium furniture and equipment, and premises to house security guards (such as a guard or gate house), gardeners, or employees;
- internal streets and roadways, and public parking areas;
- common-use recreational areas, pools, washrooms, and gardens;
- common area retaining walls and roofs, and, sometimes, the perimeter wall surrounding the complex – to verify the last, you must check the *escritura constitutiva* (establishing document);
- common-use porches, doors, paths, stairs, corridors, and patios; these are most prevalent in a vertical condominium (apartment blocks);
- common-use elevators, escalators, and freight elevators; and
- Anything else that **can be used by all condo unit owners**, and that isn't a part of any private unit.

What is Co-owned Property?

The common property is co-owned by all unit owners. However, there can also be other co-owned property in a condo.

- **In a condo apartment**, this is commonly how the walls between units are treated.

Both owners are responsible for their common wall from the centre outward.

In the case of an exterior wall, the owner is responsible from the centre inward, and the condo owns the wall from the centre outward (as common property).

- **In a gated condo**, this can apply to the perimeter wall. It's possible for this wall:
    - to straddle the property line with another property next to the condo (both properties are jointly responsible);
    - for the bulk of the wall to be on one property, with only the exterior finish being on the other; this will happen if the wall was built when one property was undeveloped, and the surface of the wall facing into this property was unfinished; any finish later applied to it by the other owner would belong to, and be the responsibility of, the other property; or
    - the entire wall (including both finished surfaces) being on one property (this is the least likely).

While the condo law deals specifically with co-ownership of the common property in a condo, another section of the Jalisco Civil Code defines the rights and obligations of co-ownership in general – *Libro Tercero* (Book Three), *Titulo Quinto* (Title Five), *Capitulo IV* (Chapter IV) titled, *"De La Copropiedad"* (About Co-Ownership).

This consists of **Articles 961 to 1000**. This section of the law will often apply to common walls between units, and walls between the condo and another property.

PART 2 – Unit Owner's Rights and Obligations

What Are the Rights of Each Unit Owner?

Chapter 5

Each condo unit owner has certain rights under the law. **Civil Code Article 1008** defines these rights.

Definition of an 'Owner'

Article 1001 first defines a *condómino* (condo owner) as the **title holder of the property.**

Then throughout the condo legislation, specific rights and obligations are given to all *condóminos* (condo owners).

This definition is important because many condos have made the mistake of assuming they know who the title owner of a condo unit is. The legal owner of the property isn't always the person living there, or even the person paying the condo fees.

Be careful! Only the title holder of the property can:

- be sued for unpaid fees;
- vote at a condo assembly; and
- serve on the Council (Board).

You have to be particularly careful with a condo on the coast that's in the Federal Restricted Zone. This will have been bought through a trust, and the beneficiary of the trust (the foreign buyer) is **not the title holder.** In this case, a power of attorney is required from the financial institution holding the trust.

This topic will be talked about further in various parts of my book – wherever it specifically applies.

From this point on in my book, whenever I use the term "*owner*," I mean "***condo unit owner*** (*condómino*)" as defined in the condo law.

Use of Common Property

Each unit owner has the right to use and enjoy the common property and common services of a condominium – **as long as** they do so according to the intended use of these facilities, and they don't do anything to restrict or impede the rights of other unit owners.

A condominium can introduce reasonable rules and regulations about the use of common facilities (such as pool rules), but it can't assess fees for use of the common property (other than to non-owners). This is because each owner owns a portion of all common property.

Quiet Enjoyment

Each unit owner has the right to peace and quiet in their private unit (house or apartment), and, therefore, each owner must use their private unit in a way that doesn't affect the tranquillity of the other condo owners.

Each unit owner is obliged to allow access to their unit for repairs and maintenance of common property (an implied easement). Access to a common perimeter wall from their garden, or access to sewer or electrical infrastructure are two examples.

An **easement** is the right to access and use portions of someone's private property for a specific purpose. There are usually easements on private lots in a condo to locate infrastructure items such as street lights or telephone connection boxes.

Proportional Ownership

Each unit owner has proportional ownership rights in the common property. These ownership rights are inseparable from the ownership of their private unit. Therefore, any transfer or disposal of an owner's private property will also include the associated rights to the common property.

What Are the Rights of Each Unit Owner?

For more detailed information on proportional rights, **see Chapter 47 – "All About Condo Fees."**

"I Don't Use Some of the Common Property"

Unit owners who don't use their own property, or who don't use some or all the common property or facilities, are not relieved from their condo obligations – including payment of condo fees.

Some owners have the misconception that if they don't use a communal pool or rec centre, for example, then they can pay reduced or zero condo fees.

This is not how it works!

The condo law requires every unit owner to pay their proportional share of the maintenance and repair of the common areas **whether they use them or not.**

This is because condo fees are not for usage, but for contributions towards the upkeep of the common property – each unit owner holds joint ownership.

Participation in the Condo Administration

The ultimate administrative body in a condominium is the condo assembly, and every unit owner is allowed to go to the assembly and vote.

It isn't legal to prevent an owner from voting at an assembly for any reason, including if they're late in paying their fees or assessments.

Every unit owner has the right to go to all council (board) and committee meetings, although they are there as an observer only, and have no vote. They can, however, speak at council and committee meetings, and ask that items be added to the agendas of these meetings.

No unit owner has the right to represent the condo, act on its behalf, or commit the condo to a financial obligation unless they're serving in the capacity of Administrator.

Equal and Fair Treatment

The condo administration is legally bound to administer and manage the condominium equitably and fairly.

Every unit owner has the right to expect due process from the condo administration, and that all rules and policies will be fairly and equally applied to all unit owners. An example would be if a complaint about a by-law violation is levied against them.

Unit owners also have the right to expect that the condo by-laws, rules, and policies will be enforced by the administration, and that they will do everything possible to properly repair and maintain the common property, and protect the well-being and security of the condo.

More Rights May be Given in the By-laws

More unit owners' rights may be contained in a particular condominium's *reglamentos* (by-laws).

It's important to understand that the condo's by-laws compliment and add to the Civil Code (which contains the condo legislation), but they can **never** contravene or change any Civil Code rule.

Article 1006 requires that these rights must be in your by-laws.

> The condo legislation in the Civil Code always takes precedence over the condo's by-laws.
>
> By-law articles that contravene or contradict the Civil Code are automatically null and void.

What Are the Rights of Each Unit Owner?

It's also important to understand that the only legal condo by-laws are the **Spanish version**. Any English translation that you have has no legal validity. You should be aware of any significant differences between the two because of a poor English translation, and correct them by issuing a better translation.

Condo unit owners must also realise that the by-laws can be changed at an extraordinary assembly. Therefore, the by-laws that existed when they bought their unit can be changed at any time in the future.

What Are the Obligations of Each Unit Owner?

Chapter **6**

As well as rights, condo unit owners also have obligations. Civil Code Articles 1009, 1010, 1010a, 1020, and 1026 outline the responsibilities of condo owners.

Comply With Condo Legislation and the By-laws

All unit owners must follow the condo legislation, as well as the condominium's *reglamentos* (by-laws).

This is one of the most basic rules of condominium living, and is definitely not unique to México. The benefits of condo ownership are balanced by slightly greater restrictions than with private property ownership. It's the nature of condominium ownership that the rights of the individual are secondary to the goals of the community.

An owner who violates the condo's rules can be fined (if allowed by the by-laws), censured by the Administrative Council (Board), and, for repeated and serious violation, have their condo unit sold at public auction (this last remedy is in the condo law).

Pay Condo Fees

Unit owners must pay condo fees to cover the expenses for maintaining and operating the common property, facilities, and services of the condo, and to set up and maintain reserve funds.

For more details on condo fees, **see Part 16 – "Fees and Assessments"**.

Hold an Annual Owners Meeting

Unit owners must meet in an *asamblea ordinaria* (ordinary assembly) at least once a year – in the first quarter of every calendar year (between January 1 and March 31).

This is an AGM (annual general meeting) where an Administrator is appointed, a new Council (Board) is elected, and the budget and fees for the coming fiscal year are approved.

For more details on condo meetings, **see Chapter 22 – "The Condo Assembly" and Part 8 – "Condo Assemblies"**.

Maintain Their Condo Units

Each owner is required to maintain their unit in such a way that it doesn't disrupt the harmony and value of the condominium. Owners must not allow their private unit to deteriorate in such a way that this could threaten the safety or security of other owners, or the property values of the condo.

It's wise to have by-law rules containing reasonable requirements for owners to keep their units tidy and well maintained, since this affects the property values of all unit owners.

Restricted Activities

Owners cannot use their unit for uses forbidden by the establishing document of the condominium regime. The most common example is a condo that's categorised as residential – in this case, no owner is allowed to conduct a business from their unit.

> Note that the intent here is that the business **does not disturb the tranquillity of the other owners**.
>
> If a home business doesn't involve the public visiting the condominium, then this restriction would be difficult or impossible to enforce. An example would be a business conducted entirely by telephone, email, or over the internet.
>
> It's also unlikely that someone would complain about such a business. It would certainly be difficult to make the case that it was disturbing them.
>
> **Article 1006** requires that any restrictions on business activity must be in your by-laws.

What Are the Obligations of Each Unit Owner?

The condo law says that unit owners and occupants of the condominium can't do any of the following without the consent of the other owners (at a condo assembly):

- do anything that affects the tranquillity and comfort of the other owners and occupants, or that compromises the stability, security, or well-being of the condominium; this also applies to deliberate acts of omission – an example would be if an owner becomes aware of a problem in or around their unit that, if ignored, could damage condo property, but doesn't report the problem;

- do anything that prevents or negatively impacts the operation of the common property, services, or facilities; or that limits or blocks the use of the common areas by other condo owners;

- change, damage, or destroy the common areas;

- cut down or transplant trees, or change the use or nature of the green areas;

- carry out work or repairs at night, except in the case of an emergency; or

- keep animals that, by their number, size, or nature, affect the security, comfort, or health of the other owners.

Violators of any of these rules, despite any other sanctions allowed by the Civil Code, are responsible for payment of damages and penalties arising from the violation (**Article 1010a**).

Changes and Renovations to Condo Units

Each owner can carry out work in their private unit, including renovations.

However, they must **not** make any change that affects the common property (structure, foundations, supporting walls, flat roofs, or residual water drainage system), or that could damage the common buildings' aesthetics, security, durability, or comfort.

Further, **all modification projects must have approval beforehand from the condominium's Administrative Council** (board).

Changes to Common Property

The Civil Code contains the following rules for work carried out on the condominium's **common property and facilities**:

- **Maintenance work** (repairs and upkeep): takes place when it's decided as being necessary by the Administrator, following instructions from the Administrative Council (Board), and **without needing the agreement of the owners**. The costs of this work is paid from the operating budget.

- **Urgent repairs** (to the common property or facilities): **must** be carried out by the Administrator **in a timely fashion**.

> **Urgent repairs** are those where the damage endangers the security of the owners or the integrity of the condo buildings, or prevents the proper operation of the common services or areas.

If your Administrator fails to make urgent repairs in a timely fashion, **any unit owner can have the work done**, without needing authorisation beforehand. The owner will be paid back the expenses for the work after justification and verification at the next assembly of the condominium.

Although not stipulated in the code, to be reasonable, the unit owner must give the Administrator notice of this intent along with a deadline.

What Are the Obligations of Each Unit Owner? 45

Although this is common sense, I recommend that you add a clause to your by-laws requiring an owner to notify the administration in writing, and to give a reasonable deadline – only after which will they go ahead and do the repairs themselves.

- **Improvements to the common property**: before these can be carried out, you must have the express agreement of the condo unit owners meeting in an *asamblea extraordinaria* (extraordinary assembly).

> **Improvements** are work or construction added to the common property that don't already exist, or where an existing common property item is significantly enhanced beyond ordinary repair or maintenance.
>
> For example:
>
> repairing broken tiles in the community pool is repairs and maintenance, while adding a jacuzzi is an improvement;
>
> repairing an electric vehicle gate that's broken down is repairs and maintenance, while replacing it with a hydraulic gate is an improvement.

Improvement work will either be supervised by your Administrator, and monitored by your Administrative Council (Board), or will be under the supervision of a special committee appointed for this purpose.

Improvement work is **not** allowed that will:

- undermine the stability or infrastructure of a building;
- decrease the security or comfort of the condominium; or

- permanently prevent the use of any part of the common property or of a common service by any unit owner – unless that owner agrees, and is compensated proportionally by all other condo owners.

Your Administrator must enforce the guarantees that are given by the contractors doing the work.

PART 3 – The Condo Administration

Makeup of Your Condo Administration

Chapter 7

As I've mentioned before, unlike condos in the U.S. or Canada, Mexican condominiums set up after 1995 are **not** a *"condo association"*, nor is there a *"homeowners association"* (HOA).

The Civil Code legislation governing a condominium regime gives you all the functions of a homeowners association, without the need for an association to be formed. In fact, it outlines a very specific structure and hierarchy for the administration of your condo.

A Four-Part Structure

The Jalisco condo law defines a condo's administrative structure:

1. **The owners assembly**: when the owners meet as a formal group in either an *asamblea ordinaria* (ordinary assembly) or an *asamblea extraordinaria* (extraordinary assembly).

   The decisions made at these assemblies take priority over any decisions made by the rest of the administration, and become directives to both the Administrator and Council (Board).

   The assembly has the power to change the make-up of the administration, or to change condo rules and policies. The owners, **and only the owners**, can approve improvements to your condo, or change your condo's by-laws.

   The owners assembly is the **supreme authority** in your condominium (**Civil Code Article 1019**).

2. **The Administrator**: either an individual or a company appointed by an ordinary assembly to help the Administrative Council (Board) carry out the day-to-day operations of your condominium, and fulfil the administrative duties outlined in **Civil Code Articles 1011 through 1013a** and your condominium's by-laws.

3. **The Administrative Council (Board)**: one or more owners who have been elected as councillors by an ordinary assembly.

   The Council works with the Administrator to make sure that the wishes of the owners assembly are carried out.

   The Council must fulfil the administrative duties outlined in **Civil Code Articles 1014 through 1018** and your condominium's by-laws.

   The Council is sometimes called the *"Condo Board"* or *"Board of Directors"*. For more information, **see Chapter 13 – "What's in a Name: Council vs. Board?"**.

4. **Committees**: these are entirely optional. **See Part 6 – "Committees."**

Relationship Between Administrator and Council (Board)

Your Administrator and Council have **separate but complementary functions**.

For example, your Council must monitor and make sure that the obligations given to your Administrator by the Civil Code and your condo's by-laws are being followed.

Your Council can ask your Administrator to give them any information, reports, and accountings that the Council feels are necessary for its work (**Civil Code Article 1017**).

> It's important to realise that the position of Administrator is not optional, and that your Administrator **cannot be a member of your Council (Board)** – or else the checks-and-balances of these two separate parts of a condo administration intended by the condo legislation are eliminated.

Your Administrator must execute the decisions of both the owners and your Council (**Civil Code Article 1012**).

Administration Salaries

An Administrator's wage is decided by the assembly where they were appointed.

If your Administrator is an owner, however, this is most often an unpaid volunteer position. The assembly can decide to pay an owner Administrator or the councillors (**Article 1016**).

If an outside Administrator is hired, the salary will usually have been negotiated by the Council (Board), and approved by the assembly.

Your by-laws could also define some sort of compensation, although I recommend that you leave this up to the assembly.

Foreigners Need a Work Permit

Be aware that if you pay your councillors or an owner Administrator, and they're foreigners, they **must have a visa that allows them to work**, they must get a tax ID number, and they must report their income on a Mexican tax return.

If they don't do all this, they're working in México illegally. A suit might be brought that cancels any authority they have and, possibly, any decisions, policies, or actions they've carried out. This might also become a loophole for a delinquent owner to try not to pay – this may or may not be successful, but it'll certainly delay your lawsuit against them (possibly for months).

An illegal foreign worker might also find themselves in a world of trouble that might include: back taxes, fines and penalties, and even deportation. Jail time is also not an impossibility in extreme circumstances.

Legal Responsibility of Your Administration

Chapter 8

Under the condo legislation contained in the Jalisco Civil Code, your Administrator and your Administrative Council (Board) together have a legal obligation to the owners to:

- make sure that your condo is administered in compliance with the Jalisco Civil Code;
- make sure that the common property of your condominium is well maintained, and kept in good repair; and
- do everything reasonable to protect the property values of your condominium.

Fiduciary Duty

A legal obligation of this kind is called a *deber fiduciario* (**fiduciary duty**):

> A **fiduciary** is a person, group, or entity who has agreed to act for, and on behalf of, another.
>
> A **fiduciary duty** is a relationship between these two parties (the condo administration and the owners) wherein one (the owners) has placed good faith, trust, and reliance in the other (the administration) to give advice, help, or protection. In most legal systems in the world, this is the highest standard of care under the law – Mexican law is no exception.
>
> A fiduciary is expected to be only concerned with the interests of the person(s) to whom they owe a **duty of care**, and must not put their own motives or agenda ahead of this duty, profit from their position, or knowingly fail in this duty of care.

Your Administrator and councillors (board members) are **fiduciaries** because they hold a position of trust that comes from being responsible for, and having control over, your condo's finances and common property.

No Excuses!

When someone accepts a position on the Council (Board), it's assumed that they understand the duties, obligations, and responsibilities of the position. Ignorance of the condo legislation or lack of experience aren't valid excuses for improper running of your condominium.

The fact that a condo is a nonprofit organisation, or that your Council (and, possibly, your Administrator) are unpaid volunteers, doesn't excuse your administration from the duty of care that they owe to the community.

It's necessary for every member of every condo's administration to learn what the condo legislation requires, what the correct procedures are, and how to avoid improper actions. You've made an excellent start by buying this book.

Common Failures of 'Duty of Care'

The most common failures of this duty of care that I've seen with condo administrations in México are:

- following procedures and policies that violate or contradict the state condo law;

- making decisions based on their own self-interest, rather than for the good of the community; and

- using their position for personal profit.

The first point is by far the most common.

Legal Responsibility of Your Administration

An administration that chooses not to follow the law exposes your condominium to all types of legal claims. These claims might result in financial losses, or in the devaluation of the property value of the homes.

While the Jalisco condo law has no such provision right now, the condo laws in other Mexican states contain stiff fines for administrators and councillors who don't handle fees and assessments properly, abuse their office, or fail to follow the Civil Code. Currently, these fines can run as high as $2,000 USD.

Sadly, the most common argument I hear for ignoring the condo law is, *"Many other condos ignore it."*

The error in this logic is huge – *"if a lot of people are selling drugs on the streets, it must be OK for me to do it too."*

The other most common "rationale" that I hear is, *"This is México – no one follows the law!"*

It always amazes me to hear such nonsense spouted by individuals who, before they retired, were upstanding citizens who wouldn't even conceive of ignoring provincial or state legislation in the country they came from. Something seems to happen to their sensibilities when they cross the border – particularly if they only live in México part-time.

Consequences of Not Following the Condo Law

"OK, so what are the consequences?" If your condo doesn't follow the condo law, there are no "condo police" that are going to come and arrest your Council (Board). You can likely skate by for years with what appears to be no consequences. Then an owner might become aware of the law, and challenge you. Possible financial exposure could be retroactive and large.

Consider this:

> A fictitious condo, *Vista del Basurero,* is a gated community with houses and lots. Lot areas vary in size by as much as 2 to 1 (not uncommon).
>
> When this condo was passed from the developer to an owner administration, they decided to collect fixed fees rather than the proportional fees required by law because it's "easier" and "other condos do it."
>
> Because of this contravention of the law, the smaller units are paying more than their fair share, and they're wrongly subsidising the larger units.
>
> The owner of the smallest lot decides that this is unfair (which it is), and files a suit. Since this is a clear violation of **Civil Code Article 1026**, the judge agrees, and awards damages in the amount of the overpayment for the length of time that this owner has been paying fixed fees (this could be several years).

Having to pay this settlement can severely impact the budget of a small condo. Other small unit owners may then decide to follow suit.

A related example with fixed fees: suppose that, rather than suing, an owner of a smaller unit who's being asked to pay more than their legal share just refuses to pay – not their entire fees, but just the illegal overage.

Therefore, they pay a smaller amount than asked, but the amount they're legally obligated to pay.

This will cause an income shortfall for the condo that, depending on how the budget is set up, may or may not be significant. Unfortunately, the condo wouldn't have a legal leg to stand on if they try to use the courts to recover this "debt."

Once the other owners become aware of this (and they will because of the Administrator's Quarterly Report), some of them might take a similar stand. This could snowball.

Your Assemblies and By-laws May Have No Legal Validity

The most common consequence of not following the condo legislation are that resolutions made at your assemblies, parts of your by-laws, or the ability of your Administrator or Council (Board) to act on behalf of your condo may have **no legal validity**.

"OK … so what on earth does this mean?"

It's quite simple. Anything that doesn't have legal validity is **not enforceable, and can be successfully challenged**.

For example, if this involved a by-law rule, no one who ignores the rule can be forced to obey it. Sanctions applied for ignoring the rule can be ignored, and aren't legally collectable.

The same applies to a resolution passed at an assembly. Suppose that you passed a resolution at an ordinary assembly that legally required an extraordinary assembly to pass it (an ordinary assembly can only deal with a few specific topics, **see Chapter 26 – "The Ordinary Assembly**).

In all likelihood, your *notario* (Civil Law Notary) would strip this item from your assembly minutes during his protocolisation process – as far as the law is concerned, it just didn't happen.

Even if your *notario* misses this, and it makes its way into the publicly registered minutes, it's unenforceable, and won't withstand a challenge.

"Can't We Avoid the Law If We All Agree?"

"If 100% of us agree to operate in contravention of the condo law, then this will be OK – right?"

Like many things in México, the answer is "yes and no."

As I've said, there are no "condo police," and you could likely get away with many things (short of criminal activity) if all owners agree – at least for a while.

The first problem is that you'd need 100% agreement of all owners – good luck! If you did manage to do this, you'll likely find it to be unsustainable.

While your current set of owners might be 100% in agreement, they're may not be continuous agreement. A condominium is a living community – owners come and go, and opinions change. There's no guarantee that a new owner who understands the condo law will agree to this, and you have no legal way to force them. Owners who originally agreed, might change their mind in future.

Any such agreement will only work for as long as every owner stays in agreement.

Because this isn't legal, you can't vote on it at an extraordinary assembly, and then publicly register the decision. Since it's in contravention of the condo law, the resolution would have no legal validity, and can never be binding on anyone.

While you could add it to your by-laws, any articles in a condo by-law that contravene a higher law (such as the state condo law) have no legal validity, and aren't binding.

You also need to realise that the issues might be more complicated than they at first appear, and definitely get much more convoluted as you choose to ignore more complex portions of the condo law.

For example, suppose you chose to charge fixed fees, rather than proportional fees.

> On the surface, this action appears to contravene only a single code requirement (**Article 1026**).
>
> In fact, it impacts seven other condo law articles (**1006 II, 1006 V, 1006 XI.a, 1009 III, 1026, 1030, and 1034**), and contravenes portions of another section of the Civil Code dealing with co-ownership (**Articles 961 through 1000**).

This situation gets further complicated because proportional fees are derived from proportional ownership, which is a fact recorded in each property's title (deed), and can never be changed.

Proportional ownership also requires proportional voting at assemblies. If you choose to charge fixed fees but continue with proportional voting, you're in an inconsistent and confusing situation that's open to question.

If you choose to disregard both legislative rules, you're entering complicated territory that might come back to bite you in the future. For example, an owner might sue to have a close vote at an assembly overturned because non-proportional voting was used.

If you decided to do something much more complex such as eliminate the position of Administrator ...

> An Administrator is such an essential part of the organisational structure defined in the legislation, that this role is linked with a significant portion of the condo law.
>
> You wouldn't be ignoring just one basic requirement of the law, but entire sections and principles.
>
> Again, you could probably get away with this for a period of time, but you'd be skating on thin ice, and risking having your whole house-of-cards come tumbling down at some point in the future – especially if your annual assembly failed to give powers of representation to another person instead of the Administrator.

Following the Law is Actually Easier

There are no parts of the condo law that are onerous or difficult to follow. They're neither random nor arbitrary.

The condo law's rules are sensible, enforce fairness, and are there to protect your community, as well as to define an administrative structure that's consistent for all condos.

Sometimes the protection given by the condo legislation is intended to protect a community from itself.

> Suppose a condo unanimously decided not to set up a reserve fund in contravention of the condo law. As a result, they wouldn't likely do regular reserve-style maintenance. They'd enjoy a short-term benefit in the form of lower fees, but, over time, property values would deteriorate, and the owners could face one or more potentially huge special assessments down the road.

Legal Responsibility of Your Administration

There are only a few requirements in the Jalisco state condo legislation that differ in any significant way from condo practices in other parts of the world (including the requirement to pay fees proportionally!).

You can waste a lot of time and energy trying to get around the law, for no benefit – it's far simpler just to run your condo properly.

Unless you're a criminal, there's never a true benefit to ignoring the law. If your actions are challenged, you'll just have to change everything anyway – and there may be significant cost involved.

Get a Quality Translation of the Condo Law

For reference, your Council should have a high quality English translation of the condo law. Some translations are inaccurate or hard to comprehend.

We recommend you use our companion book, *"Jalisco Condo Law in English."* This gives you a side-by-side translation of the condo law, along with other legislation that directly affects condos.

Whatever translation you use, don't fall into the trap of debating the semantics of the English translation. If a semantic difference actually affects something you're doing (or considering), **you must refer to the original Spanish for a resolution.**

PART 4 – The Condo Administrator

How is the Administrator Appointed?

Chapter 9

Civil Code Articles **1011**, **1013**, and **1013a** define how the Administrator is to be appointed.

The Condo's First Administrator

The first *administrador* (Administrator) of your condominium is appointed by the developer, and can only serve a single one-year term.

Appointing the Next Administrators

After this first term, the Administrator must be appointed by the owners at the **Annual Ordinary Assembly**. Administrators appointed by an owners assembly also only serve a one-year term, but this term can be renewed at the next ordinary assembly.

> The minutes of the ordinary assembly where your Administrator is appointed **must** be protocolised by a *notario* (Civil Law Notary) and registered in the local **Registro Público de la Propiedad** (Public Registry of Property).
>
> If a bond was given to guarantee the services of the Administrator, then a copy must be attached. This often happens when hiring a company.

A compound condominium must have an Administrator for each of its separate condominiums, plus a **General Administrator** appointed by a majority of all owners.

Your Administrator can be either an individual or a company. An individual doesn't have to be an owner or even a resident of your condominium. Here are some common (and legal) scenarios:

- an owner who has volunteered for the position (in this case, they must be current in their fees);

- an individual contracted by your condominium or hired as an employee; or

- a property management company.

If your Administrator is contracted, then the contract can't be for more than a one-year term (it must run out by the next Annual Ordinary Assembly), and its renewal must be approved by the owners at the next Annual Ordinary Assembly.

If the owners appoint a new Administrator, the outgoing Administrator must give the new one all condo documents **within 15 calendar days from the date of the appointment** (the date of the ordinary assembly).

These documents must include, at a minimum:

- your condo records;
- statements of condo accounts (financial records);
- securities (if any); and
- all other documents about your condo furniture, buildings, and other property that was under the Administrator's care.

Your Administrator has the single most difficult job in your condo administration. This is one of the reasons why this job is often contracted out to a management company, or is contracted to a full or part-time person who has the time to dedicate to the job.

If you're going to appoint an owner, then I strongly recommend that you only nominate someone to be Administrator who's committed, professional, and willing to work.

To help lessen the burden of an owner Administrator, some of the work can be off-loaded to an assistant or a committee.

Resignation of the Administrator

Since the Administrator must be appointed by an ordinary assembly, the Administrator can only be replaced by holding another ordinary assembly.

The reason for this is that the Administrator was given representative powers by the assembly by name rather than position. If your Administrator resigns, then the only person remaining with similar powers of representation may be the President/Chair of your Administrative Council – if this person was also specifically given these powers by the assembly. Unfortunately, the President doesn't have some of the legal authorities that the Administrator has, and can't fully act in his place.

Removal of the Administrator

The condo law is silent on removing an unpopular or incompetent Administrator from office.

Since a new Administrator can only be appointed by an ordinary assembly, I suggest that the best procedure is to call an ordinary assembly to remove the current Administrator, appoint a new one, and then give them powers of representation at the same time.

Remember that if your Administrator is an owner, they must be current in their condo fees. Therefore, your Administrator would be automatically removed as soon as they are more than 90 days in arrears. In this case, you'll have to call an ordinary assembly to replace them as soon as possible.

If the Council won't support this action by calling an assembly, a group of owners can impeach the Administrator (or Council). For more information, **see the end of Chapter 14 – "How Is the Council Appointed?"**

What Are the Duties of the Administrator?

Chapter 10

The duties and obligations of the Administrator are defined in Civil Code Articles 1007, 1009, 1012, 1017, 1029, 1029a, 1032, and 1033.

Act for Your Condominium

Your Administrator is the representative of your condominium before third-parties for administrative matters, and is also your condo's legal representative before third-parties and the courts.

Your Administrator can **not** act as a representative agent for your condo in any capacity other than for administrative and legal matters unless specifically given this power by the owners at an ordinary assembly.

When allowed by your Council (Board), your Administrator also has the right to give a general power of attorney to anyone considered pertinent to the defence and representation of the interests of your condominium in a lawsuit (such as a lawyer).

Be Responsible to Owners and Council (Board)

Your Administrator is charged with carrying out the decisions of the owners and your Administrative Council. In a compound condominium, your Administrator accepts, carries out, and communicates the decisions made by the General Administrator.

To make sure your Administrator is carrying out the obligations imposed on them by the condo legislation and your condo's by-laws, your Administrator must accept supervision from your Council.

Your Administrator must present a report about the operation and finances of your condominium to your Council once a month – this report can be given in oral or written form.

Your Administrator must also give other administrative information, reports, and accounts to your Council when asked.

Administer Your condo Finances

As far as your condo finances are concerned, your Administrator must:

- Collect condo fees from the owners, and give out receipts.
- Keep the official condo books and records.
- Give to any owner who asks for it (or have available in the administration office) **within the first 15 days of April, July, October, and January** (each quarter of your condo's fiscal year) a financial statement that includes, at a minimum:
    - a report that details condo income and any overdue condo fees;
    - a report that analyses the last quarter's expenses;
    - a list of creditors with an explanation of each credit;
    - a list of debtors with an explanation of each debt; and
    - the cash, investment, or reserve balances (if any).
- Produce a detailed statement of accounts after 90 days have passed from the due date for payment of condo fees. This report must be signed by your Administrator, with the approval of the President/Chair of your Administrative Council, and is an enforceable document. For example, if a suit for non-payment of fees is to be launched.
- Assist your Council (Board) to verify the state of the accounts and their entry into the official condo books.

What Are the Duties of the Administrator?   71

- Give to any owner who asks, a copy of the detailed statements of account for your condominium – these records must always be available for inspection by any owner.

Maintain the Common Property

Your Administrator is responsible for the day-to-day maintenance of the common property, as follows:

- Take and maintain a complete and updated inventory of all common property furniture and buildings belonging to your condominium.

- Check and arrange for the repair and maintenance of the common property, common services, and common buildings.

- Arrange for urgent repairs to the common property or facilities **to be done in a timely fashion**. Urgent repairs are defined as those where the damage puts in danger the security of the owners, or the integrity of the common buildings, or that prevents the proper operation of the common services.

    If your Administrator fails to carry out these urgent repairs in a timely fashion, **any Owner can have the work done**, without authorisation beforehand, and the owner will be repaid for the expenses of the work after justification and verification at the next Owner Assembly – the cost of these repairs will be shared amongst the owners.

- Decide when non-emergency repairs and maintenance work on common property and services will take place – make this decision according to standing instructions (or instructions specific to the issue) given by your Administrative Council (Board). It isn't necessary to have permission from the owners to carry out maintenance and repair work.

- Make payments for maintenance, repairs, and administrative expenses from the operating budget. Maintain books and documents to support all expenses – **these records must be updated within 15 working days of the expense being paid**.

- Supervise improvement work to common property and services **that's been approved by the owners at an extraordinary assembly**, while being monitored either by your Administrative Council (Board) or a special committee assigned to this task.

- Enforce any guarantees given by the contractors doing work.

Sue an Owner or Tenant

Your Administrator can sue an owner who repeatedly fails to fulfil their obligations, or unjustifiably creates conflict with the other owners. This suit takes place before a Judge of First Instance of the place where your condominium is located under terms set out in the *Código de Procedimientos Civiles del Estado* (Code of Civil Procedures of the State).

Suing an owner to sell their unit at public auction must first be approved by the owners voting in an extraordinary assembly.

With consent of the owner of the unit, your Administrator can ask a tenant who doesn't fulfil their obligations to vacate the unit. If the owner is opposed to this, then your Administrator can take legal action against both the occupant and the owner.

Other Duties

Your Administrator generally posts the call for each owners assembly (ordinary or extraordinary) – for more details on how this call is to be issued and formatted, **see Chapter 22 – "The Condo Assembly."**

What Are the Duties of the Administrator?

Your Administrator must assist any special committees that are formed to carry out a specific task – for more detailed information on committees, **see Part 6 – "Committees."**

When the seller of a private unit (or the *notario* preparing the transfer documents) asks for it, your Administrator must write a letter stating that there are no unpaid debts owed to your condominium (such as unpaid condo fees or special assessments);

As well as these duties, your Administrator must fulfil any other duties and obligations that are required by the condo law, any other applicable law, your condominium's establishing document, and your condo's by-laws.

Article 1006 requires these duties to be spelled out in your by-laws.

Remember that your condo's by-laws can add to the Civil Code by including extra duties and responsibilities for your Administrator, but these by-laws **cannot** remove or fundamentally change any of the duties outlined in the code, nor can they change the relationship between the Administrator and the Council (Board).

Administrator Can Delegate Duties - Not Responsibility

While your Administrator's **responsibilities** can't be passed to others, your Administrator is allowed to delegate any **duties** except those specifically forbidden by your by-laws or your Council. What this means is that even if your Administrator has delegated some duties to an assistant, your Administrator is still responsible, and must make sure that these duties are both carried out and carried out correctly.

Who Should be Your Administrator?

As I've mentioned, the duties of your Administrator are extensive – it's the single most difficult job in a condo administration.

You have two choices: appoint an owner as Administrator, or hire an outside Administrator – this last choice could be an employee, a contract worker, or a management company.

The decision is usually based on the size of a condo. For condos over 50 units, a paid outside Administrator is likely necessary – the size of the job is generally too much for a volunteer owner to handle, and a larger condominium has the financial resources to hire someone (can be in the range of $70K to $100K pesos per year).

A smaller condo may not be able to afford a paid Administrator, and might opt for an unpaid or minimally-paid volunteer owner.

The job needs an individual who's organised, has basic knowledge of finances and accounting, and has the time to dedicate to the job – it typically takes 20 to 80 hours a month (sometimes more).

Paying an Owner-Administrator

If you're using a volunteer owner, there's nothing preventing you from compensating this individual. I've seen compensation range from nothing, to a meal for two per month at a local restaurant, to a small salary such as $2,000 pesos per month.

> **Be careful!**
>
> If you decide to pay an owner Administrator (or your councillors), and if they're foreigners, then they **must have a visa that allows them to work,** they must get a tax ID number, and they **must report their income** on a Mexican tax return.
>
> If they don't do this, they're working in México illegally.
>
> A suit might be brought that might negate their authority and any decisions or actions they've carried out. A delinquent owner might also try to use this as a reason not to pay.
>
> They could also find themselves with problems such as: back taxes, fines and penalties, and even deportation.

If the owners do opt to pay your owner Administrator, then this fact, along with the amount and method of pay, must be recorded in the minutes of the ordinary assembly where your Administrator was appointed (or reappointed).

While not a legal requirement, I recommend that if you're going to use an owner as Administrator, you should appoint someone who's a full-time resident. This is a job that needs "boots on the ground". Note that an owner acting as Administrator must be up to date in their condo fees (**Civil Code Article 1011**).

Hiring an Outside Administrator

If you're going to hire a paid outside Administrator, then I recommend that you either contract a part-time individual or you hire the services of a management company (my preference).

Some condos directly hire an individual as an employee of the condominium, but this can have drawbacks. For more information on employees and the issues affecting them, **see Chapter 44 – "Contract Workers vs. Employees."**

Administrator Maintains Your Official Condo Records

Chapter 11

Civil Code Article 1012 says that there must be at least three separate record books kept by your Administrator as the official records of your condominium.

Required Record Books

- **Book #1** contains the minutes of all Owner Assemblies (Ordinary and Extraordinary), with attachments;

- **Book #2** contains the minutes of each council meeting (board meeting), with attachments; and

- **Book #3** contains the income and expenses records of your condominium.

If the owners assembly wants it, auxiliary records must also be kept by your Administrator. It's easiest to set this up by adding an article to your by laws at an extraordinary assembly.

Recommended Optional Records

Other records not required by the Code, but that I recommend your Administrator keep, are:

- a copy of your condo's *escritura constitutiva* (registered public document that sets up either a condo regime or an association);

- other documents from the developer including lot plans and infrastructure drawings;

- the current and past versions of your condo by-laws, plus all current rules and policies;

- committee minutes, with attachments;

- current list of unit owners and contact information (it is important to keep this up to date when units change hands);

- correspondence (such as emails, letters, etc.); documents and emails can be archived on a CD-ROM corresponding to each fiscal year, and filed in a binder; and

- quotations and executed contracts.

Attachments to Minutes

The condo legislation requires that a copy of all documents related to the minutes of either the Owner Assemblies or the Administrative Council meetings (board meetings) be physically attached to these minutes, and kept in the minute books as part of the official record. I recommend that this also be done with committee meeting minutes.

Here are a few examples of these attachments:

- any email or other written submission received from an owner, and discussed at the meeting;

- any written report presented at the meeting;

- any document presented at the meeting in support of the discussion on a motion;

- any vendor or contractor quotation or proposal that was discussed at the meeting.

Computer Records vs. Bound Record Books

While computer records are allowed for any of the optional auxiliary books, the three books mentioned above must (according to the condo law) be in the form of three separate **bound books that are signed and stamped on the first page by the local Secretary of the Town Council.**

The first two record books should be bound minute books with ruled pages, and the last record book should be a ledger book.

Administrator Maintains Your Official Condo Records

Bound *libros de actas* (minute books) are available at Office Depot and other stationery supply stores throughout México. They usually come in 50, 100, or 200 page versions.

The intent of this code requirement is that the minutes be entered into the book during the meeting, and approved at the end of the meeting. The minutes are then instantly available to any owner for examination, and, by virtue of being in a bound book with no missing pages, are guaranteed to be unaltered.

Now, I know exactly what you're thinking! *"This is the computer age – do we really need to keep handwritten condo records?"*

The answer, as you may have expected, is "yes and no."

Don't despair, I do have a more convenient way of dealing with meeting minutes that satisfies the intent of the condo law, but this is a topic unto itself. **See Part 13 – "Minutes of Assemblies & Meetings"**.

How Long Should We Keep Our Records?

It's good to have a historical record of your condo (*"How did we deal with this when it came up three years ago?"*). The condo law doesn't say anything about the length of time records must be kept.

If you have the space, I recommend as long as possible. Failing this, common practice is seven years. It's a good idea to put a minimum retention time in your by-laws.

That said, I strongly advise you to keep any publicly registered documents forever. These will generally consist of the *escritura constitutiva* (the document that set up your condominium) plus the minutes of ordinary and extraordinary assemblies.

Lessening the Burden on a Volunteer Administrator

Chapter 12

Since the job of Administrator is so extensive, there are techniques that can be used to take some of the burden off an owner doing this job as a volunteer.

Although these techniques involve your Administrator delegating some duties to others, your Administrator is still always legally responsible. Therefore, your Administrator can delegate **duties**, but cannot delegate **responsibilities** (as defined under the condo law).

Appoint an Assistant Administrator

An Assistant Administrator position can be created. This can be a volunteer owner to help your Administrator in their day-to-day duties, and act as a back-up if your Administrator is away.

It's best if your Administrator is allowed to recruit and appoint this assistant, since the two of them must work closely together, and your Administrator must have confidence in this person.

It's important to realise that the position of Assistant Administrator is **not** defined in the condo legislation. That said, I don't believe that this individual should be a member of your Administrative Council (Board). Since your Administrator isn't allowed to be on your Council (the separation between the Administrator and the Council is a Code requirement to allow a checks-and-balances system between the two parts of the administration), then it logically follows that this must also apply to the Assistant Administrator.

I recommend that if you opt for this solution, then you should consider defining this position in your condo by-laws.

Appoint a Maintenance Manager or Committee

Since your Administrator is almost single-handedly responsible for the maintenance and operation of your condo, it's common practice to appoint either an Maintenance Manager or a committee.

The choice generally depends on the size of your condo. Condos with more than 100 units may benefit from a committee, but smaller condos usually find that an individual is much more efficient.

For more information, **see Part 6 – "Committees."**

Split the Work With a Management Company

One administration model that works well for smaller condos is to delegate **some** of your Administrator's duties to a property management company.

This also avoids some issues that I'll talk about in a later section on condo bank account, taxes, and directly employing workers (**Part 14 – "Practical Matters"**).

The costs for partial management are also much less than those for full management. Indeed, some smaller management companies who are the lowest cost choice, may not be willing to take on all the duties of an Administrator.

Here is my suggestion for a list of duties that can be off-loaded to a management company (this can be used as the basis for a Scope of Work for the agreement between the management company and your condo):

- carry out the instructions of the Administrator;

- give information and account details to the Administrator when asked;

- collect condo fees from the owners, and issue receipts;

- no later than five days after the end of each month, give the Administrator a financial report for the month just ended consisting of:
  - condo income and any overdue condo fees;
  - a breakdown of the month's expenses;
  - a list of creditors with an explanation of each credit owed by your condo;
  - a list of debtors with an explanation of each debt owed to your condo; and
  - the cash, investment, or reserve balances (if any);
- cooperate with the Administrator to verify the state of the accounts;
- make payments for maintenance, repairs, and administration expenses from the operating account, as authorised by the Administrator; maintain receipts to support all expenses;
- contract wherever possible with the workers needed to maintain and support your condominium property to avoid an employer-employee relationship between your condo and these workers; administer such contracts; make payments for these contracts from the operating account, as authorised by the Administrator; maintain receipts to support all such payments;
- provide a resource for reliable local contractors; and

- when work is needed, and it's not feasible to set up a contract with the worker, directly employ the worker as an employee of the management company, and deal with all employee-related expenses and paperwork – acting as a buffer between your condo and the employee such that their relationship stays at arm's length; make payments for employee-related expenses from the operating account, as authorised by the Administrator; maintain receipts to support all such expenses.

I recommend that you formalise your agreement with a management company in a letter of agreement that clearly outlines what the duties and responsibilities of the company will be, gives them a standing authorisation to pay certain regular expenses, and requires them to not pay anything else without a properly signed Payment Authorisation Form.

A sample letter of agreement with a property management company, and a payment authorisation form, is included in your BONUS Pack.

PART 5 – The Administrative Council (Board)

What's in a Name: Council vs. Board?

Chapter **13**

Some Mexican condos refer in English to the administrative body appointed by the owners as a *"Board"* or a *"Board of Directors"*.

This is a concept that many foreigners bring with them from their condo experience in their own country. Unfortunately, it's not accurate when describing a Mexican condo administration.

In the state of Jalisco, this body is called a ***consejo de administración*** (Administrative Council), and, in most of the rest of México, a ***comité de vigilancia*** (Oversight Committee).

OK … so what's the big deal? Why not just call yourselves a *"Board"*?

Differences Between a Council and a Board

It's not only a question of semantics, but it's also a question of perceived power:

- A *consejo* (council) is a type of committee that's elected to represent and serve those who elected them (in this case, the condo owners) in an administrative and advisory capacity. It's always aware of the wishes of the electorate, which are paramount in any decisions made by it.

- A *junta directiva* (board of directors) makes policy and sets goals. These aren't powers authorised by the condo law, and are only given to the owners acting in an assembly.

    A board also makes sure that adequate financial resources are available and approves annual budgets. Neither of these are powers given by the condo law.

While a board is answerable to those who elected it, it's much more autonomous and authoritarian than a council. In fact, in most corporations, the board is the highest authority (in a condo, this is the owners).

Simply said, a Board of Directors, whether it's in Canada, the U.S. or México, generally has far greater powers and authority than does a Council.

The Intent of the Condo Legislation

Since the Jalisco condo legislation specifically refers to the members of a condo's administrative body as *consejeros* (councillors), rather than *directores* (directors), it's my opinion that the roles of council and councillor are what are intended by the Code.

> From this point on in my book, I'll use **"Council"** rather than **"Board."**
>
> My recommendation is that you also adopt the terms **"Council"** and **"councillors"** for your condo.

The Civil Code takes great pains to guarantee that condo owners are the ultimate power and authority (over and above the Council and Administrator), that a condominium is a community, that the condo administration always respects the owners' wishes, and is always subject to owner review and observation.

Setting Up a Community-Oriented Mindset

Please don't misunderstand me – calling your *consejo* a "Board" isn't illegal, and there won't be any repercussions in this area.

I strongly believe, however, that the term *"Council"* sets up a mindset that's more community-oriented and inclusive than does the term *"Board."*

Remember that unlike north of the border, your condo isn't being administered by either an association or a nonprofit corporation (both of which typically have Boards).

In my experience, many of the problems between a condo administration and the owners are because of a perceived (and, sometimes, actual) arrogance on the part of the "Board."

I've seen bitter resentment in condos when owners have the perception that their administration is detached and authoritarian – few people like to be dictated to.

A Council must do everything possible to make sure that the owners always feel included and considered.

I believe that many of the issues with condo administrations in México stem from the members of the *"Board"* believing that they have more power and authority than they do, and I further believe that referring to this body as a *"council"* and themselves as *"councillors"* goes a long way towards eliminating this misperception.

A good Council will check its collective egos at the door, and do everything possible to make sure that the owners' wishes and feelings are always considered first, that its administration is open and communicative, and that it always fosters a sense of community.

How is the Council Appointed?

Chapter 14

Civil Code Articles 1014, 1015, 1016, 1018, 1020, and 1029 set out how a Council is to be appointed.

The *consejo de administración* (Administrative Council) consists of however many *consejeros* (councillors) are required by your condominium's by-laws.

Council is Appointed at an Ordinary Assembly

The Council is elected by the owners at the **Annual Ordinary Assembly** – this is similar to an AGM.

> The minutes of the ordinary assembly where your Council was appointed **must** be protocolised by a *notario* (Civil Law Notary) and registered in the local ***Registro Público de la Propiedad*** (Public Registry of Property).

Councillors only serve a one-year term, but they can stand for re-election at the next ordinary assembly. There's no limit to the number of terms a councillor can serve (although you could limit this in your by-laws).

A councillor **must be a resident of your condominium**.

They can either be the registered title holder of the unit, or they can be an occupant of a unit (such as a renter).

If a councillor is a non-owner, then they must have written permission from the registered title holder of the unit.

Whether they're an owner or an occupant, they must be up to date in their condo fees (in the case of an occupant, the corresponding owner must be paid up).

> You must be sure that each councillor is the **registered title holder of their unit** (have them provide a copy of their deed with their name on it), or that they have written permission from the title holder.
>
> If this isn't done, your Council will be invalid, and its decisions can be called into question or overturned.

The position of councillor is voluntary, and can't be delegated to anyone else by the elected person. The owners assembly can vote to pay any or all councillors a salary.

See Chapter 7 – "Makeup of your Condo Administration" for more detail on paying wages to foreigners.

Note that your condo's by-laws can add to the Civil Code by including extra rules for your Council, but your by-laws **cannot** remove or change any of the requirements outlined in the code. For example, you can't disallow a renter from serving on your Council.

Resignation of a Councillor

A councillor can leave office before their term is up for a variety of reasons. The Council will generally want to replace each resigning councillor.

To avoid having to call an ordinary assembly (with the associated expense), your by-laws should have a procedure that allows your Council to recruit a replacement councillor from the community to serve out the remaining term.

The exception to this would be if a majority of your Council resigns en masse so that they no longer have a quorum, and cannot hold a meeting. An ordinary assembly must then be held to elect a new Council.

Two caveats:

1. If the resigning councillor will lower the number of councillors to less than the minimum required in your by-laws, your Council won't be able to pass valid resolutions once the resignation becomes effective.

   It's important, therefore, to make sure that you have a replacement councillor lined up before the effective resignation date of the outgoing councillor.

2. If the councillor who's resigning is the President/Chair of your Council, then you have a similar situation to the Administrator – powers of representation were given to the President by name (not title) at the ordinary assembly where the President was elected.

   You now have a choice:

   - call another ordinary assembly to appoint a new President/Chair of your Council; or

   - allow your Administrator to be the **only representative** of your condo in legal and administrative matters (until the next Annual Ordinary Assembly).

Removal of a Councillor

There are two ways a councillor can be removed from your Council.

- **Automatic**: if a councillor no longer meets the qualifications for being a councillor, then they're automatically removed from the Council. While your by-laws can set out other requirements for councillors, the two contained in the condo legislation are:
   - owning a unit in the condo as the registered title holder; and

- being up to date in their condo fees.

If a councillor sells their unit, then as soon as the title is transferred, this councillor is automatically no longer on the Council. Clearly, you'll want to have a replacement lined up beforehand.

As soon as a councillor is no longer up to date with their fees (defined by the condo law as being 90 days late), they'll automatically stop being a councillor.

If this is a temporary financial situation, your Council can decide to wait until the fees are paid, and then re-instate the councillor (assuming that being without this councillor won't push your Council below its minimum number or quorum). If not, then your Council should try to have a replacement lined up before the 90 days are up.

- **Recall**: the Council or some owners may wish to remove a problematic councillor. There's no specific procedure defined for this in the condo legislation, so you must put any such procedures into your by-laws.

  Here are some common practices that you can draw on for ideas:

  - **Recall by the other councillors**: your by-laws could say that a majority of the Council can vote out a councillor for cause (the cause must be listed in the motion to recall).

    Typical causes: repeatedly disruptive at council meetings; conducting a personal agenda that's against the interests of the community; or making disparaging remarks about your condo or its administration outside of the condo.

How is the Council Appointed? **95**

- **Recall by owners**: if the Council receives a written request from a number (typically, 10% or more) of the condo rights stating the reasons for such a recall, then this would trigger a recall procedure.

  If only a single councillor is involved, then the Council can act on this as above, and vote on the recall.

  If several councillors are named (or the entire Council), then an ordinary assembly must be called to deal with the issue. In this case, the recall petition would be circulated with the assembly call, and the petitioning owners should have proposed a list of owners who are willing to serve in the place of the recalled councillors.

  The Order of the Day (a firm agenda) should contain only a single item, and it must be clear that the assembly is being called to recall and replace councillors or the Council.

None of the above procedures are in the condo legislation. They're presented as ideas to allow you to develop a process that you can add to your by-laws.

Impeachment of the Entire Council (or Administrator)

If an owner recall fails (your Council might ignore the request), and if the Council is out of control, incompetent, or is impeding or jeopardising your condominium, the condo law (**Article 1022**) has a method where a group of owners who represent at least 20% of the total condo rights can petition a judge to call an assembly where a new Council can be elected or a new Administrator appointed.

If the judge agrees, he'll issue a call for an ordinary assembly – it needs the normal 15 days advance notice. In this one instance, it isn't necessary to let owners know by registered mail. The call must be put in a visible place in your condominium, published in a high circulation newspaper in the state, and published in the official government newspaper, *"El Estado de Jalisco."*

That said, if you do take such action I strongly suggest letting all owners know by email, your condo web site, and whatever other ways you normally use. To be effective and prevent possible divisiveness, you must conduct this process as openly and inclusively as possible.

Clearly, this is an extreme measure, and this group of owners must:

- have a reason good enough to convince a judge that this should be done (documentation will prove helpful); and

- have support – they need at least 20% of the total condo rights to be in the group, plus they'll need at least 51% of the total condo rights for quorum to be able to hold the assembly, plus they'll need a majority of those present to vote in favour of this action.

What Are the Duties of the Council?

Chapter
15

The duties and responsibilities of the Administrative Council and the councillors are defined in **Civil Code Articles 1009, 1010, 1012, 1017, 1029,** and **1031**.

Act for the Owners

Your Council must act for the condo unit owners in matters of their common interest, act as a general legal representative, and carry out acts of administration.

Your Council is allowed to make administrative decisions for the owners, and to direct your Administrator to execute them.

Note that there's a specific requirement in the condo legislation that your Council must carry out the administration of your condominium **under observance by the owners** – it's each owner's right to make sure that your Council is fulfilling its obligations.

> I cannot stress enough the importance of **Article 1017 V** that says that your Council must carry out its administration **under observance by the owners.**
>
> Your Council must always be open and transparent – not only because it's the right thing to do, but because **it's the law.**
>
> Note also that your Council is responsible to the owners, and that the owners' wishes are always paramount.
>
> Your Council must exercise due diligence to make sure that they aren't acting in conflict with the owners' directions (as decided at various Owners Assemblies). Decisions of an owners assembly always take precedence over any instructions given by your Council.
>
> I'll cover this in more detail in **Chapter 17 – "Your Council Must Always be Open and Transparent."**

Your Council must give an annual report to the owners during the first quarter of each calendar year (between January 1 and March 31) – this is typically done at the Annual Ordinary Assembly (AGM). This report must be on the work of the Council, the general state of your condominium, and its finances.

Your Council must approve requests from owners for changes to their private units.

Your Council must arbitrate disputes between owners. For more information, **see Chapter 57 – "Dispute Resolution."**

> The code requirement to approve requests from owners for changes to their private units is the reason why I recommend you create a set of **"Rules of Construction"** for your condominium.
>
> By doing this, all owners know what is and what is not acceptable when they plan a renovation project, and it makes the process of applying for permission to do the renovations go much more smoothly.
>
> Many condominiums appoint a **Construction Committee** to update the Rules of Construction, and to deal with the renovation/construction applications from homeowners – this practice removes this burden from your Council.

Work With the Administrator

It's the responsibility of your Council to oversee your Administrator's work make sure that your Administrator complies with the obligations given by the condo legislation, other applicable laws, and your condo's by-laws.

If there are any duties that your Administrator isn't allowed to delegate, your Council must set these out, and communicate them to your Administrator.

What Are the Duties of the Council?

Article 1017 III requires your Council to meet **at least once a month** to receive a financial report from your Administrator, and to verify the state of the accounts and their proper entry into your condo's record books. Your Council can also ask for reports and financial accounts from your Administrator as needed to carry out its duties.

> **Watch this!**
> Some condos stop having Council meetings during the "slow" season when part-time residents are absent.
> **This is illegal.**
> The Civil Code clearly requires Council meetings to occur **at least once a month** to examine your Administrator's report.

If your Administrator is unable to issue the call for an owners assembly (ordinary or extraordinary), then your Council will issue the call (usually by the President/Chair of your Council). For more details on how this call is to be issued and formatted, **see Chapter 22 – "The Condo Assembly."**

Your Council must authorise your Administrator to give a general power of attorney with judicial abilities of administration to anyone considered pertinent to the defence and representation of the interests of your condominium in a lawsuit.

Your Council can also give special powers of attorney directly to someone other than your Administrator to:

- start and stop legal actions;
- make criminal complaints;
- help the *Ministerio Público* (Public Attorney's Office);
- buy property either directly or at auction; and

- begin an *amparo* suit to stop an action by a public authority until a final determination can be made as to its legality – like an injunction.

Maintain the Common Property

Your Council must verify the proper investment of funds for repairs and maintenance, administration, and the reserves.

It must also approve the detailed statement of owner accounts sent out by your Administrator after 90 days have passed from the due date for receipt of condo fees – this is an enforceable document. It can be used, for example, if a suit for non-payment of fees is to be carried out.

If your Council has specific rules as to how your Administrator must carry out maintenance work on common property and services, they must give standing instructions to your Administrator. It must also give instructions to your Administrator specific to any issue that arises that isn't covered by these standing instructions.

Your Council must monitor improvement work to common property and services that's been approved by the owners. Your Administrator will supervise this work, and a special committee can also be appointed to monitor this work instead of the Council.

It isn't necessary to have permission from the owners to carry out repair and maintenance work, but permission from the owners at an extraordinary assembly is necessary for any improvement work.

Other Duties

Take minutes of all council meetings, and attach copies of all related documents (reports, emails, or submissions).

What Are the Duties of the Council?

If your condominium is mixed between residential and commercial, your Council must authorise any contract that involves occupation of the common property by a third-party. For example, a lease agreement to occupy a store front or office space that's part of your condo property.

Any other duties and obligations required by the condo law, any other applicable law, your condominium's establishing document, and your condo's by-laws.

Article 1006 requires these duties to be spelled out in your by-laws.

Note that your condo's by-laws can add to the condo legislation contained in the Civil Code by including more duties and responsibilities for your Council, but your by-laws **cannot** remove or change any of the responsibilities outlined in the Code, nor can they change the relationship between the Administrator and the Council.

Overstepping Its Authority

One of the most common problems in condos is when a Council oversteps its authority. The Council has no more authority than is given by the condo legislation, plus any other responsibilities (not authority) given to them by your by-laws. Here are some of the more common problems:

- Authorising work that's of a voluntary or improvement nature without getting approval from the owners at an extraordinary assembly. Your Council only has the authority to carry out maintenance and repairs, **but not improvements.**

> **Here's the test**: ask yourself if this a necessary repair or regular maintenance expense for something already existing (for example, replacing loose tiles in the community pool), or if this is a voluntary expense that adds a feature (for example, buying a thermal blanket for this same pool). The last is not allowed without an express vote from the owners at an extraordinary assembly.

- Trying to stop owners from doing something that isn't forbidden by either the condo law, your by-laws, or any existing rules. Your Council cannot make rules and infractions up as they go along.

- Trying to make policies or rules that go beyond their mandate of operating and maintaining common property – your Council has little authority in an owner's unit, apart from a few things in the condo law.

Who Should Be on Your Council?

The Administrative Council is an important body, and there's a lot of work involved. While you can't always control who'll be on your Council, here are some tips:

> I strongly recommend that you nominate people to your Council who are committed, professional, and willing to work. People with business, management, and financial experience are a definite asset.

> The Council must always think of your condo as a nonprofit business. Council meetings are business meetings. You need people who understand this, and are capable of making decisions about your condo's assets and finances in a business-like way.

They need to be able to view the operation over the long-term, and make decisions that are in the best interests of the entire community – even when these are in conflict with their personal interests.

You need people who are able to make decisions about owner requests or complaints that firstly follow your condo's by-laws and other rules and policies, and secondly benefit your condo as a whole – even if this means ruling against their friends.

I recommend that the President/Chair of your Council and a minimum number of councillors be full-time residents.

Be wary of people who are chronic volunteers. These people will be heavily into other activities, and may have spread themselves too thin to devote enough time to your Council.

You should try to avoid people who treat the Council as a social club. These people will go to all the council meetings, but will do no work between meetings.

Especially try to avoid people who mainly want to be on the Council for the "prestige" or, worse, "power." They'll tell everyone they meet, *"I'm on the Board of the Vista del Basurero condo!"* **Hint**: these are often the people who'll vehemently oppose changing the name from *"Board"* to *"Council."* These are often the type of people who will most likely try to overstep their authority.

Makeup of the Council

Chapter 16

The Jalisco state condo legislation doesn't require any titled "officer" other than a **President/Chair of the Administrative Council** – and this requirement is only to sign the quarterly statement of accounts (**Article 1029**).

You can create any other positions or titles that you feel you need. However, apart from satisfying egos, these aren't necessary.

Whatever structure you decide on should be defined in your condo's by-laws, along with the number of councillors.

Council President/Chair and Vice-President

The condo legislation mentions only a *"presidente del consejo de administración"* (Chair/President of the Administrative Council – in Spanish, *presidente* often means **chairperson**), and only for one single purpose.

There are no legal requirements for the President/Chair of the Council other than the signing of official financial statements (**Article 1029**), and this responsibility **cannot** be delegated to someone else, no matter what title they're given. This only applies to the individual elected at the assembly and named in the minutes.

Other than this one signing requirement, the Chair/President of your Council has no special powers or authority beyond those of any other councillor.

It's also important to understand that there is only a President/Chair **of the Council**, and there is no such thing as a "**Condo President.**"

That said, you can choose to give the President/Chair of your Council special responsibilities, as long as you don't give them any of the duties or responsibilities that are legislated as belonging to the Administrator, or that contradict the condo legislation or your by-laws.

The most common special responsibilities given to a Council President/Chair are:

- chairing the council meetings;
- dealing with communications to/from owners; and
- the ability to represent your condominium before third-parties for administrative and legal purposes.

These last powers of representation are already given to the Administrator by law, but not to the President/Chair of the Council. These powers can **only** be given to the President/Chair of the Council by an assembly. This is usually the ordinary assembly where your Council is elected. To be binding, this granting of powers must be recorded in the publicly registered minutes of the assembly (it is a power of attorney).

A **Vice-President** is, in my opinion, unnecessary. Most of the duties of the Chair/President can be done by any councillor, and the powers of representation are nontransferable. They're assigned to an individual by name (not the position), and they don't pass to another councillor or a successor if the person elected leaves the office part way through the term or is absent.

Why You Should Not Have a 'Treasurer'

It's tempting to have a **Treasurer**, since this is a mandatory position in organisations north of the border. However, this position **is not used in a Mexican condo.**

All the functions normally associated with the office of Treasurer are already being done by the Administrator. The condo law requires the Administrator to be a Treasurer and much more.

It's important that the name and position of "Administrator" be kept, since it has **a specific legal meaning and certain legal powers and obligations**.

Therefore, don't call the "Administrator" a "Treasurer" (or anything else) since this is the incorrect term – the specific position of "Administrator" is a necessary and important legal requirement for a condo administration, and is well-defined in the condo legislation.

Further, while one or more **duties** of the Administrator can be delegated to another person (such as an Assistant Administrator or, if you must, Treasurer), the **responsibilities** under the law cannot. You also can't legally eliminate the position of Administrator.

The Administrator Cannot Be on the Council

It's also important to realise that the Administrator can't be a member of the Council. For more information on this, **see Part 4 – "The Condo Administrator."**

Council Secretary

A **Council Secretary** (sometimes called a Recording Secretary) is an important function, since council meetings **must** be minuted by law, and these minutes form part of your official condo records. This position can be filled by either a councillor or by a volunteer who isn't on the Council.

Often this person is also given the task of managing communications to/from owners (rather than having the President/Chair of the Council do this).

Recommended Council Makeup

A Council can function perfectly well with only a President/Chair and a certain number of councillors. Therefore, I recommend that a Council consist of a President/Chair and at least two untitled councillors.

A common misconception is that it's necessary to have an odd number on the Council to avoid tie votes. **This is not true**.

There can never be an impasse, since a tied vote is no different from a failed vote – the motion doesn't pass. **Robert's Rules §44** says, *"On a tie vote, a motion requiring a majority vote for adoption is lost, since a tie is not a majority."*

In addition, not all council meetings will be attended by all councillors. Regardless of the number of councillors on the Council, you can easily have an odd number at any given meeting.

I also recommend that a **Council Secretary** be appointed to take the minutes of council meetings, and do any other clerical or communications duties that your Council sees fit – this person needn't be on your Council.

Don't paint yourself into a corner when defining the number of councillors in your by-laws – especially if you're a small condo (say, less than 50 units).

I recommend that instead of a specific number, that you set an open-ended **range** from a set minimum number (three works well) to a maximum of *"any greater number that the owners decide at an ordinary assembly."* You could also set a specific maximum.

It can often be difficult to convince people to serve on Council. You don't want to eliminate qualified and hard-working people just because you've reached an arbitrary maximum. I recommend that you appoint as many councillors as want to serve, unless this is an impractically large number – in my experience, this just doesn't happen.

You also want to avoid ending up with an illegally made up council just because one councillor leaves, they can't be replaced, and the by-laws set out a specific number that you no longer have. Any decisions made by such a Council have neither validity nor enforceability.

IMPORTANT! If your existing by-laws define a different structure than my recommendations, you must follow whatever structure is outlined in your by-laws until you decide to change them.

Your Council Must Always be Open and Transparent

Chapter 17

As I've mentioned in a previous chapter, the condo law requires your Council to carry out its administration **under observance by the owners (Article 1017 V)**. Each owner has the right to make sure that the Administrative Council is fulfilling its obligations.

It's essential that observance by the owners is both possible and simple – it must become a natural part of all administrative processes in your condo.

A good Council will always bear this in mind, and will always work in as open and transparent a way as possible.

My advice is to always try to have the mind-set of a small municipal government. Always act as if you're spending public money, and that everything you do must be under public scrutiny. The "public" in this case is the condo owners.

> Nothing encourages rumours and resentment more than the impression that Council meetings are being held secretly, behind closed doors.
>
> **This practice can give owners the feeling that your Council has something to hide.**
>
> This may not be intentional on your Council's part, but consider the following:
>
> if owners don't know when and where the meetings are held, they're being held secretly;
>
> if no one other than the Council is invited to attend, then they're closed-door meetings.

The good news is that I have several recommendations based on experience that you can use to create an open and transparent administrative process. They're all simple, and they can nip many potential problems in the bud.

Let Owners Know About Council and Committee Meetings

Send out a notice to all owners several days before each council or committee meeting (email and your condo web site are the simplest ways). Let them know the time and place of the meeting, and invite them to come if they have issues to bring up (or if they're just interested in what goes on).

Meetings are far more effective if an Agenda is prepared beforehand. So do this, and attach it to this email and post it on your web site.

Sample council meeting notices and agendas are included in your BONUS Pack.

Even if you find that few owners take advantage of your invitation, it lets the community know that you're conducting the business of your condominium in the open. The owners that do take advantage of your offer will be happy to be included, and will have greater respect for their administration and its processes.

Never Hold Closed Meetings

All council and committee meetings must be held openly, and the owners must be allowed and encouraged to be there.

The only business that can properly be conducted at these meetings is condominium business. **There are no issues involving the running of your condominium that can be legally kept from the owners.**

I can think of no topic that a condo administration or committee can be discussing that can't be talked about openly in front of the owners.

While the owners have a right to be there and observe council and committee meetings, they don't have a vote, nor can they object to the decisions being made. That said, they can be invited to contribute their input (and this is often a good idea).

For more information on in-camera meetings and executive sessions, **see Chapter 23 – "Council Meetings."**

Carry Out an Open Bidding Process

You should have a policy saying that major capital projects need three quotes based on a written scope of work. This scope of work makes sure that all your contractors are bidding on the same basis, and that their quotes can be compared.

I've heard people say that it's impossible to get written quotes – especially from small contractors. **Nonsense!** Just get them to put their price on the Scope of Work, date it, and sign it.

A sample Scope of Work is included in your BONUS Pack.

If two or three competing quotes are solicited from contractors for major repair or improvement projects (and they certainly should be), send out a summary to all owners containing, at a minimum:

- a summary scope of work on which all bids were based,
- the quotes received and the amount of each bid,
- the chosen bid, and
- the reasons for choosing the winning bid (especially if it isn't the lowest quote).

An open process removes any impression that contracts are being awarded to favoured contractors or friends, or that the owner's money is being spent without proper due diligence.

Communicate, Communicate, Communicate

One of the biggest causes of resentment towards a condo administration amongst owners is the feeling that nothing seems to be happening, or they've no idea what's supposed to be happening, or they just feel "out of the loop."

Many Mexican condos have snow-bird owners who aren't there for many months at a time, and can't see what's happening on a day-to-day basis – they want to (and need to) be told about what's going on.

As a member of the administration, it's easy to get caught up in the details of an ongoing issue, and forget that the owners don't know everything you do.

A good Council will always do their best to keep the owners informed as to what the administration is doing, and what's happening in your condo.

This process should be automatic, without the owners having to ask for the information or contact your Council.

For example, if your condo is carrying out an improvement project, the owners should be informed and updated throughout. Here is an example of the types of owner communications that should be sent out during a typical improvement project:

- when the contract is awarded, tell the owners along with an expected start date and finish date;
- if (when) these dates slip, tell them the new dates;
- when the contractor starts work, tell them this along with any changes in the schedule;

- as the work progresses, keep the owners informed of important milestones; particularly if there are pauses in the work for any reason (such as parts on order taking longer than expected) or if the work is just taking longer than expected;
- if the work restricts access to portions of your condo, tell the owners; if other arrangements have been made (parking, for example), tell them beforehand;
- when the work is finished, tell the owners; and
- if there are any special usage instructions or operating procedures for the new item (such as how to use a new entry access system) have them ready to be sent out at this time; conduct training sessions, if necessary.

Do You Need to Provide Condo Documents in Spanish?

This depends on the makeup of your ownership.

> If your condo is made up entirely of non-Spanish speaking owners, then you don't (until this changes).

> If you have at least one Mexican owner, then you need to poll all your Mexican owners to see what they want. If one single Mexican owner wants documents in Spanish, then these must be provided.

There's nothing in the condo legislation about this because it's a much more fundamental right that applies to more than just condominiums. The language of the country and the law is Spanish. Just as you'd expect a condo in France to conduct its business in French, a condo in Germany to conduct its business in German, or a condo in the US to conduct its business in English, you shouldn't be surprised that there's a fundamental right in México to have condo and legal documents produced in Spanish.

In fact, no document can be publicly registered or be binding on third parties in México if it's written in anything but Spanish.

Therefore, to avoid problems in the future, even if your community is non-Spanish speaking, the following must always be in Spanish (you can give English translations as a courtesy to foreign owners):

- the call notice for a condo assembly;
- the minutes of an assembly that are to be publicly registered;
- your condo's by-laws; and
- any legal notices.

I strongly advise you to send out the following in a bilingual format (with Spanish first), even if your Mexican owners have said that they don't need Spanish documents:

- detailed budgets and reporting spreadsheets;
- owner statements of account;
- requests for payment of fees, including collection letters; and
- any other important financial information.

The reason is that a Mexican owner who's overdue in their fees can claim that they weren't properly notified of the debt, or that they couldn't understand the request for payment.

For the rest of your condo documents, it's OK to give out English versions, and even to author them in English, but you must always give a quality Spanish translation to any owner who wants one.

Your Council Must Always be Open and Transparent 117

This could go beyond documents. Depending on the makeup of your condo, you may also be required to either conduct assemblies and meetings in Spanish, or to have simultaneous translation. If this is a reasonable request made by one or more Spanish-speaking owners, then it must not be ignored.

PART 6 – Committees

Types of Committees

Chapter 18

Committees aren't specifically defined or regulated by the state condo legislation. In general, condos will have two types of committees.

Standing Committees

Comités permanentes (standing committees) are committees that you need on a year-to-year basis. They're intended to assist your Administrative Council and Administrator with ongoing tasks.

Your condo's by-laws must define the structure and mandate of all standing committees (**Article 1006 XI**).

Examples of standing committees include: Construction Committee, By-Laws & Regulations Committee, Welcome Committee, and Social Committee.

These committees are allowed to have their own budgets (**Code Article 1006 XI**) when needed – these budgets must be approved by the owners at the Annual Ordinary Assembly, and must be included in the general condo budget.

While every part of a condo administration is responsible to the owners, standing committees are directly responsible to, and report to, your Council or Administrator (depending on the committee's mandate) unless your condo's by-laws say something different.

Standing committees must act in an advisory capacity only. They have no authority to change condo policies or rules directly. Typically, they collect information, investigate issues, and send reports and recommendations to your Council or your Administrator for further action (or not).

In a well-run condo, the Council will rely heavily on the various standing committees.

It's important that your Council not interfere with the committees, and equally important that it not ignore their recommendations or findings without a solid reason that's clearly documented in the Council minutes.

The condo law doesn't specifically require any standing committees, and they're entirely optional. There's also no legal requirement for these standing committees to be elected – the Council is allowed to appoint them.

Special Committees

Comités especiales (special committees) are committees that are set up to carry out a specific task, and generally have a limited life span – typically until the task is finished, or when a specific time-period has elapsed (such as the current fiscal year, six months, or the next board meeting). These are sometimes referred to in English as *"ad hoc committees."*

One example might be a special committee that's been created to administer a particularly large improvement project (**Code Article 1009**). This committee could: define the scope of work, receive quotes and send them to the administration along with recommendations, supervise the contractor, accept and sign-off on the work, and produce any documents that are needed.

These committees are often assisted by your Administrator (**Code Article 1012**).

If there's no language in your by-laws about the appointment of a special committee, then special committees can **only** be created by the owners at an ordinary assembly (**Code Article 1020**). Their mandate and structure will be decided at this meeting, and must be clearly outlined in the minutes of the meeting.

A separate budget can also be approved for one of these special committees. This can only be done if the committee is elected at the Annual Ordinary Meeting, and this committee budget must form part of the general condo budget also approved at this meeting.

If the ordinary assembly where the special committee was elected wasn't the Annual Ordinary Assembly, and if a separate committee budget is needed that involves funds over and above those contained in the approved general budget, then special fees to fund the committee will also have to be voted on.

Special committees elected at an ordinary assembly are by default directly responsible to the owners, and it's your Administrator's duty to directly or indirectly assist these committees (**Code Article 1012**). When their task is finished, they must send a report directly to the owners.

If a special committee is elected to assist or report to the Council, then this fact needs to be clearly spelled out in its mandate in the minutes of the ordinary assembly where the committee was elected.

When the owners approve improvement works at an extraordinary assembly, they can optionally elect a special committee to supervise these works (this is the only special committee that's allowed to be elected at other than an ordinary assembly). If an optional committee isn't set up, then your Administrator must supervise the improvement work.

The condo legislation in the Civil Code doesn't specifically call for any special committees, and they're entirely optional.

For greater administrative flexibility, I strongly recommend that specific language be added to your condo's by-laws to allow special committees to also be appointed by the Council as needed during the year. For example, to deal with an unexpected issue that comes up between Annual Ordinary Assemblies.

Your by-laws must explicitly give the Council this ability, and they should outline in general how this is done. It's costly to hold another Ordinary Meeting at another time in the year, and this should be avoided if possible.

Why Do You Need Committees?

Chapter 19

A committee is a group of unpaid volunteer owners that's been set up to assist the Administrative Council or Administrator with a specific aspect of your condo administration.

Typical Committee Makeup

Committees consist of a Chair plus zero or more members (yes, it's possible to have a committee of one). For tasks that do need more than one person, I recommend at least three committee members.

A Bridge Between the Owners and the Administration

Committees are an important link in keeping an open relationship with the owners.

They should receive and coordinate input and recommendations from owners that affect their area of work. In addition, they should be proactive by holding public meetings to actively seek input.

They should record summaries of this owner input, along with the results of meetings with owners. This should be in the form of a written report sent to both your Administrative Council and your Administrator.

More Advantages of Committees

Another advantage of committees is that they can give owners who don't have the time, wish, or skills to serve on the Council, an opportunity to be involved in the administration of your condo in another meaningful way.

Being a member of a committee can enhance an owner's pride-of-ownership and sense of community – this owner now has a feeling of being involved in the condominium.

This is important because a sense of community involvement can contribute to a successful condo. Depending on the task, it might also be an excellent way to allow part-timers (such as snow-birds) to take part.

A solid committee structure also lets people other than your Council do some of the work! Being on a council should definitely not be about doing everything yourself. A good council is skilled at delegation, and uses committees to get other owners involved in the administration of your condo.

Committees and the Administration

All committees must hold periodic committee meetings, and accurately record a summary of discussions, along with any decisions reached, in meeting minutes. They must attach all relevant documents to these minutes, and send them out as required by your condo by-laws.

Active committees should meet on a set schedule (such as twice a month, once a month, or every two months). Inactive committees can meet whenever they need to do work, but should meet regardless at least twice a year.

Committee Chairs must communicate with your Administrator as required by the committee's task. For example, the Maintenance Committee will be in more or less constant contact, while the Event Committee may have little to do with your Administrator.

The committee Chair must also go to council meetings and give a report on the status of the committee's work, along with any recommendations developed by the committee.

A copy of this report must be attached to the council meeting minutes.

Depending on the committees task, some committee Chairs should be at each council meeting, while others can go only when there is something to report.

Councillors Shouldn't Be on Committees

While not a requirement of the condo law, it's good practice to add a policy to your by-laws that stops Councillors from serving on Committees.

One of the main needs for committees is to lessen your Council's burden. This doesn't happen if your Councillors are also on these committees.

This also eliminates any perception of undue Council influence on the committees. Committees should always have an arms-length relationship with the Council.

If your condo is small, however, this just may not be practical because of a shortage of volunteers.

Common Committees

Chapter 20

I believe that each of the following committees serves an important purpose, and I encourage you to consider each one. However, you have to look at each of these in the context of the needs of your condo. In particular, consider the size of your condo. Small condos of less than 50 units likely don't have the people-power to support all these committees.

Maintenance Committee (or Manager)

Your Administrator's duties involve arranging for maintenance and repairs, and supervision of improvement work. This is a huge task. To assist your Administrator in this work, I highly recommend that you create either a Maintenance Committee or, in the case of a small condo, a Maintenance Manager (really a one-person Maintenance Committee).

If your Administrator is an owner-volunteer, then this individual has a full plate, and will certainly need the help.

If your Administrator is a management company, then this committee will provide an important liaison between the community and the management company, bringing better oversight of your Administrator than your Council alone can give.

Here are some recommended duties and responsibilities for the Maintenance Committee (not all may apply to your condo):

- work closely with the Administrator to coordinate routine repairs and maintenance of the common property; help develop a maintenance schedule for items such as elevators;
- research and recommend the best choices for repair and maintenance work to the Administrator, including getting quotes (following accepted condo bid standards and policies);

- coordinate emergency repairs with the Administrator, and make sure that they're dealt with in a timely fashion as required by law;

- assist the Council and Administrator with planning by making recommendations for future improvement work to be voted on by the owners at the next extraordinary assembly; include estimated costs and time-lines;

- meet with and involve the Construction Committee to coordinate the aesthetics and structure of any new construction, or changes to the existing construction;

- assist in the development of the yearly landscape maintenance contract; create and maintain a master landscape plan; make recommendations to the Council about new plantings, the health of existing shrubs and trees, and plan for maintenance and improvements;

- periodically look at the activities of the landscape contractor, and recommend suitable changes in the yearly landscape contract; report any problems with this contractor to the Administrator;

- look at signage, and recommend changes to condo signs (such as signs that: give directions to unit numbers; show the speed limit; or identify your condo); and

- look into pool, rec centre, gym, and meeting facilities operations to make sure that these are in good order, and that maintenance is done as needed; coordinate a schedule for pool maintenance; report any problems or observations to the Administrator.

Construction Committee

The condo law requires that your Council approve requests from owners to make changes to their private units (**Code Article 1010**).

Therefore, you should produce a set of "**Rules of Construction**" for your condominium. These must clearly outline all the restrictions in your condo. They must be given to new owners, and posted on your condo's web site.

By doing this, all owners know what is and what is not acceptable when they plan a renovation project, and it makes the process of applying for permission to do renovations go more smoothly.

The Construction Committee should update these Rules of Construction as needed, and deal with renovation/construction applications from homeowners – removing this burden from your Council.

An added benefit is that since this committee approves owner requests rather than the Council, your Council can act as an appeal body in the case of a rejected application.

A sample set of Construction Committee forms and instructions is included in your BONUS Pack.

Here are some recommended duties and responsibilities for the Construction Committee:

- assure uniformity in the architectural standards of the community by consistently applying the Rules of Construction;
- develop and carry out guidelines, and keep records of architectural recommendations to the Council; and

- recommend periodic changes to the Rules of Construction; coordinate this work with the Rules & By-Laws Committee to make sure that there's no contravention of the other condo rules, and that the formatting and language integrate with the other rules.

Rules and By-laws Committee

The best-planned regulations may not take into account all eventualities, and can turn out to be cumbersome once put into practice. Effective condo rules, policies, and by-laws need to be dynamic, and must accommodate changes in your condo, the outside community, the culture, and the laws. The most effective way of keeping on top of all this is through a Rules & By-Laws Committee.

This committee may need its own separate budget for legal opinions and translation costs. These amounts could also be included in the general budget as a line-item.

Here are some recommended duties and responsibilities for the Rules and By-laws Committee:

- recommend changes to condo rules, policies, and by-laws; report these periodically to the Council for their input; it's vital that owners be invited to attend all meetings of this committee;

- before the next extraordinary assembly, prepare a document detailing any proposed changes, and send this to the owners for their comments; based on an evaluation and consideration of owner feedback, including meetings with owners, send out the final document to the Council to be approved at least one week before the assembly;

- for significant by-law changes, community work groups (led by the committee) are a good way to both seek owner input and make sure you have community involvement; and

- recommend sanctions for violations of rules, policies, and by-laws.

Security Committee

It's important that owners feel secure and safe in your condo. To this end, a Security Committee should be appointed to design, carry out, and look into security systems and policies.

Here are some recommended duties and responsibilities for the Security Committee:

- design and recommend systems, procedures, and policies to protect your condominium property, and to lessen crime or injury on the property; develop a security program for a visible security presence in the community to help decrease burglary or vandalism;

- make recommendations to the Council for ongoing security improvements;

- monitor the performance of the security guards, and report any problems to both the Administrator and the Council;

- meet with and involve both the Maintenance Committee and the Construction Committee whenever security systems require changes to the common property;

- design and coordinate a condominium-wide Block Watch program; and

- coordinate with the local police and any condo or community security associations in the area.

Financial Audit Committee

Your Administrative Council is responsible for looking into your Administrator's handling of your condo's finances. This is an important task, and it might be more effective to off-load most of this work to a Financial Audit Committee.

Here are some recommended duties and responsibilities for the Financial Audit Committee:

- aid the Council in their supervision of the Administrator by making sure that your condominium's financial transactions are handled in a timely and accurate way, that proper receipts are being issued/collected, that the records are legal, and that all financial transactions are consistent with generally-accepted accounting principles;

- work with the Administrator to develop your condo's operating budget for approval by the Council, and for voting on by the owners at the next Annual Ordinary Assembly; during the year, look at the Administrator's budget reports and make recommendations to the Council and the Administrator, as needed;

- develop a schedule for reserve fund spending, and monitor the reserve fund; report any problems to the Administrator; and

- assist in any periodic audits.

Communications Committee

I cannot stress enough the importance of communicating what's happening in your condo to all owners. It's important that everyone feels included and "in-the-loop." This can be a strain on your Council, who already have a heavy workload. An effective way of managing this is through a Communications Committee.

This committee may need its own separate budget for printing costs – these amounts could also be included in the general budget as a line-item. With more and more documents being sent out by email and posted on your condo's web site, these expenditures become less and less.

Here are some recommended duties and responsibilities for the Communications Committee:

- coordinate and send out condo information to owners; send council and committee minutes, financial reports, condo notices, and newsletters to all owners in a timely fashion; coordinate with the Welcoming Committee to make sure that their Welcome Pack is up-to-date;

- coordinate the development of your condo newsletter, community flyers and notices, a condo web site, your condo contact list, and other general condo publications;

- update your condo contact list; contact new owners and tenants shortly after they move in to get their contact info; pass this information on to the Welcoming Committee to trigger a visit from them; and

- keep your condo web site up-to-date; recommend and suggest improvements and links to Council for approval before carrying them out.

Welcoming Committee

It's easy for a busy Council to ignore new residents. Unfortunately, this creates a rather negative first impression. An effective way of making sure that new residents are made to feel welcome, and are brought up to speed on condo rules, policies and procedures is with a Welcoming Committee.

It's difficult for newcomers to follow rules and regulations when they've no idea they exist. Remember, this information doesn't pass to them either telepathically or by osmoses.

This committee may need its own separate budget for printing costs – these amounts could also be included in the general budget as a line-item.

Here are some recommended duties and responsibilities for the Welcoming Committee:

- personally welcome each new owner or tenant to your condominium within a few days of them moving into the community; and

- coordinate the development of a welcome pack; this pack should include: a welcome letter, owner's guide, by-laws, condo procedures, budget and fees, contact sheet, minutes and reports, newsletters, and web site login instructions.

    For more details on the welcome pack, **see Chapter 55 – "Tips for Effective Communications."**

Events Committee

One of the many benefits of living in a condo is the social interaction. This leads to a general feeling of security, fellowship, and community. Events such as parties, BBQs, potluck dinners, and other get-togethers are a great way to promote greater owner-involvement in your condo.

An Events Committee is a simple way to involve people to do the party planning and to keep up the momentum by not stalling after the first event.

This committee may need its own separate budget for events – these amounts could also be included in the general budget as a line-item. Some condos don't like spending money on events. If this is the case, you can have everyone who takes part contribute food, drink, entertainment, and even a cash cover charge.

Here are some recommended duties and responsibilities for the Events Committee:

- plan and coordinate condo-wide activities such as: an annual pool party or BBQ, a Mardi Gras Party, a Christmas carolling party, or occasional pot-luck dinners and street parties; and

- coordinate with the Communications Committee to promote these events to all owners.

Nominating Committee

This is a special committee that's created before an ordinary assembly to create a list of nominees for the Council and any Special Committees to be created by the assembly.

Using an open and public process they find one nominee for each position, to be elected by acclamation at the ordinary assembly.

The Nominating Committee is disbanded right after the assembly.

For more information, **see Chapter 39 – "Recommended Election Procedures."**

Special Committees

Special committees are only created when there's a specific issue to investigate, or a specific task to be done. It's impossible to list all the reasons why one of these committees might be needed.

Recommended Practices for Committees

Chapter 21

This chapter contains some of my recommended practices for condo committees.

Set Out a Clear Mandate

Effective committees must have a structure, guidance, and a defined purpose. This can only happen when they have a clear mandate. This mandate should be created **before** the committee starts its work, and should include:

- the committee's purpose, goals, and responsibilities – stated as clearly and explicitly as possible; include limitations on the committee's scope and responsibilities; this could be in the form of a Mission Statement;

- its structure, methods for election, and term; except for special committees, the term is Annual Ordinary Assembly to Annual Ordinary Assembly;

- succession policies to replace members who leave the committee;

- reporting and communication methods;

- record keeping practices and requirements;

- in the case of a special committee, instructions for dealing with the eventuality of the committee not completing its work in its given time-frame; for example, a time extension, or the allotted time is up with no result yet;

- quorum and voting procedures;

- bid procedures (if part of the committee's work is to get quotes for work); and

- the committee's discretionary budget (if applicable, and approved by the owners).

For a standing committee, the committee's purpose, goals, and responsibilities must also be clearly expressed in your condo's by-laws.

For a special committee, this mandate and a budget (if needed) should be prepared before the assembly where the owners will elect the committee, should be given to the owners beforehand, must be referenced in the motion to be voted on, and must be attached to the minutes of the assembly.

A special committee's life is usually either the time it takes to finish a specific task (goal oriented) or a specific period of time (deadline). In either case, a special committee should last no longer than one year.

"Seems like a lot of effort ... why bother? Is this really necessary?"

Absolutely!

Without a clear mandate, committees tend to work like rudderless ships – not accomplishing much.

Without a clear mandate, it's easy for a committee to overstep its authority, only do a portion of what was expected, go off on a tangent, or not tell the Council (or anyone else) their progress.

Without communications guidelines, there may be poor communication amongst the committee members, and between the committee and your Council.

Without clear record keeping guidelines, there may be no proper or legal records of meetings – owners have the right to view council and committee minutes, and all condominium business and decisions must be recorded.

Without clear guidelines, meetings may be held without a proper quorum, or a vote may be conducted illegally – in either case, the decision or the entire meeting will have no legal validity if challenged.

Without standardised bidding guidelines, incorrect bid procedures could result in quotes that can't be properly compared because they're not all based on the same scope of work. Improper procedures might also be questioned after the fact. When dealing with "public" money, great care and due diligence must be exercised, and an open and transparent procedure must be followed.

Note that in the case of standing committees (or a special committee created by the Council, or reporting to the Council), it's your Council's responsibility to make sure that each committee follows procedures, keeps proper records, and conducts due diligence. Therefore, it's in your Council's interest to make sure that each committee has a clear understanding of its purpose, operating procedures, and general instructions. A standing committee's failure is also the Council's failure.

Special (Ad-hoc) Committee Creation

The condo law says that if special committees are to be elected by the owners, then this must be done at an ordinary assembly. It doesn't, however, say that this is the only way special committees can be created.

As I've said before, I recommend that you add a provision to your condo by-laws for your Council to appoint special committees between Annual Ordinary Meetings when there's an important reason.

This provision could read something like this:

> *"When deemed necessary by the Administrative Council, and when circumstances do not allow the issue to wait until after the next ordinary assembly, the Council may create one or more special committees to deal with a specific task.*
>
> *Such a committee is to consist of a Chair and at least two members, each of which is to be a volunteer owner not currently serving on the Council.*
>
> *The reason for creating the special committee, along with the committee's mandate and instructions, must be clearly documented and attached to the minutes of the council meeting where the committee was created."*

Committee Chairs

The Committee Chair is the liaison between the committee and your Council, and should go to council meetings to report to the Council whenever the committee has met or finished something.

The chair should also prepare the committee meeting agendas, chair the committee meetings, and make sure that committee meetings follow the agenda, stay on topic, and are conducted in an orderly way.

The Chair must make sure that committee meeting minutes are sent out to the community in a timely fashion after the meeting.

Quorum and Voting

For a committee meeting to be held, there must be a quorum of committee members.

Normally, this is considered "**a majority of the members.**" A majority always means "more than half."

Therefore, if a committee has three members, the quorum is two; if a committee has four members, the quorum is three; if a committee has five members, the quorum is also three; if a committee has six members, the quorum is four – and so on.

Unless there's an important reason to do something else, I recommend sticking with the standard definition of quorum.

When committee members vote on a resolution, the accepted practice is for the decision to carry if it receives a majority vote from the members present (assuming there's a quorum). It's also generally accepted that a tied vote doesn't pass.

Meeting Minutes and Committee Reports

An accurate record of all condominium business must be kept, and be readily available to any owner.

Any committee meeting where significant discussion or debate took place, where reports were read and debated, where owners made submissions, where contractors or bidders were interviewed, or where decisions that impact the operation of your condo were made **must** be minuted.

Good minutes don't only record decisions, but will also summarise discussions.

Recording decisions without a summary of the discussion that led up to them is all that's legally required. In my opinion, however, this is a bad practice. This makes it impossible for absentee members, owners, the Council, and future committees to understand the reasoning and history behind decisions.

Any reports or documents that were presented at the meeting must be attached to the meeting minutes.

For more details on minutes, **see Part 13 – "Minutes of Assemblies & Meetings."**

From time to time, a committee must send a progress report to your Administrative Council, your Administrator, or the owners. In the case of a special committee, a final report and recommendation on the issue for which they were created must be sent to the owners.

These reports should always be in writing. If a report outlines several choices (such as a number of different security systems), then the pros and cons of each choice (including cost and time-line) must be listed.

Any documents received by the committee that are related to the report, should be attached to the report as appendices.

Generally most committee reports, except status reports, must also contain concrete recommendations, along with the reasons behind them. The main purpose of any committee is to make recommendations.

Ex Officio Members

An **ex officio member** of a committee is someone who isn't a member of the committee, but has the same rights as a member. For example, this could apply to the Chair/President or all or some councillors.

According to **Robert's Rules** §50, an ex officio member of a committee has all the rights of a member for participation and voting, but doesn't count towards quorum.

If you want to create ex officio members of specific standing committees (or for all committees in general), you must spell this out in your by-laws.

If you want to change the rights of an ex officio member (for example, they can't vote), then this must also be spelled out in your by-laws. If you don't do this, then the standard definition applies.

PART 7 – Overview of Condo Meetings

The Condo Assembly

Chapter 22

An *assemblea* (assembly) is a temporary gathering of a condo's owners, when they're called together to make decisions affecting the administration of a condo.

While the section of the Jalisco condo law titled *"CAPITULO IV – De Las Assembleas"* ("CHAPTER IV – Assemblies") consisting of **Civil Code Articles 1019 through 1025** directly regulates assemblies, the following Code Articles also impact assemblies: **1009, 1010a, 1011, 1012, 1013a, 1016 – 1018, 1026, 1032,** and **1034**.

The Ultimate Authority in a Condo

Code Article 1019 says that the assembly of owners is the supreme administrative body of a condominium.

Terminology: 'Assembly' vs. 'Meeting'

I know what you're thinking, *"Geeez, here we go again … is it just me, or is this guy a stickler for terminology or what?"* Well, yeah … when it's important.

The correct term for a gathering of condo owners (when the purpose is to make condo decisions) is *"assembly"* and not *"meeting."* The distinction is subtle, but important.

An assembly isn't just a type of meeting – it is much more. When condo owners come together to make decisions affecting a condominium, they form an administrative body that's **a legal entity with specific legal powers** – a body in the same sense that the Council is an administrative body.

This particular administrative body is defined in, and referred to, by the condo legislation as an *"assembly,"* and it's advisable to use the same term in all your condo documents.

Therefore, while an assembly does meet (just as the Council meets), the assembly is the group that's meeting, rather than the meeting itself.

Condo owners can "meet" for many other purposes that don't have the legal powers of an "assembly." OK ... I'll step down off my soap box ... at least for now.

Types of Assemblies

Assemblies for compound and simple condominiums can be either an *asamblea ordinaria* (ordinary assembly) or an *asamblea extraordinaria* (extraordinary assembly).

The ordinary assembly can only deal with a limited number of topics, and the extraordinary assembly must be used for all others.

> This is important, since there's a significant difference in the advance notice needed, the quorum rules, and the votes needed to pass a resolution for these two very different types of assemblies.
>
> For more detailed information, **see Part 8 – "Condo Assemblies."**

A sample *"Owner's Guide to Condo Assemblies"* intended for distribution to your owners (or posting on your condo web site) is included in your BONUS Pack.

The Call Notice for the Assembly

While **Article 1012** says that it's the duty of your Administrator to call an assembly of owners, **Article 1022** adds that an assembly can also be called by any one of the following:

- the Administrator;
- the Administrative Council;

- a Judge of First Instance of the civil branch having jurisdiction in the municipality where the condominium is located; this must be requested, and this request can only be made by:

  1. a group of owners who hold at least 20% of the common property ownership rights – this could be quite different from 20% of the owners; or

  2. any one owner, when an assembly hasn't been held for over one year;

- in the case of Municipal Services Condominiums, by the mayor of the municipality where the condominium is located.

Assemblies must always take place in the municipality where your condominium is located, and in a place that allows the greatest comfort and ease of access for the owners – preferably in your condominium itself.

The call notice must be posted in a visible place in your condominium on the date of its issuance, and must be signed by the person making the call. Since this is a legal notice, **the meeting call must be in Spanish**. It's perfectly acceptable to also post an English translation, but an English-only call isn't legal.

While not required by the Code, I highly recommend that you also send a copy of the call notice to all owners (email is most convenient, although I recommend that your by-laws expressly allow this).

The call notice must show, at a minimum:

- the date and time of the assembly,
- the type of assembly (ordinary or extraordinary),
- the place where the assembly will be held, and

- the Order of the Day listing the items to be approved by the owners at the assembly.

When an assembly is called by either your Administrator or your Council, and despite what you may be told, **no publication of the notice is required by the condo law**. That said, this might be a requirement of your condo's by-laws.

Here are some other items that I recommend you consider including with your call notice:

- a brief overview of the rules of order being used at the assembly;
- a proxy form (if used), along with clear proxy instructions;
- voting instructions (if you're holding elections, and if an election procedure has been adopted) along with a void sample ballot (if you're using ballots);
- if an ordinary assembly:
  - the name of the Administrator to be appointed;
  - copy of any predetermined nominations for councillors or committees; and
  - a copy of the annual budget and fees to be approved at the assembly;
- if an extraordinary assembly, documents explaining the issues to be voted on at the assembly (such as a description of improvements and assessments, or proposed changes to your by-laws); and
- a copy of any reports to be presented (if available).

Sample Call Notices for both types of assemblies are included in your BONUS Pack, along with WORD templates.

Advance Notice

The call for an assembly must be made a minimum number of days before the date of the assembly. This advance notice period varies depending on the type of assembly.

If any owner asks for it, they must be notified by registered mail (a courier can also be used) sent to the address registered by the owner with your condo administration. This notice must be sent early enough to give the owner the same minimum advance notice **starting from the date of receipt of the notice**. Therefore, you have to take delivery time into account. Delivery receipts must be kept as proof of this advance warning, and must form part of the records for the assembly.

The exception to this mailed notification requirement is when a judicial or municipal authority issues the call for an assembly. Then, the call only needs to be published with the same advance notice in one public newspaper of reasonable circulation in the state, as well as in "*El Estado de Jalisco*" – the official government newspaper (**Article 1025**). However, a notice of the call must still be posted in a visible place in your condominium.

Terminology: 'Order of the Day' vs. 'Agenda'

While I'm sure that you're getting sick of my terminology pickiness, I can assure you that there's a good reason to call the list of topics to be discussed at an assembly an *"Order of the Day,"* rather than an *"Agenda."*

> **An agenda** isn't binding on the participants of a meeting until it's adopted at the meeting.

An Order of the Day is a list of pre-scheduled items that are considered as **orders**. For this reason, it's most commonly called the *"Orders of the Day."*

Orders are binding on the assembly, the Order of the Day predetermines the business to be discussed by the assembly, and **cannot be modified at the assembly**.

Unlike an Agenda, the Order of the Day is **never adopted by the assembly** – it already exists as a fact before the assembly, and is the reason for calling the assembly.

The condo law requires that the Order of the Day for an assembly be set before the assembly, and that it must form part of the call notice that must be issued several days before the assembly.

I've adopted the slightly nonstandard usage of *"Order of the Day"* in my book because the condo legislation uses the term *orden del día* (order of the day – singular). If you choose to use the more standard *"Orders of the Day"* I'm sure that you won't be struck by lightning, but please **do not** use *"Agenda."*

The Order of the Day Must Be Followed

Normally an assembly can't deal with any matter that isn't listed on the Order of the Day that's been published with the call notice.

There is one exception.

If an issue is raised at an assembly that is not on the Order of the Day, a vote on the issue can legally take place if **100% of the condo rights are represented at the assembly**. In my experience, this level of representation is almost impossible to achieve.

The items appearing on the Order of the Day must be carefully considered. It's important to realise that there's a limited list of items that can be legally dealt with by an ordinary assembly. All other issues **must** be dealt with by an extraordinary assembly. The reasons come from the significant difference in voting at these two types of assemblies.

As well, once the call notice has been issued, the Order of the Day is "set in stone," and can't be changed unless a new call notice is issued – triggering a new advance notice period.

> Changing the Order of the Day, say, three days after the call notice was issued, needs a new call notice to be issued, and the assembly to be re-scheduled at least three days later than the date contained in the original call notice (assuming that the original call notice used the minimum advance notice – which is common).

Resolutions Passed by an Assembly

All agreements passed by a legal assembly are binding on non-owner occupants (such as renters) and all owners, including those owners who:

- were absent from the assembly; or

- disagreed with the decision by voting "NO" on the resolution.

The decisions of the assemblies are also binding on both your Administrator (who is charged with carrying them out) and your Administrative Council (which is charged with monitoring your Administrator's actions).

Voiding the Resolutions of an Assembly for Lack of Notice

Any owner who wasn't at the Assembly, and who believes they weren't legally notified of the assembly, can demand that a court void the agreements passed by the assembly.

This must be done **within 30 calendar days after the date of the assembly**. However, during this time, this owner must not have taken any actions which suggest approval of any of the agreements they're opposing. The exception is if such actions were taken **after** they'd made it known in writing to your Administrator and Council that these specific actions don't suggest approval on their part.

Any favourable judicial decision **will only affect the person who launched the lawsuit**. Therefore, the decisions passed by the assembly would still be binding on all other owners. Although this might seem odd, it's common under Mexican civil law.

Granting of Powers

Although the condo legislation automatically gives your Administrator certain powers of representation, it's good practice to have the assembly where they were appointed formalise them, and have this recorded in the publicly-registered minutes.

This gives your Administrator a *poder* (power of attorney), and, when it's detailed and registered, there's no disputing it. Most importantly, it's binding on all third-parties.

It's also wise to give the same powers to the President/Chair of your Council as an individual, and to your Council as a body.

Here is typical wording for the granting of these powers as it could appear in a set of ordinary assembly minutes (translated into English – the legal, registered minutes **must** be in Spanish):

"The assembly bestowed upon both the Administrative Council and to its President as an individual, as well as to the Administrator, general judicial power for lawsuits and collection of money, for acts of administration, as well as for opening and closing, and making transfers of bank accounts, under the terms set by Article 2554 of the Federal Civil Code, Article 2207 of the Civil Code of the State of Jalisco, and those corresponding to the rest of the States of the Republic, with authorisation to intervene in and to cease every kind of recourse and legal action, including initiating and ceasing writs of relief [an **amparo** suit], *drawing up criminal complaints, and creating them in conjunction with the Public Ministry.*

These representatives will have authorisation to grant and to revoke powers within the bounds of the current mandate."

This granting of powers, once recorded and publicly registered, gives a power of attorney that allows both your Administrator and the President/Chair of your Council to sign contracts on behalf of your condo, deal with your condo bank account, pursue collection of overdue accounts, and represent your condo in a lawsuit.

Reading and Approval of the Minutes at the Assembly

Minutes from the last assembly are **never approved at the current assembly**. Minutes for a given assembly are always approved at the end of that assembly.

After the business of the assembly is concluded, the minutes that were being recorded during the meeting by the Secretary are read and approved on the spot.

This is necessary because the minutes must be publicly registered as soon as possible after the assembly. You can't register unapproved minutes. Therefore, it's impossible to wait until the next assembly to approve the minutes (usually a year away).

Apart from this legal requirement, this practice is also supported by **Robert's Rules §9** that says, *"Minutes of one annual meeting should not be held for action until the next one a year later."*

A Secretary of the Assembly must be appointed at the start of the assembly to record these minutes.

See Part 13 – "Minutes of Assemblies & Meetings" for more information.

Protocolising and Registering the Assembly Minutes

A representative must be authorised by the assembly to protocolise the minutes of the assembly. This means that they must appear before a *notario* (Mexican Civil Law Notary), who will format the minutes into a legal document and register it at the local ***Registro Público de la Propiedad*** (Public Registry of Property).

By law, the minutes of an ordinary assembly **must** be protocolised and registered. I highly recommend that you also do this for the minutes of all extraordinary assemblies, particularly if you've changed your by-laws.

The consequences of **not** protocolising and registering an ordinary assembly are that your Administrator may not have the authority to enter into contracts for your condo, your Council may not be able to legally represent it, and passed resolutions may not be binding on tenants and other non-owner occupants.

If an extraordinary assembly changed your by-laws, then these by-laws can't be legally enforced unless the minutes are registered.

> The term *"protocolise"* was coined by **notarios** in areas where there are a lot of foreign property owners. **There is no such English word**!
>
> It comes from the Spanish verb ***protocolizar*** – often (inaccurately) translated as *"to notarise."*
>
> The problem is that there's no English word for this process. It involves formatting the contents of a document that's to be publicly registered, and then publicly registering it.
>
> This formatting involves adding a preamble about the **notario**, another preamble about the participants in the document, the document itself, and finally adding several appendices about the registration and the legal acts surrounding it.
>
> The final formatted document is then registered with the local ***Registro Público***.
>
> Copies of the document and any original documents pertinent to it, are then put in the **notario's** protocol book.
>
> This **entire process** is what's meant by *"protocolisation."* Since this is a far more accurate description than *"notorise,"* I've adopted its use throughout my book.

This must be done as soon as possible after the assembly. The *notario* will likely need a week or two, and the public registry will need at least this much time (usually longer).

Sample minutes and WORD templates for both types of assemblies are included in your BONUS Pack.

For more information on assembly minutes, **see Chapter 40 – "Condo Assembly Minutes."**

Holding A 'Notario-Friendly' Assembly

The biggest complaints most notarios have about the assembly minutes they receive from condos, are that they:

- don't follow the Order of the Day;

- don't follow the correct sequence;
- contain irrelevant material or motions;
- are missing essential items; and
- weren't approved at the assembly.

All they want to see is a record of the motions, votes, and resolutions corresponding to the Order of the Day.

None of the debate or discussion is relevant to these minutes. None of the secondary motions used to arrive at a final motion are relevant. Including these often results in increased notario costs because of the extra time they need to "clean up" the minutes.

To avoid this, have a pre-designed, notario-friendly template for the assembly minutes, so that the Secretary of the Assembly is just "filling in the blanks." You can do this because the structure of assemblies is so rigidly defined.

The second part of this strategy is a script for the Chair that makes sure that the assembly follows both the Order of the Day and the minutes template.

By using this two-pronged strategy, you can speed up your assemblies, and save money on notario fees.

Sample chairing scripts for both types of assemblies are included in your BONUS Pack.

Chairing an Assembly

Assemblies can be chaired by any person who's been named as the *presidente de la asamblea* (Chair of the Assembly).

This is done by taking a simple majority vote of the attendees.

Unlike votes on resolutions, it's a simple show of hands or a consensus vote, and is independent of the percentage ownership of the common property held by the owners.

The Administrator is often named Chair of the assembly. The second most common chair is the President/Chair of the Council.

That said, anyone can chair the assembly with the approval of the assembly. It isn't even necessary that they be a member of the community.

Some condos use a notario or even an abogado trained in arbitration – especially if they believe that there will be highly contentious issues that might erupt into disputes or arguments.

This is an important job, and the person must be chosen carefully. They must be well versed in the Order of the Day, and understand both condo assembly procedures and the adopted rules of order. This individual is normally picked in advance of the assembly, so they can prepare.

For more information, **see Chapter 32 – "Chairing an Assembly or Council/Committee Meeting."**

Request to Record the Assembly

If an owner asks to record the assembly by audio or video, this is perfectly reasonable and must be allowed. Remember, you have nothing to hide.

However, this must not interfere with the meeting, and you may wish to set up some ground rules such as: equipment must be set up before the assembly starts, and no interruptions (such as changing batteries or media).

Holding an Efficient Assembly

Assemblies don't need to last all day, turn into verbal brawls, or degenerate into chaos. Ideally, an assembly should zip through the Order of the Day like a well-oiled machine. The keys to doing this are:

- Thoroughly air all controversial topics well before the assembly takes place, allowing public input. The idea is that all such issues will have already been debated and decided before the day of the assembly, and you have community support before the vote takes place.

- Plan the assembly meticulously, including using a template for minutes and a script for the Chair.

- The Chair must enforce the rules of order.

- Don't allow discussion of topics that aren't on the Order of the Day. The assembly is being held to carry out a finite list of administrative tasks. **It isn't a public forum for owners to vent their frustrations and complaints** – although this is a common misconception.

  If you need to do this, hold a "town hall meeting." Remember, nothing coming out of such a meeting is binding on the condo in any way. This meeting can only be used to guide the Council and committees, and any significant changes to the by-laws will need to be voted on at an extraordinary assembly.

  For more information on town hall meetings, **see Chapter 25 – "Working and Information Sessions."**

Council Meetings

Chapter
23

Procedures for council meetings aren't dealt with in the condo legislation contained in the Civil Code. That said, I can offer you some practical recommendations in this chapter.

Public Meetings With Advance Notice

Civil Code Article 1017 requires your Council to carry out its administration **under the observance of the owners**. Therefore, council meetings must be conducted publicly, and the owners must be invited.

This doesn't necessarily mean that they need to be held in your condo's meeting facilities. They can be held at a councillor's home – the most important thing is that the community is invited.

While owners must always be allowed to go to council meetings, they're only there to observe, and are not participants. They can (and should) be asked to give their input on certain issues, but they must not speak unless invited, they must behave, and they can't criticise the decisions being made by the Administrative Council.

While there's no specific requirement for advance notice of a council meeting, to comply with the law you must give owners enough notice so that they can plan on being there if they want to – 10 days to two weeks is ideal. Don't forget to explicitly invite them! As a courtesy, you may also want to ask that all owners who'll be at the meeting let the Secretary know, so that copies of meeting materials can be prepared for them.

A meeting agenda should always accompany the notice of a council meeting. For some emergency situations, it's just not possible to give this much notice – for example, quotes have just been received for some emergency repair work, and your Council must meet quickly to choose one and go ahead with the work.

Sample council meeting notices are included in your BONUS Pack.

One suggestion that'll help both councillors and owners prepare for the next meeting is to set a regular schedule for council meetings. For practical reasons, they'll likely be held in the last half of the month – your Administrator needs time to close off the month before, and prepare the financial report. You might, for example, decide to hold regular meetings on *"the 25th of each month,"* or *"the last Friday of each month."*

Although it's a source of frustration for many Councils when turn-out at council meetings is low or nonexistent, the community must always be given the opportunity to be there. Their lack of response isn't a reason to stop inviting them. Apathy on the part of the community is a common problem with condos in general, and isn't unique to México.

A positive way of looking at this is to view it as a measure of your success. People most often turn up at council meetings to complain about something. If you have no one showing up, then you just may be doing your job to everyone's satisfaction.

Minimum Frequency of Meetings

Civil Code Article 1017 requires your Council to meet **at least once a month** to receive your Administrator's monthly financial report.

> ### Watch this!
> Some condos stop council meetings during the "slow" season when snow birds are absent, or during the Christmas season.
>
> **This contravenes the condo legislation.**

Your Council can meet more often if needed. For example, there might be an issue that needs immediate attention, but can't be resolved in one sitting because more information or research are needed.

Don't Hold In Camera Meetings or Executive Sessions

An "in camera" meeting is a closed meeting.

These are most often held to talk about sensitive matters. The intent is to discuss issues that won't be recorded in the minutes, and which will keep the discussions private. These are also called "executive sessions."

This must never be done!

A condo Council is not a private corporation – it's a public body. There's no issue that your Council can discuss that does not concern the community, and no issues can be legally hidden from the community. No motions passed by your Council in such a session can ever have any legal validity, or be binding on the community in any way.

"Ah," you say, *"but what about financial matters and delinquencies? Aren't these matters of privacy?"*

> The funds your condo collects through fees are not the Council's money, nor even the condo's money – they're the owner's money, held in trust by the administration. Your Council and Administrator must **publicly** manage the owner's money, and no financial decisions can be made without the owner's knowledge and, in some cases, approval.
>
> If an owner is delinquent, this isn't a privacy issue. Delinquency details are publicly reported and made part of your condo records by law.

This is a fact of life in a condo, and if an owner finds this embarrassing, then they should pay their fees.

"OK, OK ... but what about employee issues? Are these not sensitive?"

Again, a condo isn't a company. Neither your Councillors, committee members, nor any owner are employees.

No issues or problems with actual employees (such as gate guards or maids) can ever be hidden from the community.

Remember, the owners (as a body) are the employer, not your Administrative Council.

I've challenged proponents of "executive sessions" to give me an example of a topic that must only be discussed in a closed session, along with the reasons for keeping it from the owners – so far, I've yet to hear one.

Yes, your Council represents and acts for the community, but it's required by law to always do this openly, under the oversight of the owners.

Meeting Agenda

An agenda should always be prepared before each meeting, and sent out to the community along with the meeting notice.

This makes meetings more structured and efficient, helps councillors prepare for the meeting, and allows residents to decide if they want to be there or not.

If you receive feedback on the agenda, or requests for other items to be discussed, and if there's enough time, a new agenda can be sent out as late as two days before the meeting (this isn't a legal requirement, but just a matter of courtesy).

Don't, however, let the possibility of changes hold up issuing the initial agenda and meeting call. There should always be reasonable advance notice of the meeting for both councillors and members of the community.

Any new item that doesn't make it onto the agenda will have to be dealt with under *"New Business."*

> **Don't abuse this.**
>
> A "New Business" agenda item must not be used to discuss a sensitive topic that the Council wanted to discuss all along without putting it on the agenda – to avoid "tipping off" people before the meeting.
>
> This is improper conduct.
>
> A Council must never be afraid to address controversial issues head-on, and under full community scrutiny – as difficult as this sometimes can be.

A special council meeting doesn't need an agenda if it only deals with one specific topic (which is both usual and recommended).

While there's nothing in the Jalisco condo law specifically about council meeting agendas, here are the standard topics that normally appear on meeting agendas (in standard order):

1. Adoption of the agenda

    Here is where items that didn't make it onto the agenda can be added under "New Business."

2. Adoption of the minutes of the last meeting.

    Although draft versions of the minutes should be sent out to the community shortly after each meeting (**see Part 13 – "Minutes of Assemblies & Meetings"**), these minutes aren't official until they're adopted at the next meeting.

3. Reports from the Administrator, standing committees, or councillors

4. Reports from special committees

5. Special Business

    This is business that's required by the by-laws.

    For example, if you're replacing a councillor or a committee chair, or dealing with any other issue that has specific procedures outlined in your by-laws.

6. Unfinished Business

    These are issues for which discussion was started at a previous meeting, but didn't finish – for example, more research was needed.

    To help you manage this, I highly recommend you use an **Unfinished Business Report**.

    This is just a list of all items that the Council has started discussing, but for which no decision has yet been reached. This prevents topics from "falling through the cracks" – this can easily happen without some way of tracking them.

    The report should list each unfinished item and include: the name of the item, the date of the meeting where it originated, a brief description of what's been discussed and actions pending (this section must be updated if the issue carries over to several meetings), a brief description of the reason for delaying a decision along with the person assigned to resolve it – *"councillor Reese will get a quote for replacing the broken terrace roof tiles"*.

The goal is to deal with each item on this list at each meeting until it's resolved and removed from the report.

7. New Business

    Self-explanatory. These are topics that have not been discussed before, and are coming up for the first time at this meeting.

There are items that I've seen on meeting agendas that don't need to be there. These are standard, routine, and expected administrative functions, and aren't meeting business agenda items. They happen at the meeting, and are in the minutes, but they should not appear on the agenda:

- Roll-Call
- Call to Order
- Next Meeting
- Adjournment

A sample council meeting agenda is included in your BONUS Pack.

Quorum

Quorum is the minimum number of councillors needed to legally hold a meeting. If this number isn't achieved, the meeting can't be held. Remember that if this happens, at least one council meeting must still be held in each month.

The Jalisco condo law is silent on quorum for a council meeting. If there's nothing in your condo by-laws, standard meeting practice is that a quorum is **a majority of councillors** – this means **more than half** of the councillors.

As an example, here are the quorums for some typical Council sizes:

Size of Council	Quorum
3	2
4	3
5	3
6	4

If you want to create a nonstandard quorum, such as three councillors for a seven-member Council, then this must be in your by-laws.

Voting on Motions

As with quorum, the Jalisco condo law is silent on voting at council meetings. If there's nothing in your condo by-laws, standard meeting practice is that for a motion to pass, it must receive the approval of **a majority of the councillors at the meeting** (assuming you have a quorum).

This means **more than half** of the councillors **at the meeting** – not more than half of all councillors.

> For example, you have a seven-member council. Five are at the meeting (this is a legal meeting since quorum is four). A vote would need at least three councillors voting in favour to pass.

When Decisions Must Be Made Outside of a Council Meeting

Emergency situations need a quick decision, and there may be no time to call a council meeting. For example, a portion of the perimeter wall has collapsed, must be repaired **now**, your Council has three quotes, and wants to get the work started right away.

In these situations, your Council may have little choice but to make a decision by telephone or email discussion.

A majority of your Council must be in favour, and the community must be notified of the decision at once.

At the next council meeting, this issue must be put on the agenda, ratified with a motion and vote, and recorded in the minutes.

Conflicts of Interest

A conflict of interest is when a councillor is personally affected by the outcome of a council vote.

> An example would be if your Council was discussing a complaint against this councillor as a property owner, or some other matter that affects a councillor's private unit.

> Another example might be if a councillor's family member was associated with a contractor that's bidding on work your Council is voting to contract out.

It's important to realise that a conflict of interest doesn't mean that there's any wrongdoing on the councillor's part. It's just a fact – a situation that exists.

It's standard practice for councillors who have any interest in the outcome of a vote to abstain (not vote). They also must not take part in the discussion before the vote. They needn't leave the meeting – they just can't take part in this one issue.

You must also apply this if a third-party might reasonably believe that a councillor might be biased or benefit from a vote on a particular issue because circumstances make it look like they could. This should be decided by a council vote before discussion on the issue starts. This is called a **perceived conflict of interest**.

When a councillor abstains from voting, the reasons must be recorded in the minutes.

Councillors must not abstain from voting for any reason other than a conflict of interest. Not voting isn't a legitimate form of protest. If councillors oppose a motion, they should speak against it and vote against it. If the motion passes, and they feel strongly about the issue, their objection can be recorded in the minutes.

Rules of Order

Council meetings should be conducted with relaxed rules of order for efficiency. Basic rules of order are still needed, however, to prevent chaos. **See Part 9 – "Rules of Order"** for more information.

Meeting Minutes

Minutes must be taken at all council meetings, and these, along with any attachments, must form part of your condo's official records (**Code Article 1012**). Minutes must be available to all owners at any time.

I highly recommend that you make a practice of automatically distributing the draft council minutes to the community shortly after each meeting. For more information on council minutes, **see Chapter 41 – "Council Meeting Minutes."**

Sample council meeting minutes are in your BONUS Pack.

Committee Meetings

Chapter 24

Procedures for committee meetings are also not mentioned in the Jalisco condo law. Any that you adopt, should either be formalised as a policy, or added to your by-laws.

All the comments from the last chapter on council meetings apply to committee meetings, **with the exceptions noted in this chapter.**

Public Meetings With Advance Notice

Any special committees struck directly by an assembly, must always report to the owners, and their meetings must be open. As with council meetings, owners are only there to observe.

Since standing committees are part of your condo's administration, and report to your Council, it follows that their work must also be done openly.

Therefore, the community must always be told about all committee meetings, and be invited to be there. There's no specific legal requirement for advance notice, but, I suggest 10 days to two weeks.

A sample committee meeting notice and agenda are included in your BONUS Pack.

No Minimum Frequency of Meetings

Committees don't have to meet on any particular schedule. They meet when they have an issue to deal with.

That said, I strongly recommend that you set up a minimum meeting frequency for each standing committee – for example, *"once per quarter"* or *"twice per year"* in your by-laws.

This allows the committee members to keep in touch, serves to remind them of their mandate, and allows issues to be raised by committee members and owners during the meeting. Often these issues don't surface until a meeting is called.

Meeting Minutes

Committee meetings should always be minuted.

Committee minutes don't have to form part of the official condo records according to the condo legislation, but I highly recommend that you file them in the records.

Committee decisions affect your condo, and it's a good idea to have a historical record of what they did and why. This is helpful to future committees when dealing with a similar issue to one that's come up in the past.

Working and Information Sessions

Chapter **25**

Working and information sessions, along with town hall meetings, are powerful tools for a condo administration. They're not dealt with in the condo legislation, but this chapter has some recommendations.

Working Sessions

Sometimes it's more efficient for a committee (and occasionally the Council) to hold a working session, rather than an official meeting.

A working session is a roll-up-your-shirt-sleeves event where formal rules of order are dropped, and brainstorming and discussion prevail.

These sessions usually have a narrow and specific focus – they should be used to carry out only a single task or solve a single problem.

They aren't minuted, and no motions or decisions are made (they would have no validity if they were). At a subsequent formal council meeting, decisions can be made and ratified based on the results from the working session. Each would be voted on and minuted.

As with any other meeting dealing with issues affecting your condominium, the community must be invited. Don't look on this as a negative. Owner participation can give you powerful insight into a tough problem. Sometimes a committee or Council can become stagnant on an issue or stuck in a particular mind-set – a fresh viewpoint can often break the log jam loose.

You might be amazed at how many good ideas can be put forth from members of the community-at-large.

In my experience, more members of the community are likely to go to a working session than a council meeting.

Information Sessions

These are meetings where interested owners are invited to hear a presentation by your Administrator, Council, or a committee – usually followed by a question and answer session.

This is not an assembly, and there can be no voting.

These sessions might be held to explain a new operating procedure or policy, to review various choices that a committee is considering, or to present and discuss a draft of a proposed budget before its approval at the annual ordinary assembly.

It's important that these sessions are focused and specific. The presenter or session chair must keep a tight reign to keep the meeting from drifting off-topic, or turning into a complaint session.

These sessions aren't minuted, and there can be no motions made or voted on. You can poll the people there for a consensus opinion, but this isn't a vote, and is not binding on the community. The session is informational only.

Feeling the owners out on a subject can sometimes help in making certain administrative decisions. However, you must also bear in mind that this might only be a minority opinion (depending on the demographics of the turn out for the session).

Town Hall Meetings

These are meetings where owners are invited to express their opinions about controversial issues in the condo in a forum.

They must be carefully controlled by a Chair or facilitator, or they can degenerate into chaos.

They aren't minuted (meeting notes are highly recommended), and no motions or decisions can be made. They are a tool for the Council to understand and get owner feedback on these issues.

Council can then modify policies at a council meeting – being careful not to overstep their authority by putting into a policy something that should be in the by-laws.

Council may also decide to forward suggestions to a By-law Committee for possible changes to the by-laws. These by-law changes can only be made at an extraordinary assembly.

PART 8 – Condo Assemblies

The Ordinary Assembly

Chapter 26

The ordinary assembly is used to renew the condo administration, and to approve the annual operating budget for the next fiscal year. It's the only assembly that's required annually (all others are held as needed).

Advance Notice

The call for an ordinary assembly must be made **at least 15 calendar days before the scheduled date of the assembly.**

Minimum Frequency

An ordinary assembly must be called **at least once a year**, in the first quarter of the calendar year (between January 1 and March 31).

This is usually called the *asamblea ordinaria anual* **(Annual Ordinary Assembly)**. This is an AGM (annual general meeting).

For planning reasons, I recommend that your annual assembly be held in March – around the 20th of the month is best. This allows time for a second call if you can't achieve quorum on your first call. Other ordinary assemblies can be called at any time in the year, if needed.

Subjects That Can Be Dealt With at the Assembly

Only six subjects can be dealt with in an ordinary assembly, and these **cannot** be dealt with in an extraordinary assembly **(Article 1020)**.

1. A general report on your condominium must be presented at the annual assembly by the outgoing Administrative Council.

    This is not just about finances – it must also be about property and services. Normally your Administrator will give the financial portion, but this is not required by the condo law.

2. The election of the members of the Administrative Council and, if applicable, the amount and method of paying their salaries.

3. The election of any special committees to be appointed by the assembly. These are for a specific purpose or task.

4. The appointment of the Administrator, and, if applicable, the amount and method of paying their salary.

5. The approval of the income and expense budget for the next fiscal year (April 1 through March 31).

6. The setting of your condo fees, and the method of paying them. In Municipal Services Condominiums, when the owners can't agree, the setting of fees will be made by the treasurer of the municipality where your condominium is located.

It's important to understand that **no other issues or decisions are allowed to be made at an ordinary assembly**. Any issue that isn't on the list above **must be dealt with at an extraordinary assembly**.

Although unusual, other ordinary assemblies can be called during the year if they are needed.

> One possible situation would be to deal with the resignation of either your Administrator or a majority of your Council.

> These special ordinary assemblies normally deal with one topic – it must be a topic from the list above, or else an extraordinary assembly is required.

If the assembly decides to contract an outside Administrator, the Council will have to execute the corresponding contract according to the resolution of the assembly. The term of this contract can't be longer than one year, and can only be renewed at another assembly with the approval of the owners.

Quorum for the First Call

Quorum is the minimum amount of common property ownership rights that must be represented at the assembly so that the assembly is legally made up, and can go ahead and conduct its business.

For an ordinary assembly to be legally formed on its first call, owners representing **at least 51% of the total common property ownership rights** must be present (**Article 1023**). If your by-laws allow proxies, then these are normally counted towards this quorum.

Note that this could be quite different from 51% of the owners or 50% plus one owner.

> For example, consider a sample condominium, *Vista del Basurero* – a condo with 22 lots and houses. The common property ownership rights are shown in the following table:

Unit #	% Ownership	Unit #	% Ownership
1	6.20%	12	3.59%
2	3.80%	13	3.51%
3	7.15%	14	4.34%
4	6.24%	15	4.03%
5	3.94%	16	3.62%
6	3.74%	17	4.34%
7	4.34%	18	4.34%
8	6.32%	19	3.78%
9	3.68%	20	4.39%
10	3.86%	21	3.52%
11	7.67%	22	3.60%

> Notice that the largest lot (#11 at 7.67%) is 2.2 times the size of the smallest (#13 at 3.51%) – a large difference like this isn't uncommon in horizontal condos.

Based only on the number of owners, either 51% or 50%-plus-1 would be 12 owners. However, quorum is based on common property ownership rights:

> If all the large lot owners showed up, it would only need the highest 9 of them to meet the quorum requirement.

> If only the smaller lot owners showed up, it would need the lowest 14 of these owners to make a quorum.

Both quorum and voting are based on percentage of ownership of the common property – often called **condo rights**.

This number is contained in the title documents for each owner's private unit, and represents the percentage of the common property owned by that owner.

In some condominiums where the size of lots or apartments is very close, there is little variation. In other condos, however, the difference can be significant.

Taking our example condo: the smallest lot is 291.05m^2 (3,133ft^2 or 3.51%), the median lot is 373.25m^2 (4,018ft^2 or 4.51%), and the largest lot is 635.15m^2 (6,837ft^2 or 7.67%). The difference between largest and smallest is 2.2 times!

Yes, this means that the owner of this largest property counts more towards the quorum, and has a larger vote than the owner of the smallest property.

While this might at first glance seem unfair, it's perfectly fair and logical:

The owner of the large lot owns more of the common property than the owner of the small lot.

Since this percentage also affects the amount of the owner's condo fees, the owner of the larger lot pays more than twice as much to maintain the common property.

Since this owner owns more of the common property and pays higher fees, it's only reasonable that this owner has a greater say in deciding how this property is managed and maintained – in direct proportion to the percentage of the common property owned.

The Second Call

If the quorum requirement of 51% of the total ownership rights of the condominium is not met, a second call must be made for a new assembly to be held in **no less than 7, and no more than 15 days from the date of the failed assembly.**

This new assembly can then be held with any percentage of ownership rights that are represented – it has no quorum requirement.

There's a common misconception that if there's no quorum, then the meeting can be held anyway, as long as you wait some arbitrary period of time (such as 15 minutes) before calling the meeting to order with whomever is in attendance (or some minimum number that has nothing to do with the condo law).

This is incorrect, and isn't a valid or legal procedure.

Common sense should tell us that if this were an acceptable practice, then the original quorum requirement is pointless. If you're saying that you can wait 20 minutes, and then proceed with whomever is there (or 20 people), you're actually saying you have no quorum (or your quorum is 20).

It's permissible to delay the meeting while you beat the bushes for more owners, but if you still cannot meet your quorum then you cannot proceed. **You must wait at least 7 days, not a few minutes.**

Turn Lemons Into Lemonade

If your ordinary assembly fails because of the lack of a quorum on its first call, I recommend that you take advantage of the opportunity. While you can't pass resolutions, you can still hold an informal town hall meeting (**not** assembly) with the owners who did show up.

For example, you might use this opportunity to:

- talk about any contentious issues (the budget and fees are generally the only contentious issues that come up at an ordinary assembly);
- get valuable feedback on the owners' perceptions of your administration; and
- socialise to build a better sense of community.

Be careful! This is not an assembly, and no votes can be taken or decisions made.

Passing Resolutions

Resolutions are decisions made by the assembly that affect the operation or maintenance of your condo. They must be listed on the Order of the Day that was attached to the assembly call notice.

Resolutions, when passed at an assembly, are binding on all owners, **whether they were at the assembly or not**.

Resolutions can only be passed by an ordinary assembly if they receive a favourable vote from a **majority percentage of the common property ownership rights that are represented at the assembly.** A majority means *"more than half."* A common misconception is that this is 51% – **not so!**.

> For example, assume that ***Vista del Basurero*** has owners at the assembly who represent 71.92% of the total condo rights – this gives us a quorum (more than 51%).
>
> For a resolution to pass at this ordinary assembly, it must receive at least 35.97% of the condo rights voted in favour of it.

"How'd you come up with that magic number?"

Half of the 71.92% represented at the meeting is 35.96%. More than half (a majority) is 0.01% more – **not** 1% more, because condo rights are expressed to two decimal places. "More than half" means half, plus one more of the smallest increment you are measuring.

Meeting Plan for a Typical Ordinary Assembly

- **Appointment of the Chair, Secretary, and scrutineers**: the Chair is most usually your Administrator or the President/Chair of your Council, but it can be anyone. It's not necessary that they be a member of the community. Some condos will have a notario or an *abogado* trained in arbitration chair an assembly if they believe that there are highly contentious issues that could erupt into disputes or arguments.

  A Secretary is needed to record the minutes.

  Two scrutineers must be appointed to take the roll-call and to oversee the voting.

  These are all dealt with by announcing the person, and continuing if there's no objection – this is a consensus vote (election by acclamation or general consent).

  If there is an objection, then there must be a vote by a simple show of hands, and not proportional voting (**Article 1024**). This is because the assembly hasn't yet been called to order, and this vote actually takes place outside of the assembly.

Note: all items before *"Call to Order"* are pre-assembly administrative tasks – the assembly is not yet in session. Be careful not to make any motions or call for any formal votes before the assembly has been legally formed by being called to order.

- **Roll-call and Determination of Quorum**: the scrutineers now conduct a roll-call, and announce the total percentage rights represented at the assembly. If this is enough for quorum, then the Chair can call the assembly to order. If not, a second call is needed, and the next assembly can take place with a minimum wait of 7 days, and no more than 15 (**Article 1023**).

- **Introductory Remarks**: before the assembly gets under way, the Chair may make introductory remarks about procedures or the rules of order.

- **Call to Order**: the Chair calls the assembly to order, and reads the Order of the Day.

  From this point on, business can be conducted, and resolutions can be passed.

- **Presentation of the General Report**: this is a report presented by the Council (usually by the President/Chair of your Council) about the accomplishments of the past year, the state of repair and maintenance of your condo, and its financial status – this last section of the report is often turned over to your Administrator.

  Since this is just a report, and not a resolution, there's no point in having either a motion or vote. Once the report is given, it's given – this is a fact requiring no vote. The minutes will note that the report was received by the assembly.

You can, although not necessary, have a motion to file the report with the minutes – if so, this should be approved by general consent.

- **Approval of the Budget and Setting of Fees**: your Administrator will present the budget for the coming fiscal year, along with the fees needed to support it. The assembly will vote on its approval.

  Ideally, this vote should only be a formality – the budget presented at the assembly should have been thoroughly reviewed and discussed by the community before the assembly was held. You must make sure that this was an open process, where every owner had an opportunity for input.

  If you don't have a majority support for the budget going into the assembly, you run the risk of having to make changes to it at the assembly. Because this would happen without the ability to do research or carefully consider the consequences of these changes, you might wind up with an unworkable budget.

  Regardless, the assembly must approve a budget in some form. **Without a budget, your condominium cannot function.**

  If there's no way to pass a new budget, amended or not, then you may have to revert to the previously approved budget from last year – this is a less than ideal situation.

  Approval of the budget needs a formal roll-call vote.

- **Election of the Administrative Council**: self explanatory. **See Part 12 – "Elections"** for the procedures.

- **Appointment of the Administrator**: the assembly must approve the appointment of the Administrator. The Administrator is normally chosen by the Council before the assembly, and the vote is a formality typically passed by general consent.

- **Granting of Powers**: the assembly should formally give powers of representation (a power of attorney) to the Administrator and President/Chair of the Council. This is not a resolution, and there is no vote. More on this later.

- **Election of Special Committees**: this is only needed if you need to create a special committee to deal with a specific issue. Committees can be elected by acclamation from a preselected set of nominees, elected from nominees who come forth at the assembly, or you can just elect a Chair, and leave it up to this individual to beat the bushes for committee members.

- **Compilation, Reading, and Approval of the Minutes**: the Secretary finishes the minutes (you can take a brief recess for this, if needed), then reads them to the assembly. If anyone objects, their input is considered and the minutes might be modified.

  The end result are the official minutes adopted by the assembly, ready to be translated, protocolised, and publicly registered. This adoption is by general consent, since objections have been asked for and dealt with. There can be no resolution because the business is already over.

- **Designation of a Representative**: after the minutes are approved, the assembly must give one or two people the authority to appear before a notario to protocolise and register the minutes. This is normally done by acclamation.

- **Adjournment**: the assembly is now over, and the Chair declares the assembly adjourned.

    Important: just declare the assembly adjourned, **do not ask if there's any further business**. Unless you have 100% of the condo rights represented at the meeting (this is extremely rare), you cannot legally discuss any business that wasn't on the Order of the Day.

    Also be aware that the items mentioned above are the only topics that can be addressed at an ordinary assembly. If you have anything else not listed in this plan, then it must be dealt with at an extraordinary assembly.

Sample chairing scripts for both types of assemblies are included in your BONUS Pack. Your BONUS Pack also includes a sample guide, "*How to Chair a Condo Assemblies.*"

A sample "*Owner's Guide to Condo Assemblies*" intended for distribution to your owners (or posting on your condo web site) is included in your BONUS Pack.

Assembly Minutes

A Secretary of the Assembly is appointed at the start of the assembly to take the minutes. The minutes are read and approved by the assembly at the end of business so that they can be publicly registered.

If a Council is elected, or if an Administrator is appointed at an ordinary assembly (this **always** happens at an annual ordinary assembly), then the minutes of this ordinary assembly (along with the attachments) must be protocolised by a *notario* having residence or jurisdiction in the municipality where your condominium is located (**Articles 1013 & 1018**).

To help your case against a delinquent owner, you should also register the minutes of an ordinary assembly where a budget and fees were approved.

Always register the minutes of your Annual Ordinary Assembly.

This protocolisation must contain, at a minimum:

- Data about the *escritura constitutiva* (the public document that set up your condominium regime), to include at a minimum:

    - the place and date of the registration,

    - the authorising *notario*,

    - the registration number of this instrument,

    - the generic property that's affected, its location, and the details about its registration in the *Registro Público de la Propiedad* (**Public Registry of Property**).

- Any amendments that have been made to the *escritura constitutiva* or to these by-laws.

- Any abilities or powers that, according to your by-laws or expressly by the assembly, have been given to the counsellors independent of those set out in the law.

- A transcription of the approved assembly minutes (in Spanish).

The first few items will be taken care of by your *notario*, and the last item is what the Secretary of the Assembly has produced, and was approved by the assembly. If this was done in English, it must first be translated into Spanish.

This transcription of the assembly minutes must also be recorded in your condominium's minute book – Book #1 kept by your Administrator.

The only official version is the Spanish version. If you did them in English, you can include the English version as a courtesy "translation" for the foreign owners – it should be clearly marked as such.

The legal document that contains the protocolisation of these minutes will be registered and recorded in the registration of your condominium that's kept in the Public Registry of Property.

Your *notario* will also keep a copy in his protocol book, and an official copy of the registered minutes will be available from the *notario* after they've been registered – this copy must form a part of your condo's official records.

The consequences of **not** protocolising and registering an ordinary assembly are that your Administrator may have no authority to enter into contracts on behalf of your condo, your Council may not be able to legally act for it, and the validity of your budget and fees may be challenged during the process of going after a delinquent owner.

For more information, **see Chapter 40 – "Condo Assembly Minutes."**

Sample minutes and WORD templates for both types of assemblies are included in your BONUS Pack.

The Extraordinary Assembly Chapter 27

The extraordinary assembly is used to vote on all the issues and topics that affect a condo which aren't allowed at an ordinary assembly.

Advance Notice

The call for an extraordinary assembly must be made **at least 20 calendar days before the scheduled date of the assembly.** This is 5 days more notice than is required for an ordinary assembly.

No Minimum Frequency

Unlike the annual ordinary assembly, there's no regular requirement to hold an extraordinary assembly. You only need to call one whenever your condo needs to make a decision on a subject that can only be dealt with at an extraordinary assembly.

Sometimes an extraordinary assembly is held right after the annual ordinary assembly. This is most commonly done when:

- the by-laws need changes;
- improvements need approval; and
- special fees to pay for these improvements need approval.

Subjects That Can Be Dealt With at the Assembly

An extraordinary assembly must be called at any time when a decision on any of the following issues is required (**Article 1021**):

1. Changes to your condominium's by-laws.

2. Carrying out voluntary work that's beyond normal maintenance and repair of common property – such as improvements to the property (installation of a new gate, or extending the club house terraza are examples).

The means of paying for this work must also be approved at this assembly (usually a special fee).

3. An owner might have paid for emergency repairs to common property if your Administrator failed to make them in a timely fashion. After hearing justification from the owner for this expense, the extraordinary assembly can approve paying back this owner. This reimbursement must not be unreasonably withheld.

4. To get permission to ask a judge to force a delinquent or troublesome owner to sell his condominium rights at public auction under **Article 1032**. This action uses a nonstandard vote – **see Chapter 37 – "Voting At an Assembly"** for more information on this.

5. To get permission to evict a non-owner tenant.

6. To transform or dispose of any part of the common property.

7. To incorporate new property into your condominium regime, or to remove property from it.

8. To decide on the extinction of your condominium regime.

9. **Any other decisions that concern the owners meeting as an assembly.** This would be any issue not listed above and not on the limited list of topics allowed at an ordinary assembly.

Improvements to Your Common Property

All improvements need approval of the owners at an extraordinary assembly.

Neither your Administrator nor your Council have the authority to go ahead with improvements to the common property without having sought and received the approval of the owners at an extraordinary assembly.

When an extraordinary assembly approves voluntary or improvement work, the basis for paying the costs for this work must be set out in the wording of the resolution of the assembly. For example:

> *"That three speed limit signs be provided including installation and mounting hardware. This will be funded by a special fee of $1,200 to be collected on July 1.".*

Forcing an Owner to Sell

The condo legislation contained in the Civil Code gives you a legal method to deal with a delinquent owner or an owner who repeatedly causes problems in your condo.

This is a drastic action and should be your last resort. It involves bringing suit before a judge to force the sale of the owner's unit at public auction to the highest bidder.

Once the owners approve of this action at an extraordinary assembly, the papers filed with the court must contain, among other things, an official copy of the registered public document that contains the protocolisation of the minutes of the assembly that decided to take this action against the owner.

Dissolving Your Condominium

If the buildings comprising your condominium regime are damaged to an extent that represents at least 75% of their value, any owner can ask for the division of the common property.

However, if the damage represents less than 75% of the value, then reconstruction can be voted on at an extraordinary assembly. If such a resolution passes, then the owners who voted against it are obligated to contribute to the reconstruction in the proportion that corresponds to their condo rights, or to sell their property to the other owners according to an expert valuation.

There's No Quorum and No Second Call

Unlike an ordinary assembly, **there's no quorum needed to legally hold an extraordinary assembly.**

The assembly can be held with **any number of owners who show up**. Therefore, there's never a circumstance where a second call is needed for an extraordinary assembly.

Passing Resolutions

Resolutions are decisions made by the assembly that affect the operation or maintenance of your condo. They must correspond with the Order of the Day that was attached to the assembly call notice.

Resolutions, when passed at an assembly, are binding on all owners **whether they were at the assembly or not.**

Because the decisions made by an extraordinary assembly can have more impact on your condo than those made by an ordinary assembly (which are largely administrative), the number of votes needed to pass a resolution is much greater.

Resolutions can only be passed by an extraordinary assembly if they receive a favourable vote from at least **75% of the total common property ownership rights.**

> For example, assume that you have a set of owners there who represent 71.25% of the condo rights.

> For a motion to be approved at this extraordinary assembly, it must receive at least 75.00% of the condo rights voted in favour.

Did you notice something strange? The vote required to pass a motion has **nothing to do with the number of rights represented at the meeting**.

You need at least 75% of the condo rights **no matter how many rights are actually at the meeting**.

"OK ... OK ... so, how on earth can this possibly work?"

I said the meeting can be held with however many show up, and in my example this was 71.25% of the condo rights. Doesn't this mean that the assembly is pointless because no motion could ever receive 75% of the condo rights?

Because of the rather strict need for 75% of the total condo rights to pass a vote, the condo law gives us a solution to this seeming dilemma:

> If not enough votes are received on a given motion for it to pass, and if the common property rights that aren't represented at the assembly would make a difference (as in our example), then the absentee owners must be contacted **in the 30 calendar days after the meeting** to:
>
> - declare themselves to be genuinely knowledgeable of the issues and the motion; and
>
> - to cast a vote.

A sample request for these absentee votes is included in your BONUS Pack.

If this process results in extra favourable votes that push the votes from the assembly above the 75% threshold, then the motion passes.

There's **one exception** to the 75% condo right voting requirement, and it's in **Code Article 1032**:

> When an assembly considers suing an owner to force them to sell their property at public auction, this decision needs the agreement of *"more than half of the total of the owners."*

This is a nonstandard vote that's significantly different from a normal vote at an assembly, since this special vote does not involve condo rights – a show of hands will meet this requirement.

Note that this requirement refers to **all owners**, rather than just those at the assembly. Therefore, in a 30-unit condo, you must receive a positive vote from at least 16 owners, regardless of the number of owners at the assembly. The 30-day period to contact absentee owners after the assembly still applies.

Meeting Plan for a Typical Extraordinary Assembly

- **Appointment of the Chair, Secretary, and scrutineers**: as with the ordinary assembly, a Chair, Secretary, and scrutineers must be appointed. This is normally done by acclamation. For more details, see the ordinary assembly plan.

  > **Note**: as with the ordinary assembly, all the items before *"Call to Order"* are pre-assembly administrative tasks. Don't make any motions or conduct any formal votes. For more detail see the ordinary assembly plan in the last chapter.

- **Roll-call and Determination of Quorum**: as with the ordinary assembly, the scrutineers will now conduct a roll-call, and announce the total percentage rights represented at the assembly for recording in the minutes. For more details, see the ordinary assembly plan in the last chapter.

- **Introductory Remarks**: before the assembly gets under way, the Chair may make introductory remarks about procedures or the rules of order.

- **Call to Order**: since there's no quorum needed, the Chair must call the assembly to order **regardless of the outcome of the roll-call**.

After this, the Chair reads the Order of the Day, and then deals with each business item in turn.

- **Business Items for an extraordinary assembly**: this is where the resolutions to be decided at the extraordinary assembly are voted on. Unlike the ordinary assembly plan, I've not listed specific items.

This is because the items I listed in the ordinary assembly plan are the **only** items that can be discussed at an ordinary assembly, and **all others** must be discussed at an extraordinary assembly. Therefore, the potential list of topics is almost unlimited.

The most important things to remember are:

- Every topic must appear on the Order of the Day that was issued with the assembly call. Note that it's OK to list "Voting on Improvements" on the Order of the Day, rather than listing each one.

- Every topic must have a motion and a formal roll-call vote.

I highly recommend that the Chair precede each motion with a brief introduction.

For example, if you're proposing an improvement: describe the improvement, and why it's needed; describe the scope of work; describe the benefits of the improvement to the community; and include the estimated cost, as well as how you plan to recover these costs (generally by an extraordinary fee). This is for the benefit of the assembly (none of this appears in the assembly minutes).

I also highly recommend that you conduct a very open and public process beforehand for any complex resolutions such as changes to your by-laws. This process must have input, review, and comment from all owners.

Your goal is to make sure that every owner has had multiple opportunities to have their concerns addressed **before the assembly**, so that the final changes are supported by almost the entire community.

To do this, you should follow a process something like this (by-law changes are used in the example, but this can also apply to any complex items that need approval):

1. Unless you feel the number of participants would be too large, hold a series of workshops. Invite all owners who are concerned about your by-laws to take part.

   If the numbers are large, you might also consider holding multiple workshops, with a different set of owners at each one.

2. Summarise the comments and recommendations from the workshop groups into a report for your Administrative Council.

3. Hold a special council meeting to talk about the comments and recommendations of the workshop groups. The end result should be a proposed set of changes approved by your Council.

4. Send out a document to all owners outlining all the proposed by-law changes.

   If there are a lot of changes, you should also send a DRAFT version of how the new by-laws would look (the current by-laws with all the recommended changes applied).

   Invite every owner to examine this document, and to send any concerns or suggestions to your Council for consideration.

   Give the owners a reasonable time to respond – 10 days is good. A sample of a request for input from the owners is included in your BONUS Pack.

5. Once the deadline has passed, hold another special council meeting to discuss owners' comments and suggestions. Encourage those who sent suggestions to attend this meeting.

   Make every effort to incorporate owners' suggestions into your by-laws – although this isn't always possible. Formally approve a final set of recommended changes to be voted on at the assembly.

6. Send out a final document to all owners outlining all the recommended changes. Again, if there are a lot of changes, also send a DRAFT version of how the new by-laws would look.

Include a brief summary of the reasons for rejecting each owner-submitted suggestion that wasn't incorporated.

An open and public process is important because these types of changes are usually far too complex to change in any meaningful way at an assembly. Time and resources are limited, and there's no opportunity to thoroughly think through the consequences of even a seemingly small change.

Therefore, you need to do enough groundwork before the assembly so that all significant objections have been dealt with, and the assembly vote becomes a formality.

Don't be surprised if one of the people who sent in a suggestion that was rejected makes an issue of it at the assembly. Even if your reasons for not including it were perfectly sound, some people can't accept their ideas not being used.

Deal with it at the assembly, and when they see that the majority doesn't support them, they'll usually back down. Try not to antagonise this person! Rather, try to get them to accept the majority viewpoint. Ideally, you want to avoid having them vote "NO."

Sadly, there can be people who have refused to take part in your public process in any way, but will still try to sabotage the hard work of everyone else by torpedoing the resolution at the assembly by unexpectedly voting "NO."

It's unfortunate, but there's nothing you can do but accept the result and move on. If the resolution is defeated, and it was important, you can try again next year with greater pre-assembly salesmanship.

Don't forget the absentee vote – a resolution that was barely defeated at the assembly may yet be saved.

- **Compilation, Reading, and Approval of the Minutes**: as with the ordinary assembly, the Secretary finishes the minutes, then reads them to the assembly for adoption. For more details, see the ordinary assembly plan in the last chapter.

- **Designation of a Representative**: as with an ordinary assembly, the assembly must give one or two people the authority to appear before a *notario* to protocolise and register the minutes of the assembly. This is normally done by acclamation. For more details, see the ordinary assembly plan in the last chapter.

- **Adjournment**: as with an ordinary assembly, the business of the assembly is now finished, and the Chair must declare the assembly adjourned. For more details, see the ordinary assembly plan in the last chapter.

Sample chairing scripts for both types of assemblies are included in your BONUS Pack.

Assembly Minutes

While there's no Civil Code requirement to protocolise and register the minutes of every extraordinary assembly, I strongly recommend that you do this so they become binding on third-parties.

The following are circumstances where you **must** register your extraordinary assembly minutes:

> If you've changed your by-laws, then you must register the minutes of the extraordinary assembly so that your by-laws become binding on all concerned.

If you've approved improvements and their funding, it's a good idea to register the minutes of the extraordinary assembly to be able to enforce payment of any extraordinary fees.

If any other issues have been decided at an extraordinary assembly that affect fees, have impact beyond your condo's walls, or affect tenants and other non-owner occupants, it's also wise to go through this process.

Sample minutes and WORD templates for both types of assemblies are included in your BONUS Pack.

PART 9 – Rules of Order

Introduction to Rules of Order

Chapter 28

There have been volumes written about rules of order, and I've no intention of covering this topic in such depth. If you're interested in the excruciating details, this information is readily available elsewhere. However, I feel that a basic understanding of this topic is important.

This part of my book gives you an overview of the more common aspects of rules of order, along with basic concepts. It also makes practical recommendations on applying these specifically to condo owner assemblies, as well as council and committee meetings.

Do We Really Need Rules of Order?

Certain group dynamics can hinder, or even sabotage, the achievement of a group's goals. Since group dynamics are an inherent part of human nature, systematic rules of procedure for meetings have evolved over centuries.

Rules of order govern the conduct and procedures at meetings so that they are orderly and fair. They also make sure that, while decisions are made by the majority, everyone is heard and respected.

These basic rules are followed by almost all formal meetings.

They're used by clubs, associations and societies, organisations, legislative bodies, and almost all other deliberative assemblies – such as a condo owner's assembly. They should also be used for council and committee meetings (although modified, as we will see).

What is a Deliberative Assembly?

> "*A group of people meeting to talk about a common topic, and to decide a common action about it.*"

The characteristics of a deliberative assembly are:

- The group meets in a single location that allows simultaneous communication amongst all those taking part (or under conditions that equal this).

- The group is big enough (usually more than 12) where formal rules are needed to make the meeting efficient.

- Those who take part are free to act according to their judgment.

- A member who disagrees with a decision of the group continues to be a part of the group.

- If there are absent members, the members who are at the assembly act for the entire membership – except where limitations have been set out in the body's governing rules (such as by-laws and the condo law).

The deliberative assembly is a well-established concept. It was coined by Edmund Burke (a respected 18th century statesman, author, orator, political theorist, and philosopher) in 1774 to describe the English Parliament. In fact, the parliamentary procedures of the British House of Commons are the originating source for most rules of order used today.

Parliamentary Procedure

Parliamentary procedure is part of the common law originating in the practices of the House of Commons of the British Parliament – this is the origin of the name.

> You may also hear parliamentary procedure called: parliamentary law, parliamentary practice, legislative procedure, chairmanship, chairing, the law of meetings, conduct of meetings, procedure at meetings, or, just rules of order.

Basics of Parliamentary Procedure

Rules of order make it easier for people to work together effectively, and help groups carry out their goals. Rules of order, therefore, should assist a meeting and not hinder it.

To this end, all rules of order (or parliamentary procedures) abide by six basic principles:

1. **A meeting can deal with only one matter at a time.**

    Rules of order allow for various types of motions (proposals for action) to be made during the meeting. However, at any given time only one motion can be discussed or voted on. The different types of motions are given an order of priority to help this happen efficiently.

2. **All participants have equal rights, privileges, and duties.**

    One of the chair's main responsibilities is to use their authority to make sure that everyone at the meeting is treated equally — for example, the chair must not allow a vocal minority to dominate debate (discussion).

3. **A majority vote decides an issue.**

    Each participant agrees to be governed by the vote of the majority. Rules of order are designed to efficiently allow a meeting to discover the wishes of the majority of those taking part.

4. **The rights of the minority must be protected at all times.**

    Although the final decision on any matter is decided by the majority, all participants must have the right to be heard and the right to oppose the majority without any consequences.

> Protecting the rights of every participant (majority or minority) is important to everyone taking part. This is because any participant can be in the majority on one motion, but in the minority on the next.

5. **Each matter presented for a decision must be discussed fully.**

   > As important as the right to vote, is the right of each participant to express their opinion on any issue put forth for a vote.

6. **Each participant has the right to understand each issue, as well as the impact of each decision.**

   > Any participant must have the right to ask for more information on any proposal they don't understand.

The main concept is that while the majority's wishes always take priority over the minority's, rules of order help arrive at this majority viewpoint effectively and efficiently. They do this while making sure that there's fairness towards the minority, and that each person taking part has been allowed to voice their opinion.

The goal is to allow deliberation (that's why it's called a "deliberative assembly") on all matters of importance to the organisation, and to arrive at an agreement about these issues. Almost all self-governing bodies (such as a condominium) follow parliamentary procedure to discuss issues and reach group decisions, with the least possible disruption.

How Do These Rules Apply in a Condo?

There are two levels of rules of order: formal rules for assemblies, and streamlined rules for committee and council meetings.

- **Assemblies**: an assembly is open to all members of an organisation, and normally meets to make the most important decisions about the organisation. It's normally mandated to do this by the organisation's by-laws.

    As I've mentioned earlier, a condo assembly has an even greater mandate for the enforceability of its decisions. This mandate is given to it by the state condo legislation – which has much greater authority than your by-laws.

    A condo assembly should follow formal meeting procedures so that there's decorum, efficiency, and fairness. The larger your condo, the more important this becomes.

- **Committees**: a committee is

    "a small deliberative assembly that is answerable to a larger deliberative assembly."

    Therefore, a committee consists of only a few of the members of an organisation, and is usually appointed by the entire assembly.

    Committees are appointed by the larger body to more efficiently carry out a specific purpose.

    The most common example of this in a condo (although perhaps not the most obvious) is the Administrative Council. Your Council is appointed by the owners at the annual ordinary assembly to work with your Administrator to manage the common property over the coming fiscal year.

    Your Council (and any other condo committees) should follow more relaxed rules for their meetings. The numbers are small, and relaxed rules are just more efficient.

What Do the Rules of Order Consist of?

Rules of order usually consist of a standard parliamentary authority that's been adopted by the organisation.

These rules typically dictate that business conducted at an assembly or meeting is done by way of motions (proposed actions). Members bring business before the assembly by introducing these motions, which are then debated (discussed) and, finally, voted on.

Recommended Authority - Robert's Rules

I recommend that you adopt the single most widely accepted authority on parliamentary procedure – **Robert's Rules of Order Newly Revised**. First published in 1876, it's now in its tenth edition (published in 2000).

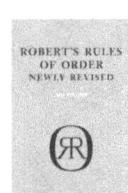

> Throughout my book, I'll call **Robert's Rules of Order Newly Revised** (RONR) just *"Robert's Rules."*
>
> Note, however, that the *"Newly Revised"* part is vitally important.
>
> Any book that's just called *"Robert's Rules of Order"* is an old edition that's in the public domain. The 3rd edition (1893) is the latest of these.
>
> A *"Revised"* edition appeared in 1915, this 4th edition is also in the public domain. The latest version of this work is the 6th edition (1951).
>
> The *"Newly Revised"* edition first appeared in 1970, and has been significantly changed to reflect modern meeting practices. **The most current version is the 10th edition (2000)**, and is significantly different from all older editions.
>
> If you're going to adopt an authority, it's important that it be the currently recognised version, or confusion will result.

The two other authorities with the most recognition are: *"The Standard Code of Parliamentary Procedure"* and *"Demeter's Manual of Parliamentary Law and Procedure."* However, neither enjoys the widespread use of Robert's Rules.

Adopting an Authority

You can just agree to use a given authority at meetings and assemblies, or (better) you can formally adopt one in your by-laws. Once you do either of these, the order of priority becomes:

1. state condo law;
2. your condo's by-laws; and then
3. the rules of order.

If you don't formally adopt an authority in your by-laws, it's important that you send a notice to all owners before an assembly saying that you will be using Robert's Rules (or whatever other rules of order you've chosen). This is so that they know how the meeting will be conducted, how they're expected to behave, and they can be prepared for both – this is the fair thing to do.

You should also consider announcing which rules of order you're using at the start of the assembly – so that all participants are operating under the same assumptions, and on the same basis. This can avoid a lot of disagreements and arguments over procedure.

Condos Should Adopt a Scaled-Down Version

After all that, I don't recommend that you **fully** adopt Robert's Rules (or any similar authority).

A scaled-down version is more suited to condos, since there are motions in Robert's Rules that are at odds with the Jalisco condo legislation. Assemblies are so tightly controlled by the condo law that it's just not possible to follow all of Robert's Rules.

In **Chapter 31 – "Rules of Order for Council & Committee Meetings"**, I'll go into this issue in detail, and give you some concrete suggestions.

Rules of Order Explained

Chapter 29

The edition of Robert's Rules now in use runs to over 650 pages in paperback. I've extracted the most important concepts, and presented them in a simple and understandable summary form.

When a 600+ page work is summarised in around 25 pages, there's clearly a lot of detail missing. This chapter isn't intended to replace the reference manual for Robert's Rules (your condo should have at least one copy), but is meant to give a basic overview of a topic that can become complex.

Fortunately, many of the complications are unnecessary for a condo assembly or meeting.

> Remember that rules of order are a means to an end, and not the means itself.
>
> The goal of using them is to control an assembly so that it doesn't descend into chaos, make sure that everyone's views are heard, and to democratically make decisions.
>
> The rules are only a tool to carry out these goals, and it can be highly counter-productive to get bogged down in the detail of the finer points of parliamentary procedure – leave this for parliamentarians to debate (and they will).

Keep in mind that your condo assemblies and meetings are meant to administer a community, and that the participants (who make up this community) are your friends and neighbours.

Unlike the condo legislation or your by-laws, rules of order don't have the authority of law. They should be regarded only as guidelines to be used to make your meetings efficient and fair.

Robert's Rules Citation Conventions Used in This Book

The latest version of Robert's Rules is divided into 61 sections. When citing a reference from Robert's Rules, I've included the section number (using the section symbol – '§') plus the page number. When I do this in this book, I'm referring to **Robert's Rules of Order Newly Revised (RONR) tenth edition.**

Overview of Motions and Resolutions

All business in an assembly or a meeting is carried out by debating (discussing) motions, and then voting on them.

> A **"motion"** is a formal proposal asking the assembly to carry out a particular action, and is usually made by two participants (a mover and a seconder).

> A **"resolution"** is a motion that's been approved by a vote of the assembly, and which describes a course of action that is binding on the entire membership (whether they were at the assembly or not).

A main motion is any motion that brings business before the assembly. Because the assembly can consider only one subject at a time, a main motion can be made only when no other motion is pending.

Here is the life-cycle of a main motion:

1. A participant makes a motion by proposing a course of action on an issue that needs a decision by the assembly. The Chair can also ask a participant to make a motion to formalise something.

2. Another participant seconds the motion. This seconder doesn't need to be in favour of the motion, and seconding a motion does not suggest this.

3. The Chair "states the question" to the assembly by repeating the motion, often putting it into clearer wording.

4. Debate on the question then follows (the motion is discussed).

5. The Chair "puts the question" to the assembly by repeating the original motion, and asking for a vote.

6. The assembly votes on the question.

7. Based on the outcome of the vote, the motion will either fail or will become adopted as a resolution.

When a main motion has been made by one participant, seconded by another, and repeated for the assembly by the chair, the group can't consider any other business until that motion has been disposed of, or until some other motion of higher priority has been proposed, seconded, and accepted by the Chair.

A main motion ranks lowest in the order of priority of motions – all other types of motions (more on these later) can interrupt or change a main motion.

Wording of Motions

A lot of time can be wasted when a motion is carelessly worded. For this reason, unless a motion is short and simple, it should be crafted in writing. Having to write the motion usually forces more careful wording. The Chair (often working with the Secretary) should do this before stating the question to the assembly, and after the maker of the motion has agreed to the wording.

In fact, for condo assemblies where the motions are known from the Order of the Day, I recommend that the motions be prepared beforehand.

The Chair reads the motion, and asks for a mover and seconder. If the motion is amended for some reason, the pre-written motion just needs to be edited.

Discussion Before Making a Motion

Strict adherence to parliamentary procedure requires that an assembly not discuss any matter unless it's been put before the group in the form of a motion stated as a question by the Chair.

In practice, however, there are times when it can be useful to allow limited discussion of a general topic before a motion is introduced. This is particularly true for smaller assemblies and committee meetings, and is allowed under **RONR §4. 33**.

Preliminary discussion on an issue can sometimes uncover the best action for the assembly to take. Presentation of a motion without this can sometimes result in a poorly worded motion, or in a proposal for action that proves inadvisable after formal discussion.

Such a departure from strict parliamentary procedure must be used with caution, and the Chair must be careful not to let it get out of control.

Once preliminary discussion has reached a point where a motion has become clear, the Chair must call for a motion and discussion can then continue based on this motion.

Debating a Motion (Discussion)

Once a motion has been made, and the question has been stated by the Chair, it's opened to debate (discussion). Every participant is entitled to express their opinion before the motion is voted on, and the Chair must make sure that this happens.

The maker of the motion always has the right to speak first.

After stating the question, the Chair must ask if the maker of the motion wants to speak, if not, the Chair can then give the floor to the first person asking for it.

In formal meetings (such as a condo assembly), speakers rise to show the Chair that they wish to speak. The Chair (or another person) must keep track of the order in which they rise, and "give them the floor" (allow them to speak) in the same order.

Only one person can speak at a time, and no one who "has the floor" can be interrupted (except in the case of some special motions – more on this later). Again, the Chair must control this.

Normally, a participant can only speak twice to a given motion, except for the mover, **who also has the right to close the discussion** by speaking last.

The Chair must make sure that those who have not yet spoken for the first time are given priority over anyone who rises to speak a second time. If two or more people rise to speak at the same time, the Chair must call first on the one who hasn't spoken yet.

If, however, an important part of a participants's speech has been misinterpreted by a later speaker, the original participant may speak again to clarify the point. However, the Chair must make sure that no new material is snuck in during the explanation.

Mover Can't Oppose Their Own Motion

The mover of a motion can't speak against their own motion, although they **are** allowed to vote against it. The mover doesn't need to speak at all, but, if so, it must always be in favour of their motion.

The seconder of a motion **can** be in opposition to the motion at the time they seconded it, can speak against it, and can vote against it.

Handling Problem Speakers

Another important function of the Chair is to interrupt a speaker who's drifting off-topic, and bring them back on point.

> Off-topic speakers (I call them *"drifters"*) can be a significant time-waster and often frustrate the other participants.

> There's also the speaker who, while they stay on topic, seems to need 100 words to say what most would say with 10 (I call these people *"lecturers"*).

A suggestion that may help with verbose speakers is to adopt rules limiting the time a participant can speak in any one discussion—for example, five, three, or two minutes. Without anything else in your by-laws or procedures, Robert's Rules sets a maximum of ten minutes (**RONR §4. 41.**).

The Chair must keep track of the time each speaker has used (or appoint someone else to do this), and remind the person when they've, say, one minute left, and then tell them to wrap up when the time is up (cutting them off after, say, 30 seconds overtime).

Another annoyance is the person who rises repeatedly to say the same thing, without contributing anything new to the discussion (I call them *"repeaters"*).

This can be eliminated by the Chair strictly enforcing the "only speak twice on one motion" rule, and, on the second time, interrupting the speaker to ask if they've anything new to say.

Amending a Motion

Once a motion has been put to the assembly and discussion starts, it can become obvious that the motion needs to be changed (amended) before it's voted on.

If this happens, a participant (possibly at the invitation of the Chair) can make a motion to amend the motion before the assembly.

The amendment must be pertinent to the motion under discussion, and must be seconded.

The amendment is then read to the assembly as a question by the Chair, can be discussed (but only as to the change itself), and voted on. If the vote passes, the motion has been amended. Discussion can then continue, but on the motion as amended.

See the later discussion of the subsidiary motion "Amend" for more details.

Voting on a Motion

At some point it will become obvious that discussion on a motion has either finished or is going nowhere. At this time, the Chair must call for a vote by putting the question to the assembly.

The Jalisco condo legislation requires somewhat different voting at a condo assembly than that dictated by Robert's Rules. The condo law has considerably higher authority than the rules of order, and **the law must be followed**.

See Chapter 37 – "Voting at an Assembly" for more details on how condo voting must be done under Jalisco state law.

Voting Rights of the Chair

Robert's Rules requires the Chair to abstain from voting except to break a tie (**RONR §4. 50-51.**) – this is to guarantee impartiality.

However, if the Chair is a condo owner, then, by law, they have the same right to vote as anyone else at a condo assembly. For convenience, I recommend that if the Chair has a spouse or partner, then this person cast the vote for their unit.

Resolutions Passed by General Consent

It's neither necessary (nor desirable) to hold a formal vote on every motion – particularly those of an administrative nature. You can avoid this by passing some resolutions by *"general consent."* This is also called *"unanimous consent"* or *"acclamation,"* and just means that no one is opposed.

This must only be done for basic and noncontroversial tasks that are unlikely to be opposed or need discussion. That said, this is a useful tool for speeding an assembly through some of the administrative or housekeeping votes. The items that are commonly passed by general consent at an assembly and at council meetings are listed in detail in other chapters.

Passing a resolution by general consent (**RONR §4. 51-52.**) is done by having the Chair say something like,

> *"If there are no objections, [NAME THE ITEM] will be adopted ... [PAUSE FOR OBJECTIONS] ... Approved by general consent."*

If you ask for general consent and there **are** objections, then a motion must be made, discussion must take place, and a vote must be held.

Note that for a condo assembly there are some motions that are a formality, and **must not be defeated**. This means that no discussion or vote should take place (**details are in Chapter 37 – "Voting at an Assembly"**).

Secondary Motions

Secondary motions are special-purpose motions that can be made only while a main motion is being debated (discussed).

When a main motion has been made and repeated by the Chair, no other main motion may be made until the current main motion is disposed of (typically, by voting on it).

Secondary motions take priority over the main motion being discussed.

When a secondary motion is made, it becomes the immediate concern of the assembly, and the main motion is put on hold until the secondary motion has been dealt with. To complicate things further, certain secondary motions take priority over others. At any given time, there can be only one motion being discussed by the assembly, although there could conceivably be several on hold (much like the layers of an onion).

There are thee types of secondary motions: privileged motions, subsidiary motions, and incidental motions – they're described in more detail in the following paragraphs.

This can become as complicated as it sounds. The good news is that for most condo assemblies there's no need for this.

If you have one or more participants at your assembly who fully understand Robert's Rules, and, if they're so inclined, they can make things difficult for others or even dominate the assembly. This is not the purpose or intent of the rules of order.

You don't need to memorise or learn all these secondary motions. The Chair needs to be aware of them in case someone makes one. In later chapters dealing specifically with condo assemblies and other condo meetings. I've suggested ways you can avoid some of them altogether – some of these motions are just not suitable for a condo assembly.

If your eyes are already glazing over, you can safely skip to "Appealing Rulings Made by the Chair." You won't need this information unless one of these motions comes up at an assembly or meeting. However, if you're planning on chairing either, then I'm afraid that you really should read on!

Privileged Motions

This group of secondary motions has the highest priority.

Privileged motions are special because they don't relate to the business currently under discussion. They involve matters of immediate and overriding importance, and are allowed to interrupt anything else.

The five privileged motions are listed below in order of priority (each motion takes priority over all motions listed after it):

1. **Fix the Time to Which to Adjourn** (RONR §22. 234.)

   During the discussion of a main motion, the assembly might want to set a date and time for another assembly to be held before the next regular assembly.

   This doesn't adjourn the assembly, and discussion on the main motion continues after this motion.

   It can't interrupt a speaker, must be seconded, isn't debatable, is amendable only as to the date and time, and must be voted on.

2. **Adjourn** (RONR §21. 225.)

   This will end the assembly. A participant rises and says, "*I move to adjourn.*"

   It can't interrupt a speaker, must be seconded, isn't debatable, isn't amendable, and must be voted on.

3. **Recess** (RONR §20. 222.)

    Unlike adjourn, this doesn't end the assembly, but just pauses it for a short break. A participant rises and says something like, "*I move to recess for 15 minutes.*"

    It can't interrupt a speaker, must be seconded, isn't debatable, is amendable only as to the length of the recess, and must be voted on.

4. **Raise a Question of Privilege** (RONR §19. 216.)

    If a situation comes up that affects the convenience, comfort, rights, integrity, or privileges of the assembly or an individual participant (such as poor ventilation, noise, or a concern over the reputation of a participant or of the assembly), a participant can raise a point of privilege.

    To do this, the participant must interrupt the assembly by rising and addressing the Chair with a *"question of privilege."* The Chair must give this participant the floor right away to make their urgent statement, request, or motion.

    The Chair must first try to resolve the issue informally (for example, by asking someone to open a window). If the issue isn't simple enough to take care of informally, the Chair must make a ruling.

    A point of privilege can also be used to seek permission to present any motion of an urgent nature.

    It can interrupt another speaker, must be seconded, isn't debatable, isn't amendable, and is ruled on by the Chair with no vote by the assembly.

5. **Call for the Orders of the Day** (RONR §18. 211.)

   If Orders of the Day or an adopted Agenda exist, and aren't being followed, a participant can rise to interrupt the assembly and ask that the agenda be followed. The Chair must enforce the Orders of the Day or the Agenda even if only a single participant asks.

   It can interrupt another speaker, doesn't need to be seconded, isn't debatable, isn't amendable, and the Chair must enforce the motion with no vote by the assembly.

Subsidiary Motions

This is the other category of secondary motions, and these all have a lower priority than the privileged motions.

They are called subsidiary motions because they help the assembly deal with (or dispose of) a main motion.

The seven subsidiary motions are listed below in order of priority (each motion takes priority over all motions listed after it):

1. **Lay on the Table** (RONR §17. 201.)

   Sometimes the assembly wants to put a motion aside temporarily without setting a specific time to resume it, but with the understanding that it can be taken up again whenever the majority decides. A participant rises and says, "*I move to lay the motion on the table.*"

   This motion delays action on a main motion. If a subsequent assembly doesn't lift the question from the table, this motion will prevent action from ever being taken on the motion – this is sometimes the intent.

It's important to know that this motion also affects all other motions under the main motion, including amendments.

It can't interrupt a speaker, must be seconded, isn't debatable, isn't amendable, and must be voted on.

2. **Previous Question or Call for the Question** (RONR §16. 189.)

   This is a tactic to end debate on a question.

   It should only be used when the debate has been overly long or repetitious. A participant rises and says: "*I move the previous question*" – also acceptable are, "*I call for the question,*" or "*I move we vote now.*"

   The confusing thing about the name of this motion is that **it refers to the current question**, and not the one previous to it.

   It can't interrupt a speaker, must be seconded, isn't debatable, isn't amendable, and must be voted on – this motion requires a two-thirds majority vote to pass.

   This stringent voting requirement protects the democratic process. Without it, a momentary majority of a single vote could deny all the other participants the opportunity to discuss any measure that this "majority" wanted to adopt or to defeat.

   If this motion passes, the Chair must call a vote on the question that was being debated right away, and **the maker of the motion loses their right to close debate with the last word.**

   If the motion is defeated, debate continues as if nothing had happened.

A common misconception is that participants can simply yell out, "*Question!*" to get the Chair to call the question right away. If this happens, the participant calling out "*Question!*" must be ruled out of order by the Chair – this isn't only an improper motion, it isn't even a motion at all!

3. **Limit or Extend Limits of Debate** (RONR §15. 183.)

   A motion to limit debate changes the normal rules of debate.

   It could, for example, limit the time of the entire discussion on a motion ("*I move that debate on this motion be limited to 15 minutes*"), or it could limit the time taken by each speaker ("*I move that debate on this motion be limited to two minutes per speaker*").

   A motion to extend debate allows greater participation and time than is usually permitted.

   It can't interrupt a speaker, must be seconded, isn't debatable, is amendable, and must be voted on – this requires a two-thirds majority vote to pass.

4. **Postpone to a Certain Time** (RONR §14. 172.)

   If the assembly wants to consider a main motion later in the assembly (or at a subsequent one), it can move to postpone a motion to a certain time (which must be set out in the motion). A participant rises and says something like, "*I move to postpone discussion on this motion until after the discussion on cats on leashes.*"

   This motion can be moved regardless of how much debate there's been on the motion it wants to postpone.

   A motion can be postponed either to a specific time, or until after some other item of business has been dealt with.

When the time to which a motion has been postponed arrives, the Chair must read the postponed motion to the assembly for its immediate consideration. If another item of business is being discussed at that time, the Chair must present the postponed motion right away after the other business has been concluded.

It can't interrupt a speaker, must be seconded, is debatable, is amendable as to the time, and must be voted on.

5. **Commit or Refer** (RONR §13. 160.)

    If it becomes obvious that the assembly doesn't have enough information to make a proper decision, or when it seems advisable to have a small group work out details that'll take too much time in the larger assembly, a participant can move, *"that the question be referred to a committee"*.

    It can't interrupt a speaker, must be seconded, is debatable only as to the advisability of the referral, can be amended (within limits), and must be voted on.

    If a motion to refer is passed, the committee to which the matter is referred must report on the question at a subsequent assembly. Sometimes the motion to refer will include a specific date or time when this report is needed.

6. **Amend** (RONR §12. 125.)

    An amendment is a motion to change another motion.

    This change is usually made to clarify or improve the wording of the original motion, and it must be pertinent to that motion.

    A participant rises and says something like, *"I move to amend the motion by adding a requirement to clean up the pool area after each use."*

It can't interrupt a speaker, must be seconded, is debatable (if the motion to be amended is debatable), may itself be amended by an amendment to the amendment (I know … I know … my eyes are glazing over too!), and must be voted on.

The Chair must allow full discussion of the change – being careful to limit debate to the amendment only, and not the original motion.

A vote must then be taken – again, on the amendment only, making sure the participants know that they're voting on adopting the changes, and not the original motion.

If the amendment is defeated, either another one can be proposed, or discussion can resume on the original motion.

If the amendment passes, the assembly doesn't necessarily vote on the "motion as amended" right away. There might still be participants who want to speak on the issue raised in the original motion that was interrupted by the amendment.

Other amendments can also be proposed, as long as they don't alter or negate the amendments already passed.

Once all discussion and amending (including amending the amendment to the amendment) has finished, the assembly must vote on the *"motion as amended"* or, if all amendments were defeated, on the original motion.

Good news – in practice, this isn't as convoluted as it seems!

7. **Postpone Indefinitely** (RONR §11. 121.)

    The name of this motion is misleading, since it doesn't postpone. **It kills the current main motion** (this is the *"indefinitely"* part).

This can be used by a participant to dispose of a question without bringing it to a vote.

It can't interrupt a speaker, must be seconded, is debatable, isn't amendable, and must be voted on.

If passed, the motion kills the matter under consideration. If the intent is to actually postpone a motion, rather than kill it, you must use *"Postpone to a Certain Time"* instead.

Incidental Motions

This is the final category of secondary motions. They're unique in that they have no priority – they're triggered by circumstances.

Incidental motions are for dealing with questions of procedure that come from another motion or an item of business.

With few exceptions, incidental motions are related to the motion being discussed right then (not necessarily the main motion), and must be decided right away before business can continue.

Each particular incidental motion can be used only in its special circumstance. These circumstances could be a feature of the current motion, or something that happened during the assembly.

An important distinction between incidental and subsidiary motions is that subsidiary motions can usually be applied to any main motion over the entire time that it's being discussed.

The eight **most common** incidental motions are (there are 11):

1. **Point of Order** (RONR §23. 240.)

   This motion lets a participant draw the Chair's attention to what they believe is an error in procedure, or to a lack of decorum in the discussion.

The participant must rise and say, *"I rise to a point of order,"* or *"Point of order."* The Chair must recognise the participant right away, who must then state their point of order. This is not the same as *"Point of Information."*

The Chair must then make an immediate ruling on the issue involved, and must give reasons for the ruling. If the ruling is thought to be wrong, the Chair can be challenged.

It can interrupt another speaker, doesn't need to be seconded, isn't debatable, isn't amendable, and the Chair must make a ruling with no vote (unless the Chair is in doubt or the ruling is appealed).

2. **Suspend the Rules** (RONR §25. 252.)

    Sometimes an assembly may want to take an action, but is prevented by one or more of its rules of order.

    The assembly can vote to suspend the rules that are preventing it from taking the action it wants to take. A participant rises and says, *"I move to suspend the rules that interfere with* [description of action that's not allowed]."

    It's important to note that **only rules of order can be suspended**. An assembly **cannot** suspend rules of either the condo legislation or its by-laws.

    After the assembly has taken the action it wanted to take, the rules that were suspended automatically come back into force.

    It can't interrupt a speaker, must be seconded, isn't debatable, isn't amendable, and must be voted on – this requires a two-thirds majority vote to pass. It may also be passed by general consent, but if there is even a single objection, then a formal vote must be taken.

3. **Objection to the Consideration of a Question** (RONR §26. 258.)

   If a participant believes that it would be harmful for the assembly to discuss the main motion, they can raise an objection to the question when it's first put before the assembly.

   A participant rises, and, without waiting to be recognised, says, *"I object to the consideration of this motion."* They then must give the reason. The Chair responds, *"The consideration of the motion has been objected to. Should the motion be considered?"*

   It can interrupt another speaker (but only if debate has not begun, or a subsidiary motion has not been accepted by the Chair), doesn't need to be seconded, isn't debatable, isn't amendable, and must be voted on – this requires a two-thirds majority vote to pass.

   This strict vote is required because the decision amends the agenda.

4. **Consideration by Paragraph or Seriatim** (RONR §28. 266.)

   If a main motion is complicated, and contains several paragraphs or sections (very unusual for condo business), and if it's felt that these would be more efficiently handled by opening the paragraphs or sections to amendment one at a time (before the entire motion is finally voted on), a participant can propose a motion to consider the motion by paragraph (or seriatim).

   It can't interrupt a speaker, must be seconded, isn't debatable, is amendable, and must be voted on.

5. **Division of the Assembly** (RONR §29. 270.)

   If a participant doubts the accuracy of the results of a show of hands vote as announced by the Chair, they can demand a division of the assembly – a standing vote.

   A participant rises and says, "*I call for a division,*" or, simply, "*Division!*"

   It can interrupt another speaker, doesn't need to be seconded, isn't debatable, isn't amendable, and requires no vote – the demand of a single participant forces the standing vote.

6. **Motions Relating to Methods of Voting** (RONR §30. 273.)

   A participant can move that a vote be taken by roll call, by ballot, or that the standing votes be counted (if a division of the assembly is visually inconclusive, and the Chair doesn't order a count).

   They can't interrupt a speaker, must be seconded, aren't debatable, are amendable, and must be voted on.

7. **Motions Relating to Nominations** (RONR §31. 275.)

   If your by-laws don't say how nominations are to be made (they should), and if an assembly hasn't collected nominations before an election, any participant can (while the election is pending) move to set out one of several methods by which candidates can be nominated, or to close nominations, or to re-open them.

   They can't interrupt a speaker, must be seconded, aren't debatable, are amendable, and must be voted on.

8. **Requests and Inquiries** (RONR §33. 280.)

    1. **Parliamentary Inquiry** (RONR §33. 281.): a request for the Chair's opinion (not a ruling) on a matter of parliamentary procedure as it relates to the business at hand.

    2. **Point of Information** (RONR §33. 282.): a question about facts affecting the business at hand, directed to the Chair who, in turn, can get opinions from others.

        A participant rises and says, *"Point of information."* This is not the same as *"Point of Order."*

    3. **Request for Permission to Withdraw or Modify a Motion** (RONR §33. 283.): Robert's Rules says that until a motion has been accepted by the Chair, it's the property of the mover – who can withdraw it, or change it as they wish. Common practice, however, is that once the agenda has been adopted, the items on it become the property of the assembly.

        A person can't, therefore, withdraw a motion by themselves. They can do this only with the consent of the assembly, once it has adopted an agenda showing this motion.

        A person also can't, without the consent of the assembly, change the wording of any motion that's been sent out ahead of time to those present at the assembly – for example, emailed before the assembly, or printed on the agenda.

        Usually, the mover will ask the consent of the assembly to withdraw the motion or change the wording.

        If no one objects, the Chair announces that since there are no objections, the motion is withdrawn or that the changed wording is the motion to be debated.

If anyone does object, a motion must be made and seconded to allow the participant to withdraw (or change) their motion – a vote decides.

A two-thirds majority is needed for permission to withdraw a motion, since this has the effect of changing the agenda.

4. **Request to Read Papers** (RONR §33. 286.).

If any participant objects, another participant can't read from any paper or book as a part of his speech without permission of the assembly.

This rule is designed to protect against using reading as a way of prolonging debate, and delaying business (filibustering).

It's usual, however, to allow participants to read short, pertinent, extracts during discussion, as long as they don't abuse this.

The participant says, while speaking in debate, something like, *"If there's no objection, I'd like to read a short excerpt from the Jalisco Condo Manual."* The participant then starts to read, unless another participant objects. If so, it must be voted on.

5. **Request for Any Other Privilege** (RONR §33. 287.).

This is a catch-all category to allow a participant to make a request that isn't covered by one of the other four types of requests listed above.

The participant rises, addresses the Chair, and makes his request. Although they can interrupt another speaker to make this request, they must never do this unless the urgency justifies it.

Usually these requests are settled by general consent, but, if there is an objection, then a motion must be made and voted on to grant the request.

If an explanation is needed, it can be asked for or given, but this must be brief, and not turn into a discussion.

Incidental motions can interrupt a speaker (if they need immediate attention), don't normally need to be seconded, aren't debatable, and aren't amendable.

Parliamentary Inquiry and **Point of Information** are responded to by the Chair (or by a participant, at the direction of the Chair), with no vote. The remaining requests must be voted on.

Appealing Rulings Made by the Chair

Some of the motions above are ruled on by the Chair, with no vote of the assembly. To avoid arbitrary control of an assembly by the Chair, there's another incidental motion called *"Appeal"* (**RONR §24. 247.**).

A participant rises and says, *"I appeal the Chair's decision."*

It's **applicable only to rulings made by the Chair.**

An assembly can't use the appeal motion, for example, to overturn a by-laws provision by making an appeal motion, and then voting to interpret your by-laws to mean something other than their obvious meaning.

If such an appeal is moved, the Chair must rule it out of order right away, without opening it to debate, or putting it to a vote.

No appeals can be made against rulings by the Chair that come out of obvious or known facts, or established laws, rules, or regulations (such as the condo law or your by-laws).

An appeal can, however, be made against rulings by the Chair that are based on their personal opinion, judgment, or discretion.

It can interrupt a speaker (but only at the time of the ruling), must be seconded, is debatable, isn't amendable, and must be voted on.

If there's a tie vote, the Chair's ruling is upheld.

Summary of Rules

A *"Table of Motions"* summarising all the most important motions (according to Robert's Rules), is included in your BONUS Pack.

Communicating Your Rules

As part of your condo's communications plan, a brief guide to the rules of order used at an assembly is useful to send out to all owners (and post on your condo's web site).

Remember that your owners come from a wide variety of work and life experiences, and may not be familiar with Robert's Rules.

You might also find that there are those who **believe** that they understand Robert's rules, but have some misconceptions.

A quick reference guide will help you avoid problems and misunderstandings.

A sample *"Owner's Guide to Assemblies"* is included in your BONUS Pack.

Specific Recommendations

The next chapters deal with streamlining Robert's Rules for condo assemblies and council/committee meetings.

Rules of Order for Assemblies

Chapter **30**

To make sure that assemblies don't get out of hand, that they run efficiently, and that everyone's opinion is heard, formal rules of order must be used.

However, not every rule of order is suitable for condo assemblies in the state of Jalisco.

While I recommend that you adopt **Robert's Rules** for your assemblies, it can't be fully adopted. You must adopt a slightly changed version.

Recommended Changes to Rules of Order for Assemblies

Your by-laws (or a notice sent out before each assembly) can just say the following:

> Owners assemblies are governed by Robert's Rules of Order Newly Revised, with the exception that the following motions are not permitted:
>
> 1. Adjourn
> 2. Lay on the Table
> 3. Previous Question or Call for the Question
> 4. Postpone to a Certain Time
> 5. Commit or Refer
> 6. Postpone Indefinitely
> 7. Objection to the Consideration of a Question
> 8. Motions Relating to Methods of Voting

Explanations for Excluded Motions

Here's a detailed explanation of why each motion on this list has been disallowed:

1. **<u>Adjourn</u>**

    This motion will end the assembly without any further business being discussed.

    This motion can't be allowed for a condo assembly because the assembly is legally obligated to finish all items on the Order of the Day that was published with the assembly call.

2. **<u>Lay on the Table</u>**

    This motion delays action on a main motion until a future assembly.

    This can't be used in a condo assembly, since all items on the Order of the Day must be decided at the current assembly.

3. **<u>Previous Question or Call for the Question</u>**

    This motion ends debate on a motion and forces a vote.

    While this motion doesn't violate the condo law, I recommend that you don't allow a forced end to discussion.

    A condo is a community of friends and neighbours, not a corporation. A motion that stifles people from expressing their opinion is counter-productive to the goal of building an inclusive community (which is what a condominium should be).

    This motion can also be easily abused by some to prevent opposing views from being heard.

Rules of Order for Assemblies

The Chair is perfectly capable of asking the assembly if they're ready to vote when debate seems to have become pointless.

4. **Postpone to a Certain Time**

   If the assembly wants to consider a motion later in the assembly (or at another one), this motion will postpone the affected motion to a certain time (which must be set out in the motion).

   Not only is this unlikely to be useful for a condo assembly, it violates the Order of the Day – which must be strictly followed.

5. **Commit or Refer**

   If the assembly feels that it doesn't have enough information to make a decision, or when it seems advisable to have a small group work out details that would take too much time in the larger assembly, a motion can be made *"that the question be referred to a committee"*.

   Although this motion itself doesn't technically violate any law, it has little use at a condo assembly. By law, all issues must be resolved the same day at the same assembly.

   This could possibly be used if the committee only needs a short period of time, and the assembly is able to recess for this same amount of time. However, if you use an open process to publicly work out key resolutions before your assembly, this shouldn't be necessary.

6. **Postpone Indefinitely**

   This motion **kills the current main motion** without bringing it to a vote.

This motion can't be allowed at a condo assembly, since the assembly is legally obligated to deal with each item on the published Order of the Day.

7. **Objection to the Consideration of a Question**

   If a participant believes that it would be harmful for the assembly to discuss the main motion, they can raise an objection.

   This motion can't be allowed at a condo assembly since the assembly is legally obligated to decide on all matters contained in the Order of the Day.

8. **Motions Relating to Methods of Voting**

   A participant can move that a vote be taken by roll call, by ballot, or that the standing votes be counted.

   This motion can't be allowed at a condo assembly, since the voting methods are strictly set out by the condo legislation and, possibly, your condo's by-laws.

Preventing Nominations From the Floor

To help avoid election problems at an assembly, it's a good idea to expressly forbid nominations from the floor.

You can add the following to your modified rules of order, *"Assembly elections must be by pre-nomination only. Nominations will not be accepted at the assembly."*

Better yet, you should also include this in your by-laws.

For a complete discussion of this issue, **see Chapter 39 – "Recommended Election Procedures."**

Dealing With Secondary Motions at Assemblies

The condo law requires proportional voting on any resolutions passed by an assembly. Therefore, a roll-call vote is necessary. If a secondary motion is made, however, then a simple vote is all that's needed (**see Chapter 37 – "Voting at an Assembly"**).

These motions only affect the progress of the assembly itself, and are a way of arriving at the final resolution.

> For example, if someone moves to amend the main motion, then, after discussion, the Chair can say, *"We have a motion to amend the main motion to read "xxxxx", does anyone object?* [PAUSE] *So amended by general consent."*
>
> If there's an objection, then a vote must be taken, but it can be a show of hands vote that'll pass with a simple majority.

Be careful! Whenever you're voting on a final resolution that's to become binding on all owners (as opposed to a secondary motion that only affects conducting the business of the assembly), then you **must** conduct a proportional roll-call vote.

Resolutions that require a roll-call vote are easily identified, since they correspond to the Order of the Day.

Discussion on Motions

Smaller condos (say, less than 50 units) can benefit from relaxed rules of order about discussion of motions.

Larger condos, however, need to pay attention to this to make sure that assemblies don't get out of hand. The larger your condo, the more important it is to strictly adhere to "one speaker at a time with no interruptions," and "each speaker can only speak twice."

Time-Limiting of Speakers

Again, small condos can relax this, although I don't recommend eliminating it. Even small condos can have people who just love to hear the sound of their own voice, and monopolise everyone's time. For a small condo, it may be wise to set a limit of 10 minutes.

Larger condos have potentially more speakers. Therefore, it's probably wise to have a shorter time limit of, say, five minutes.

This also prevents speakers from regaling the assembly with the entire history behind an issue. This doesn't interest the assembly since this information should have been circulated before the assembly. Remember that the assembly is only interested in short and concise reasons to vote "YES" or "NO" on a specific resolution.

A sample guide, *"How to Chair a Condo Assemblies"* is included in your BONUS Pack.

Rules of Order for Council & Committee Meetings

Chapter **31**

Councils and committees are much smaller and more informal groups than condo assemblies. For groups of this size, formal rules of order can be more of a hindrance than a help. I recommend, that you use a relaxed set of rules of order for your council and committee meetings.

Relaxed Rules of Order for Council & Committee Meetings

Robert's Rules calls for small groups (typically less than 12 members) to meet using relaxed rules (**RONR §1. 9.**). Your by-laws, or the Council or committee's Terms of Reference, can just say the following:

> Council and committee meetings are governed by Robert's Rules of Order Newly Revised as it applies to small committees of less than 12 members. Specifically, there are the following six differences between assemblies and small meetings:
>
> 1. Councillors or committee members are not required to have the floor before making motions or speaking, and may stay seated while doing so.
>
> 2. Motions need not be seconded.
>
> 3. There is no limit to the number of times a councillor or committee member may speak to a motion, and motions to limit or end debate are not allowed.
>
> 4. While no motion is pending, informal discussion of a topic is allowed.
>
> 5. All proposed actions of the Council or committee must be voted on, but the vote is by a simple show of hands.

6. The Chair need not rise while putting questions to a vote, may speak in discussion without rising, may make motions, and may vote on all questions.

Abstaining From Voting

If a councillor or committee member abstains from voting, the reasons must be recorded in the minutes.

Councillors can't abstain from voting for any reason other than a conflict of interest, since they have a fiduciary duty to address all issues brought before the Administrative Council, regardless of their personal feelings or opinions.

Chairing an Assembly or Council/Committee Meeting

Chapter **32**

The role of the Chair is vital to conducting a successful meeting or assembly. Many people believe that the Chair just opens and adjourns the meeting, and stops the occasional argument. **There's much more to it than that!**

Goal of the Chair

The primary goal of the Chair is to make sure that the assembly or meeting achieves its goals.

> Condo assemblies are called to carry out specific tasks that have been set out before the assembly (in the Order of the Day that's published with the call).
>
> Other condo meetings (council and committee) should also be called for a specific purpose.
>
> > The Council will have regular monthly meetings, as well as special meetings to deal with a specific issue.
> >
> > Committees generally meet when there's either something specific they need to deal with, or as a "catch-up" if they haven't met for some time.
>
> In both cases, a draft agenda should have been circulated before the meeting, changed as needed, and adopted at the start of the meeting.

As Chair, it's your responsibility to steer all discussion at the assembly or meeting according to the Order of the Day or the adopted agenda. This might seem obvious and sound simple, but, in practice, it can often be a challenging task.

Skills Needed to Chair

The skills needed of you as Chair include:

- **Impartiality**

    A Chair is somewhat like a judge. Regardless of your personal views or feelings, you must make sure that all participants have an opportunity to express their point of view.

    Believe me, it's difficult to leave your personal opinions at the door, but if you can't stay impartial, you shouldn't chair a meeting or an assembly.

    It's especially important to handle conflicts impartially, and conflicts are inevitable.

    When introducing an agenda item, just announce the topic, and, if necessary, give a background summary (be brief!). Never blame anyone, and always try to talk about the issue in a constructive way.

- **Knowledge of the Rules of Order**

    The Chair must be familiar with at least the basics of the rules or order in use at the assembly or meeting, and, preferably, understand the finer points as well.

- **Assertiveness**

    As Chair, you must make sure that everyone is heard.

    Unfortunately, this almost always involves preventing one or two individuals from dominating the discussion – you mustn't allow a vocal minority to overpower less assertive participants.

    The more contentious the issue is, the more you'll likely need to be firm.

Chairing an Assembly or Council/Committee Meeting

Don't misunderstand this, you don't need to be rude, patronising, or dogmatic. A tactful, but assertive, Chair becomes a facilitator, and the end result is an effective meeting.

Try to be proactive. If only one or two people always seem to be the main participants, specifically ask for other views. If some people always seem to be silent, draw them out by asking for their opinions.

When there's dissent over an issue, the Chair must encourage and promote cooperation. This can be done by clarifying or summarising what people have said, and then asking the participants to propose specific solutions.

Heated arguments need to be nipped in the bud, and might even need a short break to allow the participants to cool off. You must keep profane language and personal attacks in check.

At an assembly, the Chair must make sure that speakers are given the floor in the order they asked for it (by observing the audience), that speakers aren't interrupted, and that each attendee has a chance to speak at least once before someone who's already spoken is given the floor for the second time.

At a relaxed rules meeting (such as a council or committee meeting), the Chair should try to use phrases such as, *"I think we should hear from John on this"*, or *"can we have some comments from Derek on this issue?"*.

Once you give a participant this opening, you must make sure that there are no interruptions while the next speaker has their say.

- **Keeping on Track**

    Meetings naturally tend to drift away from the agenda – this is human nature. As Chair, you must always keep foremost in your mind the reason the current agenda item is being discussed, and the goals the group are trying to achieve.

    Part of being able to do this is being familiar with your adopted rules of order, and their procedures for the type of meeting that you're chairing.

    You need to assess the importance of each item on the agenda, and allot time to each topic based on this. If time is a major constraint, you can always name someone as timekeeper.

    Listen carefully, and prevent participants with nothing new to add from repeating a point they've already made.

    If one issue begins to take up too much time, the Chair must take control. You could suggest delaying the item to a future meeting, or that the main parties involved continue the discussion at the end of the meeting.

    If, however, the issue needs to be resolved at this meeting (an assembly, for example), then you must end the discussion and call for a motion – especially if you feel that further discussion is pointless, repetitive, or going nowhere.

    Throughout the meeting, you must be alert to make sure that each issue is given an adequate and impartial hearing, in a reasonably allotted time.

- **Summarising**

    Summarising is a tool that a Chair can use to end a topic, to end a discussion, to limit the need for discussion, and, at the end of the meeting, to make sure that everyone has an understanding of what took place and what actions are now needed.

    You may want to give a short summary of how each issue was resolved before moving on to the next agenda item. In this summary, you should make sure that the participants understand what the group has just agreed to.

    You should consider ending the meeting with an action summary – an even better idea is to send out an Action Plan within a day after the meeting.

    Meetings generally fail because people are either not held accountable, or they don't feel accountable – it's important that they own any issue they're tasked with. Avoid assigning tasks to "someone."

    In either your verbal summary or (better yet) the Action Plan, you should summarise the actions that group members have agreed to carry out, and make clear the deadline or time-frame for each action. Remember, **the only way to get a true commitment from someone is to clearly assign them a task with a clearly set out deadline.**

    The ability to summarise is a valuable skill for a Chair to have.

    Summarising needs active listening skills – you must restate <u>concisely</u> what was said (*important* – don't take as long for your summary as the discussion itself!), say this in an impartial way (don't interject your own personal opinion or bias), and end with a clear statement about what's expected to happen next.

While it does take practice to summarise well, it's a skill that's worth developing.

Things to Avoid

There are also a number of things that you must avoid when chairing an assembly or meeting:

- taking sides;
- being overly verbose;
- manipulating the meeting in favour of your personal agenda;
- criticising the ideas or values of others;
- being overly verbose;
- forcing your own ideas on the group;
- making decisions without asking the participants for agreement; and
- being overly verbose.

Tips for Effective Chairing

- **Before the meeting**

    As Chair of any condo-related meeting, whether it be an assembly, a council meeting, or an information session, it's important to do your homework before the meeting:

    - familiarise yourself with the issues, and assess the priority and potential for divisiveness for each agenda item; allot time to each agenda item based on: these priorities, decisions needed, the number of people who'll be there, and any time constraints on vital participants (for example, our lawyer must leave by 2:00pm);

Chairing an Assembly or Council/Committee Meeting

- read emails and other submissions;

- gather together all the materials relevant to the Order of the Day or the Agenda; have copies printed and available for the meeting; and

- make sure that all interested parties have been notified; try to make sure that any people needed for the meeting (for example, the Chair of a committee responsible for an agenda item, or a person who's done some research on a topic) will be there.

For an assembly, it's wise to prepare a script based on the Order of the Day so that everything runs smoothly and doesn't deviate from the Order of the Day (**it cannot!**).

- **Starting the meeting**

    It's a good idea to set up a rapport and level of comfort with the participants. Guests from the community (especially if they're at a council or committee meeting for the first time) might be tentative and guarded during the first few minutes of a meeting.

    Greet people before you sit down. If it suits your personality, break the ice with some **suitable** humour.

    Have coffee and muffins, if appropriate – it's amazing how people bond around food and drink.

    Always start on time, and don't wait for stragglers (unless they're needed for a quorum). Once the advertised starting time has arrived, call the meeting to order as soon as you have a quorum.

    If you begin and end on time, you'll condition the participants to be on time.

Before officially getting under way, make the group aware of any time constraints. For example, you could say something like, *"We have only one hour today, and Vick has to leave at 1:30."*

In the case of an assembly, the Chair should make preliminary remarks that give an overview of the assembly. As well, give a brief summary of the most common aspects of the rules of order (such as rising to be noticed, or only one person speaks at once).

- **During the meeting**

  The Chair must:

  - focus on the decisions needed to be made at this meeting vs. issues that can be delayed if time doesn't permit (this doesn't apply to an assembly);
  - make sure that everyone is given adequate time to express their opinion;
  - decide when to end discussion on each issue;
  - use suitable questions to get information and opinions from the participants, or to re-direct the discussion;
  - control heated discussions, personal attacks, and profane language;
  - listen carefully to all opinions; and
  - clearly summarise the proceedings including the decisions taken, and future plans.

- **Ending the meeting**

  Do your best to make sure that the meeting finishes on time – pay attention to time constraints that participants might have.

Chairing an Assembly or Council/Committee Meeting

> **IMPORTANT!**
> If one or more council or committee members have to leave the meeting, make sure that you still have a quorum after they leave – if you won't, then you must adjourn the meeting as soon as they go.

- **Outside of meetings**

    Try to get feedback from others about your role as Chair. Ask them what they think your weaknesses were, and ask them for suggestions on where you can improve.

    While this can be difficult (no one enjoys criticism), remember that this solicited constructive criticism will help you improve. When their opinion is solicited, few people will be rude or abusive.

    Pay attention to how others chair meetings. Analyse both their good points (incorporate them), and their bad points (avoid them).

Other Responsibilities

Other responsibilities of the Chair are detailed in **Chapter 29 – "Rules of Order Explained"** in the context of each procedure.

A sample guide, *"How to Chair a Condo Assemblies"* is included in your BONUS Pack.

PART 10 – Proxies

The Problem With Proxies

Chapter 33

It might just be me, but the title of this chapter reminds me of the classic Star Trek episode, *"The Trouble With Tribbles"* – which is fitting, since the recommendations contained in this section of my book seem to stir up controversy with some. I'm about to boldly go where no condo administrator has gone before...

What is a Proxy?

A proxy is a legal power of attorney that allows someone who's physically present at a meeting to act for an absentee who's entitled to take part in the meeting.

The proxy form allows this representative to vote on resolutions instead of the absentee owner.

Proxies are also used to count towards quorum, so that the absentee owner's condo rights are included as part of the quorum at an ordinary assembly during roll-call.

What Does the Condo Law Say About Proxies?

The Jalisco condo law is silent on proxies. Since they aren't explicitly forbidden, there's nothing that seems to prevent their use.

However, you shouldn't use proxies without fully understanding them and formalising them in your by-laws – your by-laws may already have a clause or two about proxies.

That said, the use of proxies (or their non-use) can also be a highly controversial subject.

"Why controversial?", I can hear you say...

Disadvantages of Proxies

Proxies have two well-known disadvantages:

1. One or a group of owners might hold a number of proxies from absentee owners to create a voting block to further their own agenda.

2. Proxies eliminate the advantages of a deliberative assembly where owners discuss issues before voting on them. An absentee vote is an uninformed vote, because the voter isn't part of these discussions. Nor do they have knowledge of any changes made to the resolutions.

   It's largely for this reason that the **10th Edition of Robert's Rules of Order Newly Revised** doesn't allow proxy voting unless state law or the organisation's by-laws require it.

Let's look at these problems in more detail.

Problem #1 - Voting Blocks

You've likely seen voting blocks in action – one person or group holds enough proxies to force the outcome of a contentious vote to suit their agenda. It is seldom in the best interests of your community to allow the will of a minority to become binding on all owners.

The most effective defence against this tactic is to not allow general proxies.

All proxies should be limited by having the voting intentions of the proxy giver clearly shown, rather than allowing the proxy holder to vote in any way they want.

Problem #2 - Uninformed Voting

This is by far the bigger problem of the two.

Have you ever gone to a meeting and expected to vote one way on an issue, but were swayed to vote differently because of points raised by others during discussion at the meeting? An owner who votes by proxy gives up the fundamental right to change their mind based on new information or points of view.

> For example, suppose there's a vote on an improvement to upgrade your condo's entry gate, to be paid by special fees. The proposal put forth at the assembly is minimum. At the assembly, there's discussion about increasing the gate's security and reliability. Coming out of this is an amended motion to add some extra-cost features to enhance the original proposal. This amendment is approved at the assembly.
>
> The proxy givers couldn't possibly know about any of this when they voted on their proxy ballots.

The fundamental issue here is that because of an absentee owner's lack of participation in the discussion, this owner's pre-meeting vote was based on different information than people who were physically present at the meeting.

Even if the proxy holder was given permission to vote as they saw fit (a general proxy), they couldn't possibly know how the absentee owner would have voted if they'd heard the discussion. If, after the meeting, the absentee owner disagrees with how the proxy holder voted on their behalf, they have no recourse. This is another reason not to use general proxies.

Robert's Rules' Position on Proxies

Robert's Rules is a set of rules that allow meetings and assemblies to proceed in an orderly fashion (**see Part 9 – "Rules of Order"**). It's become the most commonly adopted and recognised authority on meeting procedures in the US and Canada.

The **10th Edition of Robert's Rules of Order Newly Revised** says this about **absentee voting using ballots** (such as the ballot on a proxy form):

> "It is a fundamental principle of parliamentary law that the right to vote is limited to the members of an organization **who are actually present at the time the vote is taken** ... The votes of those present could be affected by debate, by amendments, and perhaps by the need for repeated balloting, while those absent would be unable to adjust their votes to reflect these factors. Consequently, the absentee ballots would in most cases be on a somewhat different question than that on which those present were voting, leading to confusion, unfairness, and inaccuracy in determining the result."

Robert's Rules says this about **proxy voting**:

> "Proxy voting is not permitted in ordinary deliberative assemblies unless the laws of the state in which the society is incorporated require it, or the charter or bylaws of the organization provide for it ... Ordinarily it should neither be allowed nor required, **because proxy voting is incompatible with the essential characteristics of a deliberative assembly...**"

Because of these issues, proxies are only used either by shareholders, or in elections where the slate of candidates is fixed and can't be changed at the meeting.

The Use of Proxies at an Assembly

Chapter **34**

As I've covered previously, the two types of condo assemblies work differently:

1. **ordinary assemblies** need a quorum, only a limited set of administrative issues can be dealt with, and votes on resolutions are counted only at the assembly;

2. **extraordinary assemblies** have no quorum requirement, potentially contentious issues are dealt with that could result in much discussion, and votes on resolutions must be solicited from absentee owners in the 30 days after the assembly.

Based on this, let's look at proxy use at each type of assembly in detail.

Proxies at an Extraordinary Assembly

I'll deal with the extraordinary assembly first, since it's the simplest. I recommend that you **do not accept proxies for an extraordinary assembly**.

"Hey! Wait a minute ... aren't you taking away our democratic rights?"

No, exactly the opposite ... here's why:

- Since no quorum is needed, you don't rely on proxies to give you the numbers needed to legally hold the assembly.

- The condo legislation (**Article 1023**) nicely resolves all the problems with proxy voting.

    For any motions that didn't pass at an extraordinary assembly, absentee votes must be collected up to 30 days after the assembly, unless this would make no difference to the outcome.

This process gives the absentee owners the opportunity to learn what happened, and talk with owners who were present about: the assembly, the issues, the discussions, and any other or changed motions. They can then cast an **informed** vote (which cannot be done before the assembly takes place).

This Jalisco condo law provision is there to protect absentee owners from the cancellation of their voting rights that comes with the use of proxies.

If an absentee owner gives someone their proxy, they give up their rights under this provision of the condo law. In my view, this is too important a right to give up – the right to make an informed vote after-the-fact based on what happened at the assembly.

Proxies at an Ordinary Assembly

In my opinion, proxies are a useful tool for an ordinary assembly. I do, however, recommend that proxies be specific rather than general (I'll talk about this difference later in this section of the book).

Since these assemblies need a quorum of at least 51% of the total condo rights, proxies can be a useful tool to achieve this and allow the assembly to go ahead.

Only four things are allowed at an ordinary assembly that could potentially need a vote:

- **Presentation of the General Report**. A report is a report – it is what it is. The report should be accepted by acclamation. It just doesn't make sense to have a formal resolution. Since there's no formal vote, this doesn't concern the proxies.

- **Approval of the budget and the fees**. your proposed budget and fees should have already been through a community review process, and the final version incorporating the community's input should have been sent to all owners before the assembly.

  In this case, a proxy vote is possible by simply having "approval of the budget and fees" shown on a limited proxy form for the absentee owner to mark with a "YES" or "NO."

  If the community input process has been handled correctly, this vote should only be a formality.

- **Election of the Council and any special committees that might be needed**. This is something that can, but not necessarily, need a motion and a vote (or even an election).

  If an election is needed (**see Part 12 – "Elections"**), limited proxies must contain a ballot, and the proxy giver must clearly mark their vote.

  If you've eliminated nominations from the floor in your by-laws or rules of order, and if you have preselected a slate of candidates (usually done by a Nominating Committee), then you only need an item to "approve the recommended candidates" on the proxy form.

- **Appointment of the Administrator**. This is usually an appointment of an individual or company that's passed by acclamation.

  If for some reason you need an election, then the limited proxy forms must have a ballot.

A sample proxy form for an extraordinary assembly, a WORD template, and a sample instruction sheet, are included in your BONUS Pack.

Adopting the Use of Proxies in Your Condo

Before you can use proxies, you must add the ability to use them (along with any other limitations or requirements) to your by-laws – or change your existing by-law proxy policy if needed.

Legal Requirements for Proxies

Chapter 35

In México, as in most countries, a proxy is a legal document. In fact, it's a limited power of attorney. In México, these are called *poders* (powers).

Minimum Legal Requirements

Because of this, the proxy form itself has more rigid requirements in México than in the U.S. or Canada. To avoid problems, the following are the minimum requirements for a proxy form to be legally binding document:

- Legal documents must be in Spanish. It's possible, however, for the form to be bilingual – English-only, however, could result in an invalid proxy (especially if challenged).

- The names of the proxy giver, proxy holder, and the witnesses must appear, and all must be full legal names.

    In the case of a Mexican, these will be the given names, followed by the *apellido paterno* (**father's family name**), and, finally, the *apellido materno* (**mother's family name**).

    In the case of a foreigner, this must be the name as it appears in the person's passport. If the passport includes a middle name or initial, then the person must use it. If the passport doesn't include a middle name, then the person must **not** use it.

- A proxy must be from the currently registered title holder.

- The meeting for which the proxy is being given. Also consider including the common property ownership rights represented.

- A clear statement of exactly what powers are being given, along with any and all limitations on them. If this is a limited proxy, include a ballot for specific motions with clear "YES" or "NO" choices, and include a ballot for any needed election voting.

- A place for the signatures and printed names of the owners giving the proxy, along with the date and the place where the proxy was signed (municipality, state/province, and country). **Signatures should always be made with a blue pen.**

- A place for two witness signatures along with their printed names. There must be two separate witnesses regardless of the number of owners who signed. **Signatures should always be made with a blue pen.**

- If the proxy form is longer than one page, then the proxy giver must sign all pages that don't contain the signature block in the right-hand margin (lengthwise).

As with many legal matters, you can get away with ignoring these practices for years. They only become a problem for you when someone complains about the process or disputes a proxy.

A sample proxy form for an ordinary assembly, a WORD template, and a sample instruction sheet, are included in your BONUS Pack.

Proxies Must Be From the Title Holder of the Property

Before accepting a proxy, you must know for a fact that the proxy giver is the current legal title holder of the property. **Don't assume anything!** You may be surprised.

There's no guarantee that either the person living in the unit or the person paying the condo fees is the registered owner of the condo unit. Get a copy of the current title for the unit. The legal owner will be shown on the title document

The proxy form must be from either the title holder or a person who has a legal power of attorney from the title holder.

In this last case, you must also get a copy of this power of attorney. I advise you to show this to an ***abogado*** or ***notario*** to make sure that it gives the person the right to exercise the condo rights for this unit.

Failure to make sure that the proxy giver has the power to issue a proxy could result in illegal voting at an assembly. One or more resolutions passed at this assembly could be overturned.

Proxies Should Be Submitted to an Authority

Owners should send their filled-out proxies to a single responsible person – name this individual before the assembly is held. Often this will be one of the scrutineers (name them as Chief Scrutineer).

There must be a deadline to receive proxies, and the day before the assembly is typical.

A copy of the filled-in proxy should also be sent to the proxy holder.

General vs. Limited Powers

A general proxy is one that lets the proxy holder vote on the proxy giver's behalf in any way the proxy holder sees fit. If the proxy giver disagrees after-the-fact, there is nothing they can do.

This isn't only a surrendering of rights and responsibilities by the proxy giver, the proxy might also be abused.

If you use a general proxy, then the proxy form must expressly name the individual who'll act for the proxy giver at the assembly. The proxy holder doesn't have to be another owner or even a resident of your condo, unless your by-laws say differently.

While it's legal to give general powers, I don't recommend it. A limited proxy is preferable.

It allows the proxy giver to specifically mark their vote on individual resolutions, and to vote for candidates in an election (if any).

The limited proxy is legally binding. It must contain clear instructions from the proxy giver in the form of an absentee ballot both for the resolutions to be voted on, and for any candidates at an election.

If your proxies are limited (preferred), the authority to which they were sent (such as a Chief Scrutineer) must be named as the proxy holder.

The votes will be taken directly from the proxy forms by the scrutineers, rather than asking anyone to repeat them. This procedure is more efficient, and removes the possibility of errors or voting irregularities.

Proxies Can be Dealt With by Email and Fax

The simplest way to deal with proxy forms in the 21st century is to send the forms to the absentee owners as an email attachment (PDF is best). They should also be available on your condo web site.

The proxy giver can then print it, fill it in and sign it, have it witnessed, scan it, and email it back. Failing this, you should have a fax number for them to use.

It's a good idea to allow both email and fax receipt of filled-in proxy forms in your by-laws.

"I Changed My Mind!"

If the proxy giver changes their mind, they must send in a new proxy form. Verbal changes cannot be accepted, and the written form must always take priority over any subsequent verbal instructions.

To make this process practical for absentee owners, I recommend the following:

- Any change made to a proxy form up to two days before the assembly must always be in the form of a new proxy.

- Changes made one day before the assembly can be accepted in the form of an email sent from the proxy giver to the authority to which the original proxy was sent. This email must: clearly express this wish, be attached to the proxy form at the start of the assembly, and stay attached to the proxy form for the official records.

Adoption of a Proxy Policy

If you want to use proxies at your assemblies, then the rules, procedures, and limitations **must** be spelled out in your by-laws.

While every owner has the right to give anyone else a power of attorney to act on their behalf, if there's no by-law procedures, there's no guarantee that the assembly will accept a power of attorney.

If the rules of aren't spelled out anywhere except in the power of attorney itself, there's no consistency – different powers of attorneys may give different owners different rights.

Unless proxies are allowed in your by-laws, you should avoid using them, especially if you don't want to be open to all type of claims and problems. Problems such as,

> "What are the proxy rules, and where are they written?", or "I think they should work this way – where does it say I'm wrong?".

Remember, you can't fall back on Robert's Rules, since they forbid the use of proxies unless state law requires them (which it doesn't), or if they're required by your by-laws (my point).

Recommended Proxy Policies

Chapter 36

I recommend that you accept proxies for an ordinary assembly, but not for an extraordinary assembly – the detailed reasons are covered in the previous three chapters. Based on this, here are some general procedures and policies dealing with proxies.

Avoid General Proxies (...again!)

As you should have gathered by now, I urge you to **never use a general proxy**.

A general proxy gives no indication as to how the proxy giver wishes to vote on either a motion or in an election. Instead, it gives discretionary power to the proxy holder to vote as they see fit.

In my opinion, this is an abrogation of responsibility on the part of the proxy giver, and a potential for abuse on the part of the proxy holder.

All this runs against the spirit and intent of a deliberative assembly, and is unfair to those who are actively participating.

Validating Proxies at an Assembly

Proxy forms must be given to the scrutineers at the start of the assembly by the authority to whom they were sent (often the chief scrutineer).

Each proxy form must be validated by the scrutineers before it's accepted. This is done just before the assembly starts. If any proxies are in contravention of your by-laws or your proxy policy, then they must be invalidated and not used.

Possible reasons why a proxy might be rejected:

- the proxy holder's name is unclear or incorrect;
- if this is a limited proxy, the ballots aren't clearly marked;

- the proxy isn't signed by the proxy giver; and
- there aren't two different and valid witness signatures.

Dealing With Changed Proxies at an Assembly

If the holder of a limited proxy claims that the proxy giver has changed their mind on one or more votes, then an email explaining the change must have been sent in before the assembly. The email must make clear the intent to change the proxy (as well as the exact nature of this change), and it must be attached to the proxy form before the assembly begins.

Never accept, *"Trust me, I'll bring it by later."*

Failing any of the above, if the proxy is valid, it must be accepted at **face value** (unchanged).

Dealing With Proxies for Quorum at an Ordinary Assembly

At an ordinary assembly, the scrutineers must include the voting rights represented by the proxy forms in the roll-call to find out if quorum has been met.

The scrutineers must announce the attendance percentage (including the proxies). This percentage must be recorded in the minutes.

Recording a Proxy Vote

During the assembly, the scrutineers must record the proxy giver's vote directly from all limited proxy forms for any vote on a resolution, or for any election that's held. The proxy form will serve as the proxy giver's ballot.

Avoid copying the votes from proxy forms to another ballot, or relying on the proxy holder to tell you what the vote is (unless you accept general proxies, and this is a general proxy).

Destruction of Proxy Forms - Don't!

Once the assembly is over, the proxy forms must never be destroyed. They're legal documents that must be kept as part of your condo records.

Sample Proxy By-law Article

Here's a sample of what your by-laws might include if you want to use proxies at assemblies:

- proxies can be used at ordinary assemblies, and will be counted towards the quorum for the assembly;
- proxies must not be used at extraordinary assemblies;
- filled-in proxy forms can be received by mail, email, or by fax;
- proxies must be sent to the chief scrutineer no later than 3:00pm on the day before the assembly;
- proxy forms must be filled-in according to the instructions, and must be signed by two independent witnesses; and
- invalid proxy forms may be rejected.

PART 11 – Voting

Voting at an Assembly

Chapter 37

As I've mentioned before, voting on resolutions at an assembly is generally done by using condo rights. This is called proportional voting. While I've touched on this type of voting in previous chapters, it can be a difficult (and sometimes contentious) concept, so I'll go into more detail in this chapter.

What are Condo Rights?

In a condominium, each title holder owns not only their private property, but also a portion of the common property.

Your condo rights are the percentage of the common property that you own. This percentage is spelled out in the title documents of your private unit (your deed), and are normally different for each owner. These differences are sometimes large. However, it's also possible for them to be small – the most common example of this last situation would be a block of condo apartments where each apartment is almost the same size.

This percentage ownership of the common property is set up for each private unit when your condo regime was created, and cannot be changed, sold, transferred, or separated from the title of the private unit. Therefore, they're often called *"indivisible rights."*

These rights are always expressed as a percentage representing the area of your lot or apartment out of the total area of all lots or apartments in your condo (this total would represent 100.00%).

These rights are essential to the functioning of your condo, and are used for the following purposes:

- to form the basis of paying condo fees and special assessments; each owner must pay fees in direct proportion to their ownership of the common property; therefore, smaller lots/apartments must pay lower fees than larger ones;

- to achieve quorum at an ordinary assembly – at least 51% of the **total condo rights** must be represented for the meeting to be legally held;

- voting on resolutions at an ordinary assembly – for a resolution to pass, a majority of the condo rights represented at the assembly must vote in favour of it; and

- voting on resolutions at an extraordinary assembly – for a resolution to pass, at least 75% of the **total condo rights** (regardless of the amount of rights represented at the assembly) must vote in favour of it.

Scrutineers: Their Duties and Functions

A scrutineer is an individual who monitors voting to make sure that the correct voting rules and procedures are being followed.

I recommend that you appoint two scrutineers at each assembly. This is usually done beforehand. Unless your by-laws say differently, these can be anyone – including non-owners. Ideally, they should be trustworthy people who have an eye for detail, and know how to use a basic spreadsheet.

Scrutineers cannot vote (a serious conflict of interest), so sole owners are not good candidates.

The scrutineers take the assembly roll-call, tally the property rights for those owners represented at the assembly, and announce the total rights represented. This is recorded in the minutes, and the Chair of the Assembly uses this number to see if quorum has been met for an ordinary assembly.

For an ordinary assembly, the scrutineers then work out the minimum voting threshold for a motion to pass based on the rights represented at the assembly – this would be a majority (more than half of the rights present).

For an extraordinary assembly, this number is fixed at 75% of the total condo rights.

During any vote to pass a resolution, the scrutineers will carry out the roll-call for the vote, and record the property rights for each favourable vote.

If absentee owners have voted by general proxy, the scrutineers must ask the proxy holder for the vote.

If absentee owners have voted by limited proxy, the scrutineers must record the vote from the proxy form. The proxy-holder cannot change the proxy-giver's vote unless the proxy form specifically allows this by using a general proxy.

They must then tally the total percentage rights voted in favour of the motion, and announce it to the assembly. This number is recorded in the minutes, and the Chair of the Assembly announces whether the resolution has passed or is defeated.

Determining Quorum at an Ordinary Assembly

In my experience, the most foolproof way to record the percentage rights for a quorum count at an ordinary assembly is to use a spreadsheet that lists:

- each unit by number,
- the name of the registered title holder, and
- the percentage of common property ownership belonging to this condo unit.

The scrutineers can use this spreadsheet to do a roll-call at the start of the ordinary assembly. If the total of the common property percentages of those represented at the meeting meets or exceeds **51% total rights of the condo**, then you have quorum and can legally hold the assembly.

Even though there's **no quorum needed for an extraordinary assembly**, I strongly recommend that you record the rights represented at the assembly in the minutes (for the record).

A copy of my voting spreadsheet as well as a sample set of scrutineers' instructions is included in your BONUS Pack.

Proportional (Roll-Call) Voting Must Be Used For Resolutions

Because of the legal requirement to use proportional voting, the only practical method of voting on resolutions at either an ordinary or an extraordinary assembly is by **roll-call**. This means calling out unit numbers, and recording the vote announced by the designated voter for the unit. This must be a registered title holder or or a legal representative of a registered owner.

While a few people might be concerned about open voting, and might prefer a secret ballot, this is just not practical.

A condo assembly is a legal proceeding, is public (within your condo), and the minutes must be publicly registered – including the results of each vote on a resolution. There can be no expectation of privacy, nor is this practical to achieve.

Potential misunderstandings can be easily headed off if owners understand one important concept **before** the assembly:

> With proportional voting (which is required by law – this isn't an option), **there is no confidentiality of the votes.**

Apart from the impracticality of voting other than by roll-call, a vote result based on proportional votes can usually be deconstructed afterwards using basic logic. This is because there is often only one combination of unit rights that adds up to the total vote.

One Vote Per Condo Unit

When voting on a resolution starts, each owner's unit number is called out by a scrutineer.

When they hear their number, the person entitled to vote for the unit announces their vote out loud, and the scrutineers record it.

Only one vote is allowed per unit, regardless of the number of people who co-own it.

You Need to Know Who Actually Owns Each Unit

You must confirm who the registered title holder of each unit is for your records. This person (or a representative with power of attorney) is the **only one allowed to vote for the unit, or give a proxy to another**. This is also the only person you can legally pursue for unpaid fees.

For a small condo, this is simple. Collect copies of deeds from all your existing owners, and create a list of the legal title holders. Since you generally know when units change hands, you must update your records as transfers happen by getting copies of the deeds from the new buyers.

For large condos, your records can easily get out of sync with reality. Consider contacting owners for proof of title every year before your assembly is held.

For those who don't respond, or for whom you have no contact information, you can do a search of title at the local ***Registro Público de la Propiedad*** (Public Registry of Property).

It's also possible to lose track of ownership if an owner dies. Never assume to whom the title has been transferred, or even that a title change has taken place.

Insist on proof of title before an owner is allowed to vote. Have a registration process in advance of the assemblies where owners submit proof of title (a copy of the portion of their deed showing the title holder and the description of the property).

Have proxy givers supply proof of title along with their proxy.

> There's a Restricted Zone made up of all land that's inside 100 kms (about 62 miles) of any Mexican international land border, plus all land inside 50 kms (about 31 miles) of any Mexican coastline.
>
> If your condo is located in this Restricted Zone, then foreigners must have bought their condo units through a ***fideicomiso*** (trust).
>
> **It's vital that these owners get a power of attorney from the trustee** (the financial institution). This power must allow them to exercise their rights in all matters affecting their condo unit.
>
> **Article 1001** clearly states that a ***condómino*** (owner) must be the title holder of the property. Only the registered owner of the condo unit can vote at a condo assembly, and make decisions about the condo property.
>
> In a trust, **the registered owner is the trustee**, and not the foreign buyer. Without a power of attorney, they cannot exercise their rights in the condominium.
>
> Yes, the trust gives them all rights of use and enjoyment of their property, but this doesn't apply to condo rights which are governed by the condo legislation.

If Someone Votes Illegally

It's important that only the registered title holders of a unit be allowed to vote the condo rights of that unit. It's Ok to let someone vote if they have a power of attorney authorising them to act **for the registered owner**. But you cannot allow anyone else to vote.

If a resolution is passed at an assembly, and people voted in favour of it who were not legally entitled to vote, someone who found out (say, someone who opposed the resolution) could have these votes invalidated. Under this situation, it's possible that the resolution could be overturned. This could be quite a mess for your condo.

Have a Registration Procedure

You'll experience a much more efficient assembly if you have a process to register voters.

If you have a number of units with multiple title holders, or that are owned by companies, then you might consider using a form for these units that names one of the registered owners as the voter for the unit. This must be filled in before the assembly starts (a Voting Certificate).

A sample Voting Certificate is included in your BONUS Pack.

A Voting Certificate **isn't the same as a proxy**. The life of the certificate lasts beyond just the one assembly – until it's changed in writing. They must be kept on record for use at future assemblies. In addition, they cannot be used in place of a proxy.

Voting Certificates are particularly important for larger condos. They could also prove useful for a small condo where one or more units are co-owned by couples who have separated.

Regardless of whether you use a voting certificate, you must always have a registration sheet for the owners to sign-in.

This sign-in sheet becomes a valuable part of your condo records, and serves as evidence of attendance – especially if the legality of the assembly is ever questioned.

For smaller condos, a registration (sign-in) sheet should be created for each assembly, and each attending owner must fill in this sheet at a sign-in station at the entrance to the assembly. A volunteer should be there to make sure that people register.

For larger condos, you might want to consider dividing the registration sheets up into two or more separate registration stations. Each station would have the registration sheets for a portion of your condominium. These are best divided by lot or unit numbers (this works better than alphabetically by last name – this last system falls apart when there are co-owners with different last names).

Each registration station should have a sign indicating the range of lot or unit numbers that it deals with. This greatly speeds up the sign-in process.

The registration sheet should contain, at a minimum: date, time, location, and type of assembly; the unit number; printed name; and signature for each registered voter.

While only one person per unit can register to vote, other co-owners can certainly take part in the assembly, and should be allowed to voice their opinions during the discussions.

There should also be a section of the sheet (or a separate form) where the authorised receiver of proxy forms (often one of the scrutineers) fills in the unit numbers and owner names of those who are represented by proxy, and attests to this by signing it.

You can also have a separate sign-in sheet for those who are at the assembly, but aren't registering to vote.

A sample registration sheet is included in your BONUS Pack.

If you're holding an election, and use election ballots, these should be handed out as each unit registers to vote – one per unit, regardless of the number of co-owners of the unit who are at the assembly.

This should be done by the volunteers at the sign-in stations as each voter is registered. For more information on ballots, **see Chapter 39 – "Recommended Election Procedures."**

Registration sheets form an essential part of the assembly records, along with the proxy forms. If you use election ballots, and you're keeping these ballots until at least the next assembly (and you should), these will also be attached to the records.

Passing a Resolution

A resolution is a motion that the assembly votes on, and which affects the operation or maintenance of your condominium. It is binding on all owners and residents.

These must always be listed on the Order of the Day that was attached to the call notice for the assembly. The results of all resolution votes must be recorded in the assembly minutes.

A resolution passes if the "YES" votes tally:

- greater than 50% of the condo rights represented at the assembly for an **ordinary assembly**; and
- at least 75% of the total condo rights for an **extraordinary assembly**.

Note that the rights represented at an ordinary assembly are recorded by the scrutineers after they do a roll-call to see if there's a quorum.

I've covered this already, but it bears repeating. A common misconception is that *"greater than 50% of the condo rights represented"* means 51% of these rights – **this is not accurate**.

Condo rights are usually expressed to two decimal places. Therefore, the increment isn't 1%, but 0.01%, and the requirement is, in fact, 50% + .01% and not 50% + 1%.

> For example, if 82.87% of the condo rights are represented at an ordinary assembly of *Condominio Vista del Basurero* (from the roll-call), then a resolution will pass if it receives at least 41.45% of the rights voting in favour.
>
> Let's look at this in detail: 50% of 82.87% is 41.44%. Add 0.01% to this (the *"more than 50%"* part) and you get 41.45%. 51% would be 42.26%, and is not correct.

While all these calculations might seem complex, they can be easily and automatically taken care of by using a voting spreadsheet.

Exceptions to Proportional Voting

You may have noticed at the start of this chapter I said that voting at an assembly is *generally* done using condo rights – this is because there are three exceptions:

1. **The appointment of the Chair and Secretary of an assembly**, as well as the scrutineers, is done by a majority show of hands of the owners at the assembly. Bear in mind that *"majority"* is defined as *"more than half."*

The reason that a non-proportional vote is allowed for these is that these votes are always taken before the assembly is called to order, and aren't resolutions (decisions) affecting your condo. These people serve temporarily for just this assembly.

> For example, at an assembly with 78 households there, a person needs the approval of at least 40 owners to chair the assembly. This is true whether it's an ordinary or extraordinary assembly.

In practice, these positions are normally appointed by consensus.

2. **The decision to sue an owner to sell their property at public auction** is done by a majority show of hands of owners (one vote per unit) at an extraordinary assembly. For this resolution to pass, the number voting in favour must be **more than half of the total number of owners of your con**do (**not** just half of the owners at the assembly – **Article 1032**).

    > For example, in a 30-unit condo, you need the approval of at least 16 owners to go ahead with this action. This is independent of the number of owners actually at the extraordinary assembly.

3. **If a secondary motion is made**, then a simple vote is all that's needed. These motions only affect the progress of the assembly itself, and are a way of arriving at the final resolution.

    For more details, **see Chapter 30 – "Rules of Order for Assemblies."**

Items Having No Motion or Vote

There are certain assembly tasks that must be done, but for which there shouldn't be a motion or vote:

1. **Reading of the Order of the Day** – the Chair of the Assembly will begin by reading the Order of the Day. It's vital that this be exactly the same as it was when posted with the call! It cannot be changed from the call.

   Never call it the *"Agenda,"* and **never have a motion to approve or adopt an agenda or an order of the day.**

   There's no agenda for a condo assembly – it's an order of the day. There are significant differences between the two.

   While an agenda does need a motion to be adopted, an order of the day cannot be adopted. The order of the day is the reason the assembly was called, and it cannot be altered by the assembly.

   Once the Order of the Day has been read, the business of the assembly officially gets under way.

2. **Acceptance of the General Report at the Annual Ordinary Assembly** – it's a report – it is what it is, it's been presented, and can't be changed. There's no motion needed. In particular, avoid a motion to "receive the report" – this is improper. You can move that the report be filed with the minutes. In this case, it should be passed by general consent (see the next topic).

Motions That Can Be Passed by General Consent

One way to avoid a roll-call vote for every single motion involves passing some motions by general consent. This is also called: "unanimous consent," "by consensus," or "by acclamation," and just means that no one is opposed.

However, this can only be done for basic and noncontroversial tasks that are unlikely to be opposed or need discussion. This is a useful tool for speeding an assembly through some of the administrative or housekeeping votes.

The following items are commonly passed by general consent:

1. **Appointment of the Chair, Secretary, and scrutineers** – we've already covered these appointments, they take place before the assembly has been called to order. These are normally chosen beforehand.

2. **Election of the Council and Standing Committees** – no motion or formal vote is needed **as long as there are no contested positions.** For example, you have a list of prenominated candidates created by a Nominating Committee. If there are no contested positions, ask for the election of the nominated candidates by acclamation. If no one objects, then a vote isn't required.

   For more information on avoiding an election, **see Chapter 39 – "Recommended Election Procedures."**

3. **Appointment of the Administrator** – this shouldn't require a motion unless contested (very unusual) – ask for general consent.

4. **Approval of the Minutes** – these are read to the assembly at the end, and are discussed and corrected as needed at this time. Once this is done, they're adopted by general consent.

5. **Designation of a Representative to Protocolise the Minutes** – this is just an administrative decision made at the assembly, and can be passed by general consent. Don't make a motion – the assembly business has already finished.

Passing a motion by general consent is done by having the Chair say something like,

> *"If there are no objections, Sarah Connor will act as Secretary of the assembly ... PAUSE FOR OBJECTIONS ... Approved by general consent,"* or

> *"If there are no objections, the only nominee, Kyle Reese, will be appointed as President of the Council by acclamation... PAUSE FOR OBJECTIONS ... Approved by general consent."*

If you ask for general consent and there **are** objections, then a motion must be made, discussion must take place, and a vote must be held (except for those items I mentioned that take place before the assembly has been called to order – these are voted on by a basic show of hands vote).

Items That Always Need a Motion and Roll-Call Vote

The following are resolutions that must **always** be moved, seconded, discussed, and formally voted on by roll-call vote. These must **never** be approved by general consent:

- **Approval of your condo budget and the fees** – it's necessary to document the number of property rights voted in favour of the budget, so a motion and vote are needed.

- **Election of the Council, and standing committees** – whenever there are contested positions, then an election must take place.

  The election will result in a final approved list of nominees. A motion to accept this list of nominees can then be moved, and formally voted on. It's usually better to just declare them elected by acclamation (a formal vote to accept the nominees is rather pointless after an election has been held).

For more information on holding an election, **see Chapter 39 – "Recommended Election Procedures."**

- **Appointment of the Administrator** – if the Council's recommendation for Administrator is challenged, then the assembly must make a motion, debate it to a solution, and then vote.

  This should be rare, since the Council should have examined the candidates, is in the best position to make this decision, have done so openly and publicly, and there's no opportunity for research or investigation at an assembly.

  An Administrator **must** be appointed, or your condo cannot legally function.

- **Most Core Business at an extraordinary assembly** – including: approval of improvements and the method to fund them, or changes to the by-laws. The decision to sue a delinquent owner needs a formal motion, but has a nonstandard vote.

Absentee Votes After an Extraordinary Assembly

As I mentioned in **Chapter 27 – "The Extraordinary Assembly"**, you have 30 days after an extraordinary assembly to poll owners who weren't represented at the assembly and ask for their votes – assuming that this can make a difference to a motion passing or not.

To work out whether a resolution needs polling of absentee owners, you must compare the percentage rights of the absentee owners to the favourable votes received at the assembly.

Some examples might help here:

> Assume an extraordinary assembly of *Condominio Vista del Basurero* with 78.53% of the condo rights represented at the assembly. This means that 21.47% of the condo rights are **not** represented – these are the absentees.
>
> If 37.27% of the rights at the meeting voted in favour of a particular resolution, there wouldn't be a need to poll the absentee owners on this decision. The reason is that if all the missing 21.47% rights voted in favour of the resolution, the motion still would only have received 58.74% in favour – this isn't enough to pass (it needs at least 75%).
>
> If another resolution received 75.02% of the rights, there'd also be no need to poll the absentee voters, since this resolution has already passed.
>
> If a third motion received 71.08% of the represented rights voting in favour, then this resolution **must** be put to the absentee owners since only 3.92% more rights voting in favour are needed to pass (to get at least 75%), and this is clearly possible with the 21.47% absentee votes.

The simplest way to quickly work out the number of voting rights represented by absentees is with the roll-call spreadsheet that the scrutineers use.

Here's how to go about collecting the absentee votes after the assembly:

> Send an email to all absentee owners. It's not necessary to send individual emails, since this is an extension of the assembly, and should be an open process.

The email should be sent by the same person who called the assembly (typically your Administrator or President/Chair of your Council). You should cc the scrutineers.

For each motion that was voted on at the extraordinary assembly, but that didn't pass (and that could pass with absentee votes), the body of the email should contain:

- the exact wording of the motion that was voted on at the assembly (including any amendments that were made at the assembly);

- the introduction to the motion that was given at the assembly explaining the reason for the vote, and the benefits to the community;

- the PRO side of the argument; this can be material that's already been circulated, and should also include a brief summary of any other positive comments that were brought up at the assembly by those speaking in favour of the motion (don't repeat points that have already been covered in the circulated material);

- the CON side of the argument; include a brief summary of negative or opposing points that were raised at the assembly by those speaking against the motion.

It's important that you present this information in a non-biased way. The intent is to give the absentees enough information to make an informed vote (as if they had been present at the assembly).

Include instructions on how to vote.

Voting is most easily done by reply email (be sure to tell them to quote your original email in their reply) cc'd to the two scrutineers – this is done because the scrutineers must still be able to verify the vote.

If you feel that there might be potential vote fraud using email, then have votes returned by courier. However, the extra trouble and expense of this process may result in fewer (or no) absentee votes. You have to make a judgement call here.

Tell the absentees that they must clearly name each motion, and clearly vote either "YES" or "NO". It's also important to make it clear that you can only accept one vote per unit.

You must give them a deadline (30 days from the date of the assembly). I recommend that you send out two reminder notices: one week and one day before the deadline.

Include an offer to answer any questions or concerns that they have about the motions or the process. Any replies to questions must be non-biased (you must not be perceived as trying to influence the vote one way or the other), and should be cc'd to all absentee voters, as well as the two scrutineers.

If you receive more than one vote from a unit that has two or more co-owners (remember, they must be title holders), you must go back to them and explain that you can only accept one vote per unit, and that they must withdraw all votes except one.

If they can't agree amongst themselves, and you are left with more than one vote when the 30 days run out, you cannot accept any votes from this unit.

A sample request for absentee votes is included in your BONUS Pack.

Be Proactive: Get Support BEFORE Your Assembly

It's critical that all complex resolutions to be voted on at an assembly be thoroughly vetted in the community well before the assembly.

Changes to most of these types of resolutions are too complex to make spontaneously at the assembly – you can never thoroughly think through the impact of even a seemingly minor change under the pressure of an assembly.

You need to do a lot of work beforehand to make sure that major objections have been dealt with, and that the vote at the assembly becomes more or less a formality.

You need to:

1. Involve the community in the planning for any complex resolution (such as by-law changes, or approving the new budget).

2. After the community input and planning (may need multiple meetings and public reviews), send out a Council-recommended document fully explaining the details and reasons (such as a list of by-law changes, or a copy of the proposed new budget). Ask for final comments on this from the community.

3. After looking at and addressing this community input, send out a final Council-approved document for voting at the upcoming assembly (several days before the assembly).

All of these should also be posted on your condo web site.

A sample request for owner input (step #2 above) is included in your BONUS Pack.

PART 12 – Elections

Legal Requirements for an Election at an Assembly

Chapter 38

The Jalisco condo law is crystal clear on voting to pass resolutions at an assembly, but silent on voting to elect candidates to positions.

The Condo Law Has No Procedure for Election Voting

Elections can become unmanageable when using proportional voting to elect candidates. Most people prefer the simplicity of ballots for election voting. Is there a way to do this?

The condo law says that voting to pass a resolution must be proportional (a roll-call vote), but says nothing about the methods you might use to get to this final resolution.

Coming Up With a List of Candidates

You can use non-proportional voting (including ballots), or any procedure you like, to come up with your final list of candidates for elected positions. This may include a Nominating Committee who have conducted a search for candidates before the assembly is held. You just need to be careful that no motion is made during this process that becomes a resolution of the assembly (this would need a roll-call vote).

Once you've agreed on a list of people to fill each elected position, the assembly can make a formal motion to accept this list. This is a resolution, and must be voted on by using a proportional roll-call vote (or, better yet, just declared by acclamation).

Adoption of an Election Policy

There are various ways you can carry out an election – I'll cover this in detail in the next chapter.

However, to avoid problems at or after an assembly (especially if something contentious happens), I strongly recommend that you publish an election policy or procedure document.

If you plan to hold an election at an assembly, this should be sent to the community before the assembly (possibly with the call notice). This policy should also be posted on your web site.

Possible Elections at an Ordinary Assembly

- the Administrative Council; and
- a special committee needed for a specific purpose.

Possible Elections at an Extraordinary Assembly

- Any other kind of special election that might be needed, although I can't think of a reason for one. Such an election, whatever it might be for, can only be held at an extraordinary assembly, and not an ordinary assembly.

Appointments at an Assembly - These Are Not an Election

The appointment of the **Chair of the Assembly** must follow the procedure outlined in the condo legislation (**Article 1024**) – either by general consent or by a simple show of hands. This also applies to the appointment of the **Secretary of the Assembly** and the **scrutineers**.

There must never be a motion and formal vote on any of these – the assembly hasn't yet been called to order. These are just pre-assembly housekeeping.

The **Administrator** is appointed at an ordinary assembly, and **not elected**.

Legal Requirements for an Election at an Assembly

Whether the Administrator is hired, contracted, or a volunteer, they should be chosen by the Council based on qualifications – this should be done before the assembly is held. The assembly is only ratifying this appointment.

The appointment of one or two **representatives to protocolise the minutes** of the assembly must also be by general consent or a by a show of hands vote. This appointment takes place after the business of the assembly has been finished, and is not a resolution.

Recommended Election Procedures

Chapter 39

Here are some detailed procedures you can use to develop your own policy for elections at assemblies.

#1 Tip: Try to Avoid an Election!

In my experience, elections can be divisive – they have the potential to tear apart a community. If there's a way to avoid an election, I encourage you to go that route.

You can do this by coming up with a list of candidates for each position before the assembly is held. This should be an open and public process (a Nominating Committee should be used). Your goal is to end up with a single nominee for each position to be filled. This list of candidates is then elected at the assembly by acclamation (rather than a formal election process).

- **The Administrator:**

    There is no election for the Administrator. While the condo law requires that the Administrative Council and any special committees be elected, it says that the Administrator is **appointed**.

    If you hire an Administrator, this individual or company should have already been chosen by the Council or a special committee. This will most likely be the same company or person as the last year – for continuity, you shouldn't change Administrators, unless there's a good reason.

    If you have an owner-volunteer as your Administrator, then this person should have also been chosen in advance.

If you have more than one person champing at the bit to fill this job as a volunteer consider yourselves fortunate. The Council must decide on the individual impartially **based on qualifications** – this is definitely not a job where you want an assembly to choose the person based on popularity.

To nip any potential controversy in the bud, you should announce to all owners that the re-appointment (or new appointment) of the Administrator will be examined at a specific upcoming council meeting. Give the community 10 days to two weeks notice, and invite them to come to this meeting, or send in comments.

If you're looking for a new volunteer Administrator, put out the call to the community well before this meeting. Invite those who can't be there to send in any comments, suggestions, or concerns before the meeting. Explain that the purpose of the meeting is to choose an Administrator for the next fiscal year, and that they will be appointed at the upcoming assembly.

The assembly must still approve the appointment, but if the selection process has been open and public, then this should just be a formality.

- **President/Chair of the Council:**

The condo legislation doesn't require that you elect a President/Chair of the Administrative Council at the Annual Ordinary Assembly. You can just elect a Council, and let them decide at their first meeting which councillor will serve as their President/Chair for the coming year.

However, I recommend that you **do** elect the President/Chair of your Council at your Annual Ordinary Assembly because of the granting of powers:

The condo law gives your Administrator the power to represent your condo for administrative and legal matters.

It's good practice to have a backup in case something urgent comes up, and your Administrator is sick or away. Therefore, I recommend that the assembly also give these powers to the President/Chair of your Council.

To be able to do this, you must elect a President/Chair of your Council at the assembly because these powers must be granted to an individual by name.

It's important to realise that there's no such thing as a **Condo President** (a common misconception). The condo legislation mentions only a *"presidente del consejo de administración."* This translates as "President/Chair of the Administrative Council" – in Spanish, *presidente* often just means **chairperson**, and the Council is, after all, a committee.

- **The Administrative Council:**

Members of the Administrative Council (councillors) must be elected at an ordinary assembly (generally the Annual Ordinary Assembly).

Unless your by-laws say differently (and you must check this!), you should appoint a Nominating Committee to create a list of nominees for each position on the Council.

They'll start by canvassing all owners at least a month before the assembly. They should put out at least two published calls for candidates (usually by email and your condo web site).

They must include in these calls a brief summary of the duties and responsibilities of the councillors, as well as any limitations.

For example, the condo law requires that councillors be up to date in their condo fees, and your condo's by-laws could have further limitations (such as a full-time residency requirement, or only one councillor per condo unit).

The Nominating Committee should hold a meeting and invite all owners. It's important to make clear to the community that the purpose of this meeting is to choose the nominees for election to the Council at the upcoming assembly.

The calls for nominees should also mention this meeting, and the deadline for nominations should be the date of this committee meeting.

The goal of the Nominating Committee is to reach agreement on a final list of councillors before the assembly is held. Often a public cooperative discussion will result in a list of nominees that everyone is happy with.

If this proves to be an impossible task, then you have no choice but to hold an election at the assembly. This could happen if you have two "warring factions," or if a group is trying to take over your Council.

Instead of a fixed number of councillors, it's better if your by-laws call for a **minimum** number only. You can then easily accommodate one or two extra councillors.

In my experience, the greater the breadth of knowledge and experience on your Council, the more varied viewpoints you'll have at your meetings. This generally results in an effective council.

Some people become concerned about the Council becoming too big.

A good workable council is about five to seven members. Yes, Council size can be taken too far – 10 to 12 should likely be the upper limit (depending on the size of your condo).

If you're concerned about this, you can also set a specific maximum. In this case, you'd specify a range from xx to yy councillors (for example, "3 to 7").

In practice, you'll find that it usually becomes self-limiting. In a 22 unit condo, for example, it's almost impossible to get more than seven volunteers for a Council. A 200 unit condo, on the other hand, could easily achieve ten or 12, and, for a condo of this size, this could prove to be quite effective.

I'd rather have a larger council than a small one. A larger council tends to dilute minority perspectives and personal agendas (sadly, not everyone who volunteers as a councillor has the community's interests in mind).

- **Special Committees:**

    The condo law requires that any special committees to be created by the assembly be elected (**Article 1020**).

    Again, I strongly urge you to have the make-up of this committee decided and agreed to (at least by the Council and everyone who stepped up to serve on the committee) before the assembly is held. This should be another task for your Nominating Committee.

    In particular, try to get people who have some experience or expertise in whatever it is that the committee is to investigate, research, or do.

If you've created a list of nominees to fill each of your positions before your assembly is held, and, if you've done this fairly, openly, and with the participation of all candidates, then you should be able to elect your Council and any special committees by acclamation.

Disallow Nominations From the Floor

If someone (or a group) steps up unexpectedly at the assembly and puts themselves up as a nominee from the floor, you will be forced to hold an election.

Unless your by-laws say differently, the Chair of the Assembly should ask if there are any nominees from the floor. This should be done right after the Nominating Committee's list of candidates is presented.

Any nominees put forth at the assembly effectively challenge the preselected nominees, and force an election.

If you have conducted an open and public pre-nomination process, this **shouldn't** happen. Sadly, it sometimes does – never underestimate human nature. There are just some people who appear to delight in grandstanding to make a point – unfortunately, their "point" is often only obvious to themselves.

This is an unfortunate situation, since it can blind side the entire community. It frustrates everyone because there's no reason why this individual or group couldn't have taken part in the public pre-assembly nomination process.

If you've followed my advice, and have specified only a **minimum** number of councillors in your by-laws (rather than a fixed number), you can avoid an election by simply adding this person to the preselected list of candidates by acclamation.

This problem can also be easily solved by adding a clause to your rules of order or by-laws saying that candidates will be preselected by a Nominations Committee, and disallowing nominations from the floor.

Use of Ballots for Elections

If you must hold an election at your assembly, here are some considerations when using election ballots:

- <u>**Positive votes only**</u>: the ballot must contain only a single box for each candidate where the voter records a positive vote – generally by marking an '**X**'.

  An election vote is different from a vote on a resolution (motion), and under no circumstances can you allow a "YES" and "NO" choice for each candidate.

  Think about a typical ballot for a governmental election where you mark an '**X**', punch a hole, or dimple your chad beside your choice.

  Here's what Robert's Rules Newly Revised 10th Edition says about election ballots in **Chapter XIII Voting, §45. Voting Procedure**:

  > *"In elections, "for" and "against" spaces or boxes should not be used ... An election, in effect, is a vote on filling a blank, and a voter can vote against one candidate only by voting for another who has been nominated..."*

- <u>**Proxy ballots**</u>: if a limited proxy form contains an election ballot (and it should if you are holding an election), then the filled-in proxy form must be used by the scrutineers as the proxy giver's voting ballot for the election. This eliminates any errors or confusion, and saves time. Do not transfer information from the proxy form to a ballot.

  The proxy form must be clear, and must contain precise voting instructions for the proxy giver. It's a legal document, and must be crystal clear, and not open to interpretation.

If you've followed my earlier advice and avoided general proxies, then the limited proxy form **must** contain a ballot. If the proxy form is general, then it **must not**.

- **Extra space**: if your by-laws require that you take nominations from the floor at the assembly, then you should have a few blank lines so that you can write names in at the assembly. Unfortunately, the proxy ballots cannot anticipate this.

Avoid a Show-of-Hands Election Vote

While it might be tempting to want to use a simple show-of-hands vote for an election – **don't do this!** Ballots are superior to this form of voting for the following reasons:

- they guarantee that there's only one vote cast per condo unit;

- they make sure that each person only votes once for each candidate, and, if there's a limit to the number of candidates for a given position, it guarantees that no one exceeds this limit; and

- they allow verification of the voting after the assembly – if there's a dispute you can do a recount.

Avoid Partial Voting

I strongly recommend that if an election calls for a fixed number of candidates, say, five councillors, then all voters should be **required to vote for five candidates – no more and no less**.

If this is done, then any ballots with votes for more or less than the required number of candidates must be rejected.

Some voters feel that they're making a statement by not voting for someone. Unfortunately, this is a petty attitude that's anti-community, and has no place at a condo assembly.

A condominium is run by a volunteer administration. To only vote for a portion of the required council or special committee is disrespectful to those people who have stepped up to run as candidates to give to the community their time and efforts.

The fact that a voter might not personally like a candidate is a poor excuse to punish the community as a whole.

If a voter feels strongly against a candidate, then they should either run for election, or abstain from voting altogether. To only vote for a sub-set of candidates, skews the voting.

Validation of Election Ballots

Each ballot must be validated by the scrutineers before its votes are recorded, and, if a ballot is in contravention of your by-laws or your published election policy, then it must be rejected without the votes being recorded. This includes ballots on proxy forms.

For the validation process to be fair, the following must happen:

- both the ballots and the proxy form must be clear as to how they are to be filled out;
- clear voting instructions must be given to all owners in writing before the assembly (preferably, along with the proxy form and a voided sample of the ballot); these instructions must clearly define the rules which could cause a ballot to be rejected;
- clear voting instructions must be read to everyone at the assembly before the election begins; and
- the scrutineers must be given a clear procedure for validating proxy forms and ballots.

Possible reasons that a ballot could be rejected:

- the ballot is marked so that it's not clear for whom the voter is voting; both scrutineers must be in agreement on this one;
- there are five candidates running for three positions, and the voter has voted for more than three candidates; or
- there are five candidates running for three positions, and the voter has voted for less than three candidates – assuming that your election policy forbids this (I believe that it should), and that the voting instructions make this clear.

This applies to both regular and proxy ballots.

Keeping Election Ballots

You might be under pressure from some people to destroy the election ballots right after the assembly.

This should never be done!

> Destroying election records right after an election takes away the right of an owner or candidate to contest the election results.
>
> According to the **ACE** (the Administration and Cost of Elections Project, an international group of nine Canadian, Mexican, UN, and international electoral organisations), the generally accepted rule for elections is to "*...keep relevant electoral material as long as there exists an opportunity to challenge the election result.*"

How often have you seen recounts in government elections? What do you suppose the public's reaction would be if the ballots had been destroyed, and no recount was possible?

If a vote is contested after the assembly, there's no way to investigate any allegations, or to recount the votes, if the ballots have been destroyed.

I recommend that, at a minimum, you keep the ballots until the next assembly. Although this is a generally accepted election practice, it's not required by the Jalisco condo law (which makes no mention of election ballots at all).

As a comparison, keeping ballots for one year is a legal requirement for most provincial and state condo and homeowners association legislation north of the border. You can adopt this as a policy, although it may be wise to include it in your by-laws.

If you do keep the ballots until at least the next assembly (and you should), these still become part of your condo records, and are still accessible to all owners at any time.

If you want to keep the secrecy of the vote, you can remove any identifying marks – but you must make sure that the votes can still be seen. You might need to recount them if the results are contested.

That said, it's important to realise that ballots on limited proxy forms can't be destroyed or defaced in any way – these proxies are legal documents, cannot be altered or defaced, and must be kept as permanent condo records. Removing, altering, or obscuring the ballots on a proxy form is not allowed. All identifying information must stay intact for proxies.

Who Wins an Election?

While this may seem obvious at first glance, there are two popular voting methods for elections: plurality voting and majority voting.

While I believe that plurality voting makes more sense, there are those who adamantly endorse the concept of majority voting.

So, what's the difference?

A **plurality vote** is where the winning candidate is the one who receives the most votes.

A **majority vote** is where a candidate must not only receive the most votes, they must also receive a number of votes that meets or exceeds the majority of the votes cast – there's a minimum vote threshold.

For example:

Assume that four people are running for a position. The voting results are:

Candidate	Votes
A	10
B	19
C	7
D	6
TOTAL:	42

Under plurality voting: candidate B received the most votes, and would be declared the winner.

Under majority voting: there'd be **no winner**, since no candidate received a majority of the votes cast – in the case of 42 votes, this **majority threshold would be 22 votes**.

Depending on the rules, this would either be a failed election, or the bottom candidate could be dropped and another round of votes taken, or some other procedure would be followed. It's possible that several rounds may be needed before a winner is declared.

While majority voting has its proponents, I strongly believe that its problems far outweigh its benefits for a condo assembly. You mustn't forget that a condominium administration is a small group of volunteers, not a corporate board acting for shareholders in a major corporation (for whom majority voting has some distinct advantages).

For a condo, the major downside of majority voting is the possibility that there could be no winner, and that you might not be able to fill a position, or will be subjected to a complicated series of multiple rounds of voting. Most owners want an assembly to run efficiently and quickly, and not be complex and lengthy.

For an example of the possible complexity, suppose you have three positions on your Council and four candidates. With plurality voting the three candidates who receive the most votes will fill the positions. With majority voting, you'd likely need a series of run-off elections, and the complexity could become cumbersome. This also makes the use of proxies problematic, since, unlike the votes of those physically present, limited proxy votes won't change from round to round.

Another method of voting that you could consider instead of plurality voting, is **preferential voting**. In this model, each voter ranks the candidates in order of preference.

For example:

> If there are four candidates, each voter marks the numbers 1,2,3, & 4 next to each name on the ballot, in order of their preference.
>
> The candidate that received the most '1s' would be elected.
>
> If there are three positions to fill, then the candidates that received the most '2s' and '3s' would also be elected.

Recommendation: Plurality Voting

Plurality voting is, after all, the voting system used in most western democracies to elect our government representatives. **This is my preference, and recommendation for condo elections.**

PART 13 – Minutes of Assemblies & Meetings

Condo Assembly Minutes

Chapter **40**

Civil Code Article 1012 says that one of the three books required to be kept by your Administrator as the official condo records must contain the minutes of all owner assemblies (ordinary and extraordinary) along with attachments – this is Book #1.

Assembly Minutes Are Always Adopted at the Assembly

Assembly minutes are read and adopted by the assembly right after the assembly business has finished because the approved minutes must be publicly registered.

The most efficient way to do this is to create a minutes template before the assembly, and have the Secretary of the Assembly "fill in the blanks" during the assembly.

Public Registration of Assembly Minutes

The Jalisco condo legislation contained in the Civil Code requires that you protocolise and publicly register the minutes of any ordinary assembly where your Council was elected, a special committee was appointed, or your Administrator was appointed.

> **Protocolise** means that the *notario* (civil law notary) will reformat your document into a suitable form for filing with the public registry and in his protocol book.
>
> **Public registration** happens when the *notario* files the protocolised version of your documents with the local public registry office. You'll be given a certified copy for your condo records, and the original will be kept in the public records.

It's also a good idea to protocolise and register the minutes of any ordinary assembly where you approved an annual operating budget (and set the fees to be collected in support of it). This makes these decisions binding on third-parties, and collection enforceable.

Since these items are pretty well all you can deal with at an ordinary assembly, it's safe to say that the minutes of **every** ordinary assembly should be protocolised and publicly registered.

There's no specific Civil Code requirement to protocolise and register the minutes of extraordinary assemblies, **with the exception** of an assembly where your condo by-laws have been altered, or one where it's been decided to sue an owner.

That said, I strongly recommended that the minutes of all extraordinary assemblies be protocolised and registered to make sure that decisions made by the owners at these assemblies are binding on third-parties, and can't be challenged.

Protocolisation and registration must happen as soon as possible after the assembly – this is the reason why the minutes are approved at the assembly (unapproved minutes cannot be registered).

Minutes Must Be in Spanish

A document can only be publicly registered if it's in Spanish. As soon as the assembly minutes are to be protocolised and registered, they must be translated into Spanish (if they weren't originally written in Spanish).

Physical Format of the Assembly Minutes

The Jalisco condo law requires that the assembly minute book be a **bound book that's signed and stamped on the first page by the local Secretary of the Town Council.**

Bound *libros de actas* (minute books) are available at Office Depot and other stationery stores throughout México. They usually come in 50, 100, or 200 page versions.

That said, most of us would prefer to take minutes on a laptop – the fill-in-the-blanks template I mentioned earlier works this way.

How can we reconcile this with the legal requirements for a bound book?

Article 1012 of the condo legislation also says that if it's not possible to enter meeting minutes in such a book for any reason, then the minutes must be protocolised by a *notario*. If you take my advice and always protocolise the minutes of every assembly, you automatically meet this requirement.

The intent of a bound book is that, by being bound into a book that has no missing pages, the minutes are guaranteed to be unaltered from the original.

Protocolisation of the minutes also satisfies this intent, since the original minutes of the meeting will be kept not only in your condo records, but also by the *notario* in his protocol book as well as filed in the public registry office.

These original minutes must have a signature block on the last page for both the assembly Chair and Secretary to sign. Both individuals must also sign all the other pages of the minutes lengthwise in the right-hand margin –**signatures should always be made with a blue pen**. These original minutes will be kept by the *notario*, and you should keep a copy along with the registered minutes in Book #1 of your condo records.

Your condo records should also contain a copy of the assembly sign-in sheet, along with copies of any proxy forms – this way, there's an irrefutable record of the attendees. If you use ballots for election voting, they should be kept until at least the next assembly, when they can be destroyed or kept – depending on your election policy.

Any documents that were presented at the meeting (such as reports or the budget) must be included with the minutes in your condo records as attachments (**Article 1012 VI**).

Physically, Book #1 could be either a three-ring binder or an expandible archive file. The last one is my preference, because copies of the registered minutes are a little larger than legal size, and it's difficult to find a three-ring binder of a suitable size.

Archivos expandibles (expandible archives) can easily be found at any Office Depot or large *papelería* (stationery store) in México.

What You Need to Register Your Minutes

After the minutes are approved, the assembly will have appointed one or two people to protocolise and register the minutes. As soon as your minutes are available in Spanish, one of the named individuals should meet with your *notario*.

Your *notario* (civil law notary) will need the following:

1. ID of your condo's named representative. For a Mexican citizen, this will be their national ID. For a foreigner, this will be their passport and visa (*inmigrante* or *no inmigrante rentista* – formerly called an FM2 or FM3) – the *notario* will make copies.

2. The original minutes of your assembly in Spanish. These must have a signature block at the end signed by the Chair of the Assembly and the Secretary of the Assembly. These two must also sign the other pages lengthwise in the right margin. Always use a blue pen to sign legal documents.

3. The original sign-in sheets for the assembly – keep copies for your condo records.

4. The originals of any proxies used at the assembly – keep copies for your condo records.

5. If you used election ballots, your *notario* won't need them, but you should keep them in your condo records (for more details, **see Chapter 39 – "Recommended Election Procedures"**).

The *notario* will need a few days to prepare the documents for registration (protocolise them). The public registry office then usually needs several more weeks to finish the registration.

Once your *notario* has filed the documents, you'll receive a certified copy of the *escritura* containing your minutes. This document is an important part of your condo records, and must be filed in book #1 by your Administrator.

What Should Be In Your Assembly Minutes?

Assembly minutes are meant only to record the attendance plus the decisions reached by the assembly. This last is done by recording the wording of resolutions and the vote results. These minutes must not contain any summary of discussions or issues, or any secondary motions used to arrive at the final resolution.

Distribution of Assembly Minutes to the Owners

Although the Civil Code doesn't require it, I **strongly recommend** that you automatically send out the assembly minutes to all owners after the assembly (as a policy). You should also post them on your condo web site.

It's been my experience that many of the problems between a condo administration and the unit owners are caused by poor communication from the administration to the owners.

If you always keep the owners informed as to what you're doing and what's happening in your condo, the majority of them will be happy and satisfied.

Remember that the assembly minutes are official condo records, and must always be available to any owner who asks to see them.

Council Meeting Minutes

Chapter 41

Civil Code Article 1012 says that another of the three books required to be kept by your Administrator as the official condo records must contain the minutes of all council meetings along with attachments – this is Book #2.

No Public Registration of Council Minutes Is Needed

There's no legal requirement to protocolise and publicly register the minutes of council meetings. That said, it is required that every council meeting be minuted, and that these minutes form part of the permanent condo records.

Physical Format of Council Minutes

As with the assembly minutes, the condo legislation says that the council minute book must also be in the form of a **bound book that's signed and stamped on the first page by the local Secretary of the Town Council.**

> *"Great, but we'd prefer to take minutes on a laptop, rather than handwriting them in a book! You showed us how to avoid this with the assembly minutes by getting them protocolised. But this isn't practical for council minutes, and you said that we shouldn't do this. So... what do we do for council minutes?"*

Taking **Article 1012** literally, we can avoid entering council minutes in a bound book if the minutes are notarised – but **without translation, protocolisation, and public registration.**

<u>Technically</u>, this is what you would do:

> The original council minutes should have a signature block for both your Council President/Chair and Secretary on the last page. Both individuals should also sign all the other pages of the minutes lengthwise in the right-hand margin.

Signatures should always be made with a blue pen.

If you have these original minutes signed and stamped by a *notario* on each page, then you've fulfilled the legal requirement because the *notario* is certifying the document, and the *notario's* stamp, date, and signature **on each page** makes sure that the records can't have been altered after the fact – they should be accepted as valid records.

You then file these, along with any documents that were presented at the meeting (such as reports) as attachments, in Book #2 of your condo records.

Although this meets the legal requirements, it's still a lot of work, and incurs extra expense each month – this can impact the budget of a small condo.

Here's another method that doesn't strictly follow the Code, but I believe **it meets the intent of the legislation:**

Follow all the steps above **except** for having a *notario* sign and stamp each page.

This works because it would be almost impossible for anyone to alter the minutes afterwards. This would mean that the President/Chair, Secretary, and Administrator would all have to be in cahoots to deceive your condo. The President/Chair and the Secretary would have to re-sign the altered minutes, and your Administrator would have to replace the original records with the altered records. I can't envision this happening.

If you follow my advice and send out council minutes to all owners after each meeting, this would be impossible since they can't change everyone's copy.

> **IMPORTANT!** If you don't follow one of these procedures (**either** record your minutes by hand in a bound book authorised by the municipality, **or** have them notarised on each page, or sign them on each page), **then your minutes may not be valid or legal** – problems will arise if any Council decisions are challenged.
>
> If your records turn out not to be legal, then any decisions made at a council meeting will be invalid, and could be overturned by an owner seeking a legal decision.
>
> Even if an owner does not take you to court, you will have no legal basis for enforcing any invalid decisions or policies.

A word of caution, however. I strongly advise you to run this procedure and its reasoning past your *notario* to see if he agrees that you can do it.

Book #2 physically can most easily be a three-ring binder, since these minutes can be letter size sheets.

What Should Be In Council Meeting Minutes?

Since council minutes are neither protocolised nor registered, they can (and should) contain a summary of discussions on issues. Unlike assembly minutes, they don't need to only record decisions.

You should include summarised details for the following reasons:

- Apart from recording the decisions made by your Council, the minutes are also a communication tool for the community. They should contain enough information so that an owner who wasn't at the meeting (particularly absentee owners) can get a sense of the background on an issue, as well as the discussion and reasoning leading up to the decision.

This allows the owners to understand the reasoning behind decisions – especially controversial ones. This way, your Council's decisions are less likely to be questioned or resented.

- In the worst-case, the make-up of your Administrative Council could conceivably change each year. To help future councils facing the same or a similar issue, you should document the background and reasons for previous Council decisions.

Since council minutes are published and sent out (and posted on your condo web site), this is supported by **Robert's Rules §48** that says, "…**unless the minutes are to be published**, *they should contain mainly a record of what was done at the meeting, not what was said* … **When minutes are to be published**, *they should contain … an abstract or the text of each address…*"

Council Minutes Typical Outline

I've already discussed a typical council meeting agenda in **Chapter 23 – "Council Meetings."** The minutes must follow the agenda and the order of the events as they happen at the meeting.

Items listed in that chapter as being housekeeping and administrative in nature, and that shouldn't form part of the agenda, must still be recorded in the minutes.

Here's a typical layout for council meeting minutes, with a brief description of each item:

- **Roll Call**: the minutes must list the roll call of those present at the meeting. The President/Chair should be listed first, followed by the councillors in alphabetical order. Any councillors not there must be listed as absent.

    If your Administrator is present, this fact must be noted.

If the Secretary isn't a councillor, then they must also be listed.

A separate line should be included noting anyone else who's there, but who isn't a councillor (such as a committee chair or an owner there to observe). These should all be listed alphabetically.

- **Call to Order**: this is necessary to start the meeting, and can only happen if there's a quorum – if not, then the meeting cannot take place.

  There's no motion, the Chair just calls the meeting to order. Record the time the meeting was called to order in the minutes.

- **Adoption of Agenda**: the agenda should have been sent out before the meeting day, along with the notice. This advance agenda was for information only, and isn't the final agenda until it's adopted by the Council at the meeting.

  Councillors and guests can now bring up last minute items that weren't listed on the draft agenda. Except in unusual circumstances, these would normally be discussed under "New Business". The Chair must make sure that discussion on these topics is held off until they come up (such as when "New Business" is dealt with).

  Any corrections or additions to the agenda must be recorded in the minutes. The Agenda is usually adopted by general consent (acclamation).

- **Adoption of Minutes**: if you take my advice later in this chapter, the draft minutes will have been circulated to all councillors shortly after the last meeting.

Once their feedback and approval were received, they then should have been sent out to the community in draft form as a communications tool to keep owners informed of what your Council is doing.

These minutes stay as draft minutes until formally adopted at the next meeting (which is now this meeting).

Any changes needed are recorded in this section of the minutes. If the minutes have already been reviewed and commented on by all councillors, changes are unlikely. Minutes are usually adopted by general consent.

If there are changes needed to previously adopted minutes, these must also be recorded here. It's good practice to handwrite a note (initialled by the Secretary) on the copy of the changed minutes in the records. This note should be in the margins beside the issue that's being changed. It should briefly summarise the changes, and name the minutes where the changes are recorded in detail (the current minutes). **Be sure not to cross out anything on the original minutes when making this note** – the original minutes must still be legible.

- **Administrator's Report**: you can either just say that the report was given, or summarise its main points. The Administrator's report should be in writing (it will typically contain detailed financial information). It's permitted by condo law for this report to be oral (**Article 1017 III**), but I strongly discourage this.

  Make sure that the report is attached to the minutes.

- **Committee Reports**: standing committees should report first, followed by special committees.

It's good practice to always list each of your committees, whether they are presenting a report or not.

Under each committee that does present a report (this is normally done by the Committee Chair, but not necessarily), briefly summarise the report – these are most often verbal. If a committee has nothing to report, just write *"No report"* under the name of that committee.

Any written committee reports must form part of the record as attachments to the minutes.

- **Other Reports**: These would be reports by, in order, councillors, owners, or guests.

  Again, any written reports must form part of the record as attachments.

- **Special business**: if there's any business arising from procedures outlined in your by-laws, then it must be summarised here, along with details on any motions.

- **Unfinished Business**: your **Unfinished Business Report** should now be discussed, with the aim of closing as many unresolved issues as possible.

  The Unfinished Business Report is a powerful management tool, and consists of a table with the following four columns (at a minimum):

  1. **Issue** – short descriptive name for the item;
  2. **Date** – date of meeting where it came up;
  3. **Description** – brief description of the issue, along with its status; and

4. <u>**Action**</u> – brief list of who agreed to look into or deal with the issue.

To update the status on an issue, you just add another description to the description column, with a corresponding entry in the date column.

It should be your Administrative Council's goal to keep the Unfinished Business Report as short as possible by dealing with matters as they come up, and avoiding putting off decisions. If more research is needed on a matter, then it should be finished in time for the next meeting, and the matter decided and closed then. It's not good to see multiple entries for an issue in the description column, with multiple dates – this means that the issue has been put off too often. It needs to be wrapped up!

In the Unfinished Business Report, for ease of reference, it is helpful to **bold any new items that have just been added** and to *italicise any items that have been slated for deletion*. Any kind of highlighting will work, just make sure that these are easy to spot. Deleted items should stay on the report for one more cycle, and then drop off. Items marked for deletion at the meeting should be explicitly listed in the minutes as such (for tracking purposes).

I recommend that an **Action Report** also be updated and sent out. This is a useful tool to remind people of the tasks to which they agreed at the meeting. You'd be amazed (or not) at how many of these are quickly forgotten after the meeting.

The Action Report is really a condensed version of the Unfinished Business Report, and can consist of a simple three-column table:

1. Name of person assigned the task,

2. Description of task, and

3. Deadline date.

For the Action Report to be effective, it must be updated **as soon as possible after the meeting** by the Secretary, and then sent to all councillors, your Administrator, committee chairs, and anyone else at the meeting who was assigned a task.

Ideally, this should happen on the same day as, or the day after, the council meeting. It takes only minutes to update this report, and it's important that it be sent out as soon as possible after the meeting.

The Unfinished Business Report should be updated right after the draft minutes are finished, and then sent to all councillors, your Administrator, and committee chairs. This should happen within a week after the meeting.

The Unfinished Business Report and the Action Report aren't legal requirements. They're simple, but powerful, management tools that you can use to stay on top of things that have a habit of falling through the cracks because of human nature.

- **<u>New Business</u>**: this is the section where the actual business of the Council takes place.

    New items of business that are known beforehand will have been put on the agenda, and sent out with the meeting call as a point of information. Other items that councillors or owners wish to bring forth can now be brought up (these will have been added to the agenda at the start of the meeting).

    List each item in the minutes as it's discussed, and comment on each to briefly summarise the issue and any main background information.

Briefly record the reasons for any decisions made, along with the decision (motion).

If a decision on an item can't be made at this meeting, then it's good practice to include in the minutes brief details on any action needed and who's volunteered for the task. This information should also be added to the Action Report, and sent to all participants shortly after the meeting.

If any written information (email, letter, or report) has been received on one of these issues, then it must form an attachment to the minutes.

- **Next Meeting**: always try to set a date and time for the next meeting before adjournment.

  Even better, have a regular date and time for council meetings (such as the 25th of each month, or the last Friday of each month). This must be confirmed at the meeting before recording the next date.

- **Adjournment**: No motion is needed, the Chair just says, *"There being no further business, the meeting is adjourned."*

  Record the time of adjournment in the minutes.

Sample council meeting minutes and council reports are included in your BONUS Pack.

Misc. Practices

- A motion to receive a report is neither needed nor desirable. Such a motion can only cause the report to be read, which is pointless, since this is likely already the intent (reports are typically listed on the agenda). Nor can you refuse to hear a report if someone wishes to present one.

It's not proper to make any motion about a report itself once the report has been read, since it's a report, and it is what it is, It cannot be changed – it's just a matter of fact.

It is, however, proper to make motions to deal with issues raised by a report. For example, a report contains recommendations that your Council decides to carry out. Any motions dealing with issues arising from a report must be recorded in the minutes.

- When a motion is made, the mover of the motion must be recorded in the minutes, as well as the wording of the motion and the outcome of the vote ("CARRIED" or "DEFEATED").

  A seconder for a motion is normally not used for the relaxed rules of order set out for small board, council, and committee meetings. It's simply much more efficient not to second motions at a council or committee meeting.

  See Chapter 31 – "Rules of Order for Council & Committee Meetings" for more information.

- When a report, email, or other document is mentioned at the meeting, it must also be attached to the minutes (**Article 1012**). When the item is first mentioned, the minutes should say, *"(copy attached to and forming part of the minutes)."*

- While standard meeting practice doesn't require the reasons for a dissenting vote to be recorded automatically in the minutes, they must be recorded if the dissenter asks for this (sometimes they want the reason for their objection to be on the record).

- When a councillor abstains from voting, the reasons must be recorded in the minutes.

Note that under most accepted rules of order, councillors can't abstain from voting for any reason other than a conflict of interest. Especially in a condo, where they have a fiduciary duty to deal with all condo issues – this is what the job is all about.

Distribution of Council Minutes to the Owners

As with assembly minutes, I **strongly recommend** that you automatically send out your Council meeting minutes in draft form to all owners shortly after each meeting, as a policy.

The simplest way to do this is for the Secretary to finish the draft minutes within a few days after the meeting, and send them to each person who took part in the meeting for their review and input. Once the necessary changes have been made, the final draft minutes can then be sent out to the community along with the attachments.

Note that these draft minutes are for community communication only, and don't become official minutes until they're adopted at the next council meeting.

The official minutes are always the ones that have been formally adopted at the next meeting, are signed by the Chair and the Secretary, and are put in the permanent condo records. These minutes (as well as all condo records) must always be available for inspection by any owner who asks to see them.

Committee Meeting Minutes

Chapter 42

There's no mention in the condo legislation about minutes of committee meetings. Any policies that you come up with in this regard must either be documented in the form of a policy, or form part of your by-laws.

No Public Registration of Committee Minutes Is Needed

There's no requirement to protocolise or publicly register committee minutes, nor should this be done.

Physical Format of Committee Minutes

Since these minutes aren't required to be kept in one of the three record books required by law, the issues of trying to replicate the intent of a bound minute book don't exist.

These minutes can most easily be taken on a laptop, and filed in a three-ring binder with all attachments (any document presented at the meeting). They must form part of your condo records that are kept by your Administrator – committees are part of your condo administration, and their work must be able to be observed by the owners.

I do recommend that there be a signature block on the last page for the Committee Chair and the Secretary to sign. **Signatures should always be made with a blue pen.** Consider having them sign each page as well.

Distribution of Committee Minutes to the Owners

I recommend that committee minutes be sent out to the owners in the same way as council minutes.

Sample committee meeting minutes are included in your BONUS Pack.

PART 14 – Practical Matters

Your Condo Bank Account

Chapter 43

Your condominium needs a bank account to deposit the condo fees collected from the owners (along with any other income), and to pay maintenance and operational expenses.

You have two choices: open your own condo bank account, or use the bank account of a property manager (my recommendation).

Using A Commercial Bank Account

A bank account belonging to a condo must be a commercial account at a Mexican bank. While the rules for opening a commercial bank account vary from bank to bank, the following is typical:

- proof of either the creation of a condominium regime; this would normally be a copy of the *escritura constitutiva* (the registered public document that incorporated your condo regime);

- official ID of the legal representative who'll have signing authority (this would normally be your Administrator); accepted ID is normally an electoral ID card, a Mexican professional certification, or, for a foreigner, an *inmigrante* or *no inmigrante rentista* visa (formerly called an FM2 or FM3) along with a passport; an FMM tourist visa is not accepted;

- proof of address of the representative who'll have signing authority; accepted proof of address is normally an electrical or telephone bill that's no more than two months old;

- proof of the representative power of the person who'll have signing authority; this power will have been given by the ordinary assembly where your Administrator was appointed, and will be recorded in the assembly minutes; the required proof is a notarised copy of these assembly minutes;

- your condo's ***numero de Registro Federal de Contribuyentes*** or ***RFC*** number – this is the Federal income tax number given when your condo registered with the ***Secretaría de Hacienda*** (Ministry of the Treasury – the income tax department);

- a minimum opening balance (usually $3,000 to $5,000 pesos).

> If your condo **does** open its own bank account, it will first have to register with the ***Secretaría de Hacienda y Crédito Público*** (Ministry of Finance and Credit) and get an ***RFC*** (tax number).

Using a Property Management Company's Account

My recommendation is to hire a property management company to either assist your Administrator or act as the Administrator, so you can use the management company's bank account. For more details, **see Chapter 12 – "Lessening the Burden on a Volunteer Administrator."**

The advantages to this approach:

1. You can avoid registering with ***Hacienda*** (the Mexican tax department). Registering not only potentially opens up a can of worms, but it requires annual filings.

    Hacienda might also try to collect taxes on your collected fees. They shouldn't do this (a condo is a nonprofit), but, if they do, it can be a bit of an uphill battle to convince them differently.

    On January 1, 2010 a change was made to **Article 29** of the ***Código Fiscal de la Federación*** (Federal Tax Code) requiring that an annual receipt must also be given out whenever you collect partial payments during the course of year on a monthly, quarterly, or semiannually basis.

This annual receipt is in addition to the receipts you must issue for each payment. This should apply to condo fees, and is yet more bureaucracy to deal with.

2. You avoid the requirement of periodic filings involving the expense of a Mexican accountant.

3. There's no need to keep changing the account signatory at the bank every time you change Administrators (potentially annually).

4. You can deal with common area service "employees" at arms-length, by not directly employing them.

> ### *Important!*
> **Never** open a personal bank account under the name of a member of your administration, and use it for condo operations.
>
> While you might not be doing anything wrong, depositing condo funds to a personal bank account just looks bad.
>
> This could also be seen by the government as an attempt to get around Mexican income tax laws.
>
> Any single deposit of $25,000 pesos or more must have tax paid on it right away. While an individual must always pay income tax, your condo normally wouldn't, because it's a nonprofit organisation. While this can likely all be sorted out, it's a hassle and an expense. It may also take a while to get your money back.

Contract Workers vs. Employees

Chapter 44

It's my strong recommendation that you hire staff for your condominium (such as security guards, pool cleaners, or gardeners) either by contracting a company for these services, or by hiring these individuals as independent contractors – **avoid hiring them as direct employees**.

In both cases, you need a proper contract that sets up this relationship.

If there are certain jobs where it isn't practical to create a contract, then you might have no choice but to directly employ an individual.

If you hire a property management company to either assist your Administrator or to act as Administrator, then this management company could already have these people as employees. This insulates your condominium from the expenses, liability, accounting, and reporting issues surrounding employees. Your condo will have an arm's length relationship with them.

At first, it might seem that an employee is less expensive than a contracted worker, but if you include all the "hidden" expenses required by Mexican labour laws, this may not be the case.

There are other issues to consider about directly hiring employees for any position that's critical to your day-to-day operations– security guards, for example.

How do you keep up security if your guard is sick, has a family emergency or other obligation, or just wants to take holidays?

What happens to your security if your guard doesn't show up?

If your guards are contracted from a security company, the security company must send you replacements right away under any of these circumstances.

If you're considering directly employing people, your administration must be familiar with Mexican labour laws (which much more significantly favour employees and their rights than do their northern counterparts,). These laws have teeth!

Mexican Labour and Social Security Laws

There are primarily two federal laws that govern labour and employment in Mexico:

- the *Ley Federal de Trabajo* (Federal Labour Law), and

- the *Ley del Seguro Social* (Social Security Law) which controls the *IMSS – Instituto Mexicano del Seguro Social* (Social Security Institute).

The Federal Labour law contains rules and regulations that govern the relationship between the employer and employee, labour unions, and labour boards (arbitration boards). Depending on jurisdiction, labour boards can be federal or local, and have similar powers for labour issues as courts do for other issues. The decisions of these boards are enforceable by law.

Types of Employment

- <u>a specific task</u>: a well defined scope of work that has a clear end based on finishing a specific piece of work;

- <u>a specific period</u>: (for example, six months) this can <u>only</u> be used if it makes sense, based on the type of work, to set a time limit, or if this is a temporary position substituting for another worker who's taking some sort of leave of absence; or

- <u>an indefinite period</u>: this is the most common, and is the type of work that would most likely apply to a condo employee.

If you directly hire an employee, I recommend that you draw up an indefinite work period contract that captures all your expectations.

This could help prevent unexpected issues or surprises from arising. This contract must be drawn up in Spanish and, preferably, by an *abogado* (Mexican lawyer).

Payroll Deductions

Payroll deductions must be subtracted from the employee's wages and paid to a government department. Some of them also require extra contributions from the employer.

Some potential payroll deductions you need to be aware of when hiring employees:

- **Income tax**: employers must withhold personal income tax from an employee's salary, and remit it monthly to the federal government – there's no income tax for employees earning the minimum wage.

- **Social security**: it's the responsibility of an employer to register each of their employees with the *Instituto Mexicano del Seguro Social* (Mexican Institute of Social Security) or **IMSS**.

    Both the employee and the employer make contributions to IMSS, and the employer withholds the employee's contribution from their pay and remits it – at the time of writing, the employee's contribution is **5.25%**, and the employer's is **17.70%**.

    If an employee is earning the minimum wage, the employer must pay the entire contribution (currently **22.95%**).

- **Housing fund contribution**: all employers must pay an amount equal to **5%** of each employee's wage to the *Instituto del Fondo Nacional de la Vivienda para los Trabajadores* (Institute of the National Housing Fund for Workers) or *INFONAVIT*.

- **Pension contributions**: employers must make monthly contributions that, at the time of writing, are equal to **2%** of the employee's wage under the *Sistema de Ahorro para el Retiro* (System of Savings for Retirement) or *SAR*.

  These pension contributions are capped at a maximum of 25 times the current minimum wage set out for México City.

- **Support payments**: it's the responsibility of an employer to deduct from the employee's salary any support payments for spouse or children that have been decreed by a court, and to remit these payments.

> You'll need to hire a Mexican public accountant to deal with employee deductions and remittances to government departments.

Standard Employment Expenses

Employment expenses are amounts over and above the employee's wages that must be paid by the employer.

Some potential employment expenses you need to be aware of when hiring employees:

- **Seniority bonus**: employers must be paid a seniority bonus of 12 days salary per year worked over one year.

- **Vacation bonus**: as well as vacation time off, employees must also be paid an annual vacation bonus of no less than **25%** of their vacation pay.

- **Christmas bonus** (*aguinaldo*): each employee must be paid a year-end bonus equal to **at least 15 days wages**. This must be paid each year before December 20.

  A common misconception is that this is two weeks salary – no, it's 15 days. The correct calculation is to divide the weekly salary by seven, and multiply the result by 15.

- **Profit sharing**: each employee must be paid a profit-sharing bonus.

  Normally this wouldn't apply to nonprofit entities such as a condominium, but it **could** apply if your condominium has revenue over and above the condo fees. For example, if your condo rents out part of the common property for retail space. This type of income could change your status from nonprofit to profit.

General Employment Rules

Here are some employment rules you need to be aware of when hiring employees:

- **Payment of salary**: the salary period for employees doing normal labour can't exceed one week, and the salary is to be paid directly to the employee in cash.

- **Employment certificates**: each employee must be given a certificate at the end of the year that confirms the employee's seniority and the vacation time to which they're entitled.

  If an employee asks for it, the employer must give out a certificate every 15 days stating the number of days worked and the salary paid for this period.

You must give each employee a summary certificate on dismissal. It's best to use an accountant for this.

- **Working hours**: the employer and employee can mutually set the work hours, as long as these hours don't exceed the maximum allowed by the law.

  The law defines three types of work shifts:

  - **day shift**: between the hours of 6:00am to 8:00pm, with a maximum of 8 hours;

  - **night shift**: between the hours of 8:00pm to 6:00am, with a maximum of 7 hours; and

  - **mixed shift**: spans the working hours of the day and night shifts, with a maximum of 7½ hours.

  Throughout the various examples that follow, I'll use a night security guard, *Miguel*, employed by *Condominio Vista del Basurero*.

  > Assume that Miguel works from 7:00pm to 7:00am – this would be a *mixed shift*. The first 7½ hours would be straight time, and the remaining 4½ hours would be overtime.

- **Work breaks**: during any continuous shift there must be at least one 30 minute break, and time must be given for lunch. The worker can be made to skip these breaks, but only in emergency circumstances.

- **Overtime pay**: a worker can voluntarily agree to work more hours in a shift than those allowed by the law.

  > As we've seen with our night security guard Miguel, he's voluntarily agreed to work a 12-hour shift, but this means that we must pay him 4½ hours overtime per shift.

For a mixed shift, the first 45 hours worked in a week are paid at standard time (6 days at 7½ hours per shift). The next nine hours must be paid at double-time, and any extra hours must be paid at triple-time.

> *Assuming a six-day work week (normal), our night security guard Miguel would work: 45 hours at straight time, 9 hours at double time, and 18 hours at triple time – therefore, he must be paid the same as* **117 hours of straight time salary per week** *although he actually only works 72 hours.*

- <u>**Working days**</u>: employees are entitled to one day off **with pay** for every six days worked.

Although not legislated, it's normal to also give employees a day off on their birthday or other significant family occasions.

The legislation says that this rest day **should** be Sunday, but that the employer and employee can mutually agree on another weekday.

If an employee is made to work on their day off, they must get double the salary for their working hours on the day off **plus** the salary they'd have received if they had taken it off.

> *If Miguel worked seven days in a row in a given week, this would work out to the same as* **49½ hours straight time hours for the seventh day** *(7½ hours straight time plus 4½ hours at triple time, all doubled, plus 7½ hours at straight time).*

If an employee does work on Sunday, then they must be paid 25% more than their salary for any other day. If Sunday is also their normal day off, then this will be 125% of the salary mentioned in the paragraph above.

Therefore, if we made Miguel work seven days a week, his weekly salary would work out to about **238 straight time hours for 84 actual work hours.**

- **Paid holidays**: there are specific holidays that the law requires be given off with pay. They are:

  - **January 1** (New Years),
  - **February 5** (Constitution Day),
  - **March 21** (Benito Juárez Day observed – the actual holiday might vary by a couple of days to create a long weekend),
  - **May 1** (Labour Day),
  - **September 16** (Independence Day),
  - **November 20** (Revolution Day),
  - **December 1** (inauguration of a new federal government – **only happens once every six years**), and
  - **December 25** (Christmas).

  There could also be other **local** holidays that apply.

  If an employee is made to work on any of these holidays, then they must receive double the salary for their working hours on the holiday **plus** the salary they would have received if they had taken it off.

- **Vacation time**: once an employee has worked for one full year, they're entitled to a **paid holiday of at least six days**.

  This time increases by two or four days a year after a full year of service, according to a formula. For example, after five years the employee is entitled to 14 days off.

If the employee works for less than a year, then they're entitled to pro-rated holiday pay based on six days per year.

The time off must be continuous, and the employee **must be given his vacation time off**. It's illegal to pay the employee instead of time off unless the employee has terminated his employment before taking the time off.

Vacation time must be taken in the first six months of the year after the year for which the vacation time was earned.

- **Maternity leave**: all female employees must be given fully-paid maternity leave of 12 weeks – six weeks before their delivery, and six weeks after. They have the right to return to the job they left.

- **Discrimination**: an employer must not discriminate based on age, sex, race, social standing, or religious and political beliefs.

- **Minimum Age**: the minimum legal working age is 14 years old. Workers under 16 must have the permission of their parents plus a permit from the *Secretaría de Trabajo y Previsión Social* (Secretary of Labour and Social Welfare) or *STPS*.

  There are also limits on the hours they can work, there are special vacation time rules, and other special rules.

  Employees under 18 must not work after 8:00pm or before 6:00am.

- **Training**: all employers are obligated to give their employees training related to the work – including literacy training.

- **Tools and materials**: all employers are obligated to supply all tools and materials needed by their employees to carry out their jobs. This also includes uniforms, if needed.

- **Health and safety**: the work place must meet the minimum health and safety standards set by the federal government, including the installation of a first-aid station.

  A worker who has any type of accident on the job is entitled to all medical attention that's deemed necessary, regardless of whether they (or a co-worker) were negligent. Medical care is generally provided under IMSS (see "Payroll Deductions").

  Employers are required to alter the work place as needed for the health and safety of their workers.

- **Day care**: all employers are obligated to provide day care, if needed.

Some people will tell you that you don't need to bother with these rules. As with other things, you can probably skate by for quite a while – but if it catches up with you, it can bite you big time!

Others will tell you that all you need to do to avoid most of these issues and expenses is to get the employee to sign a waiver giving up some or all of these rights.

Don't do this!

This is illegal, and this waiver is unenforceable.

Any waiver given by an employee to give up any of their rights under the labour law is automatically considered null and void. This is because, as a protection for workers against unscrupulous employers, it isn't possible for an employee to voluntarily give up any of the rights enshrined in the labour laws.

While you might get away with this as long as you're on good terms with your employee, things could turn ugly quickly if you have a falling out, and they become disgruntled.

The labour courts won't respect your "agreement" with the worker, they won't look kindly on you for trying to take advantage of the employee, and the retroactive expenses and penalties could be huge.

Termination and Severance Pay

If it's necessary to terminate employment, there are a number of other issues of which you need to be aware:

- **Severance pay**: isn't needed if an employee is dismissed for cause. However, there are only a few specific causes for dismissal allowed under the law such as:

    - working less than one year,
    - completion of a written labour contract,
    - working under the influence of drugs or alcohol,
    - sabotage,
    - gross violation of safety procedures, or
    - a physical or mental disability preventing them from working properly.

    This covers the most important items, but isn't a complete list (although it's not much longer).

    To legally fire an employee for cause, an employer must give the employee written notice within 30 days of the incident that caused the firing. This notice must clearly give the reason for firing, as well as the date of the employee's termination.

    Fired employees who have been working for two or more years have a right to sue if they feel that their firing is unjustified.

If the employee wins this suit, they must be given back their job, receive full back pay, and could possibly receive punitive damages.

Severance is also not needed if the employee **quits or agrees to leave for any other reason** – but be sure to get this in writing with the employee's signature!

> It's important to realise that if work isn't specifically defined as temporary at the time of hiring, then you'll have to pay severance.
>
> **It's important to clearly set out in writing that a position is temporary**, and to explicitly define a set time or milestone for the end of the job.

If an employee is dismissed/fired/laid-off for **any reason other than those defined as a legitimate cause**, then it is without cause. The employer is then liable for **all** the following severance payments to the employee:

- three months salary; **plus**
- 20 days salary for each year worked; **plus**
- a seniority bonus of 12 days salary per year worked over one year; **plus**
- any wages due from the last pay to the day of dismissal.

The Cost of Employee Benefits

It's usually estimated that employee benefits **add between 30% to 50%** to the direct wage costs.

However, there are some "hidden" costs as well:

- Many of the payroll deduction and remittance requirements require your condo to use a Mexican public accountant. This will likely add at least $1,200 pesos per month to your condo's budget.

- There's a significant administrative burden in dealing with employees – with a volunteer administration, it isn't clear who'd look after this. It's an even greater load on your Administrator, and is impractical for an owner-volunteer. The cost of hiring a paid Administrator must also be considered.

- While not a financial cost, it can be emotionally troubling for many people to fire someone, and might be difficult for a volunteer administration to deal with.

Do We Really Need to Comply With All These Rules?

This kind of question always comes up when talking about Mexican laws.

> *"I know condos who ignore these rules, and most Mexican businesses do as well! So, why shouldn't we?"*, I've heard some of you say.

While this is partly true (it's not **most** Mexican businesses, by the way), it's definitely not right.

Although the labour boards have real teeth to go after abusive employers, this only happens if an employee makes a complaint. Many employees are too afraid of losing their jobs to complain.

As foreign guests in this country, I think we have an even higher duty to the laws and the people than do native businesses.

I sincerely hope that your condo is not the kind of employer who takes advantage of your employees just because you know you can get away with it, and you know that they're more or less powerless to do much about for fear of losing their jobs.

If so, then shame on you.

PART 15 – Condo Finances

Your Condo Budget

Chapter 45

Each year, a new budget must be approved for the next fiscal year (**Article 1020**). This is done at the annual ordinary assembly that must be held in January, February, or March of each year.

Your Condo's Fiscal Year

A fiscal year is a financial (budget) year, and is often different from a calendar year (January 1 through December 31). Condominiums are no exception.

According to the condo legislation (**Article 1012**), a condo's fiscal year must run from April 1 through March 31.

The condo legislation also requires that your annual ordinary assembly be held either in January, February, or March, **but in no other months (Article 1020)**.

You should try to hold this assembly in the same month each year, and, preferably, in the last month of your fiscal year (March).

I recommend March because there's a lot of preparation involved for the annual assembly (typically at least two months), and you'll find that not much is able to be done in December because of holidays, festivities, vacations, or visits to/from relatives. It's important that these preparations have momentum and continuity, and if you plan the meeting for, say, February, you'll find that the interruption caused by December will be a problem.

You also need as much historical financial data as possible to prepare a good budget, and you must be aware of as many upcoming expenses as possible. It's just more accurate to forecast the next fiscal year at or near the end of the current one.

You also need to consider that if you can't get quorum for your scheduled annual ordinary assembly, then you must reschedule it no sooner than 7 days and no later than 15 days (**Article 1023**).

Since the assembly must be held no later than March 31 (**Article 1020**), the first call for the assembly must be at least 7 days before March 31 in case you need a second call. For this reason, most annual ordinary assemblies are held between March 20 and March 24.

What Is a Budget?

A budget is just an estimate of the income and expenses for the coming year. Its purpose is to work out how much money is needed to operate during the coming budget year (the next fiscal year).

This is done by estimating all the expenses for the year, and then setting the income (fees) to cover these estimated expenses.

The Structure of a Condo Budget

The condo legislation requires funding for two things: maintenance/operating expenses, plus a reserve fund.

Standard budgeting and accounting practices require that the operating budget be supported by a contingency. Therefore the structure of your condo budget will be:

1. operating and maintenance expenses;
2. operating contingency;
3. reserves; and
4. income (fees).

Let's look at each of these in detail.

Part I: Operating and Maintenance Expenses

This part of your budget must list all the expected operating and maintenance expenses for the year. These amounts are normally based on historical data, assumed inflation, and contractor estimates for any planned repairs. It's important that you try to include every expense that you can reasonably predict will come up during the next fiscal year.

Here are some typical condo budget categories (not all apply to every condo, nor is this list meant to be exhaustive):

- **Payroll expenses**: if your condo has direct employees, this is the spot for payroll expenses such as:

    - wages – each employee should be a separate line item;
    - vacation pay;
    - income tax deductions;
    - social security deductions (IMSS);
    - housing fund contributions (INFONAVIT);
    - pension contributions (SAR);
    - bonuses (such as seniority, vacation, or Christmas);
    - severance pay.

    Remember that in México, employees are paid weekly (and not monthly, like north of the border). Since your budget will be on a monthly basis, remember to bump your expense projections in months that have five weeks – your annual budget must include all 52 pay periods per year.

- **Common property services**: if you do your routine maintenance using contractors (as opposed to employees), list these here. They might include:

  - security guards;
  - maids for common property areas;
  - gardeners for common property areas;
  - pool maintenance for common pools;
  - trash collection;
  - bonuses for contract workers (aguinaldo), if you pay these.

  These are typically monthly expenses, and must be shown in each month. As with your payroll expenses, watch out for contractors that are paid weekly – about five months in each year have five weeks, and the weekly expenses for these months will be higher by 25%.

- **Professional services**: any professional services you use in a given year, such as:

  - contracted Administrator or property management services;
  - accountant fees for audits, for filing employee deductions and reports, and for filing hacienda tax reports and forms; these last two will only apply if you have direct employees and a bank account respectively;
  - translation services for:
    - legal documents or any document that's to be publicly registered such as assembly minutes or by-laws;

- the call for any assembly, as well as the attached Order of the Day – these must be posted in Spanish; or
- various condo notices if you have a significant Spanish speaking population (or if you have a single Spanish speaker who asks for it);

- *notario* services (Civil Law notary) for protocolisation and registration of assembly minutes;
- *abogado* services (lawyer) for legal advice, letters to delinquent owners, arbitration, or other collection efforts.

Try to put these in the months where you expect the expense to be paid. The notario fees for assembly minutes, for example, would normally go in the month after the annual ordinary assembly. If you're holding an extraordinary assembly, the expenses should appear two months after the assembly to allow you 30 days to collect absentee votes.

- **Utilities**: common property utility charges, such as:
  - municipal water for common property areas, such as sprinkling of lawn areas or a pool;
  - telephone for common property use, such as in a guard house, meeting room, or admin office;
  - cable or satellite TV charges for common property areas such as a meeting room or a lounge;
  - electricity for common areas including such things as pool filtration and street lighting;
  - gas for common area facilities such as a BBQ, or pool or jacuzzi heater.

These can be monthly, bimonthly, or some (like gas) could be sporadic. For accurate cash flow analysis, try your best to put them in the months where you most expect the expense to be paid. For example, gas expenses for a pool or jacuzzi will likely happen less often during the rainy season, and most often during the warmer months.

- **Repairs and Maintenance**: this is where you try to capture all known repair or routine maintenance items, such as:
  - general repairs and maintenance; this line item is a catch-all for the little repairs that crop up over the year expressed as a representative monthly amount – generally based on history (for example, you can take last year's total and divide by 12);
  - recurring maintenance; this is a line item for routine maintenance that needs to be done one or more times a year (such as cleaning a common area *aljibe* – water cistern); try to put these in the months where they're expected to be paid; or
  - specific repairs; often you know beforehand that you need to fix various things in the coming year; these are listed here along with your best estimate as to what this will cost; the expense should go in the month where it's expected to be paid.

- **Supplies**: this category includes all the supplies that you need to buy for regular maintenance, such as:
  - general supplies such as toilet paper for common property washrooms, cleaning supplies, or light bulbs;
  - plant and gardening supplies like fertiliser, insecticide, replacement plants, or soil;

- pool chemicals (if not included in your maintenance contract); or

- office supplies.

While it's usually impossible to predict what these might be each month, you can spread a yearly estimate out as twelve equal monthly amounts. If you know that a specific expense is seasonal, then split it as best you can across the proper months.

- **Insurance**: any insurance carried by your condo for the common property (such as fire and earthquake, or third-party liability).

- **Web site**: annual costs for keeping up your condo web site.

- **Committees**: if any committees have been assigned a budget, then these must be included.

- **Misc. Expenses**: this is a catch-all section for those other **expected expenses** that just don't fit the rest of the categories (such as bank charges, interest, or other fees). List each of these here as a separate line item so that they can be identified and tracked. Try to figure out the months where these should go, or spread them evenly across the year.

    Do not have a general unspecified "Misc." amount – this is what the contingency is for.

A sample annual operating and maintenance budget is included in your BONUS Pack.

You Need to Allow for Inflation

Your budget must allow for inflation.

You need to look at some of your recurring expenses (particularly employees and services) to see if they'll need to be bumped in January for the final three months of the budget year.

The Mexican government increases the base salary for the minimum wage each January, and the amount is published in December.

For example, assume the average increase in base rate has historically been about 5% (this is what it is at the time of writing this book). Employee costs will need to be bumped by 5% for the final three months of your budget.

Improvements Are Not Included

You'll notice that so far we've been talking only about repairs and maintenance to existing common property elements. This is because **improvements don't form a part of the operating budget to be approved at your annual ordinary assembly.**

Improvements are expenses that are outside of the annual operating and maintenance budget, and must be specifically approved by the owners at an **extraordinary assembly (Article 1009 III)**. This same assembly must also set out how the improvement will be funded (generally by special fees), and approve this funding.

> Examples of improvements might be: a heater for the pool, a roof added to an uncovered terraza, or adding a motorised entry gate or access system.

> Examples of repairs and maintenance are: repairing an already existing pool heater, repairing an existing pool terraza roof, repairing an existing motorised gate, re-painting the buildings, pumping out septic tanks, or replacing **existing** pool furniture (buying **more** furniture is an improvement).

The funding for any improvements approved at an extraordinary assembly must be added to the approved budget as a modification to the budget.

If they're to be funded by collecting special fees, then these fees must be added to the income projection, and the cost of the improvement must be added to the expense section. Normally, these cancel out, and don't change your bottom line.

If the improvements are to be funded from the reserves (I don't usually recommend this, except in special circumstances), then the expense must be added to the planned reserve expenses section of your budget.

This updated budget must then be sent to all owners.

Part II: Operating Contingency

Part I of your budget tries to fund all normal expenses **that can be reasonably forecast for the coming fiscal year**. The contingency is just a separate amount of money set aside to deal with **unknown expenses.**

Any sound operating budget must have a contingency – this is standard accounting practice. Do not call your contingency a "slush fund" – this term has unethical or illegal connotations.

A common misconception is that a contingency is for unexpected expenses. **This is not so!**

One or more of these expenses absolutely will come up every year (I guarantee it!). You just don't know what they'll be, how many, when, or the amount.

Therefore, they aren't unexpected – **they're fully expected, just unknown**. By having a contingency, you're anticipating them.

Your contingency must accommodate any of the following expense situations that can't be reasonably forecast when preparing your operating budget:

- a budgeted item costs more than was budgeted because of circumstance; for example:
    - your pool maintenance contractor quits part way through the year, and you can't find a replacement for the same low cost;
    - you got an estimate for a repair in January when preparing your budget, and the actual quotes you receive in April are all higher than the budgeted amount;
- something happens that you couldn't have predicted; for example, your septic tanks overflow, and need pumping right away, a water main breaks, or your pool pump seizes up;
- an owner becomes delinquent, and the fees you're collecting are no longer adequate to cover your expenses.

Typically, 7% to 10% of total operating expenses is considered a reasonable contingency for general operation.

I recommend, however, that you also try to accommodate delinquencies – these are a fact of life in Mexican condos. Look at your delinquency history. If you expect in any given year to have a problem with one unit, or two, or three, then your contingency should take this into account.

> If, for example, you expect that one particular owner might not pay their fees during the year, and if their fees represent 5% of the condo rights, then I'd add this to the minimum contingency, and set it at 12% to 15%.

If you expect that two units might do this, bump it up by a higher percentage.

It's important to realise that, unlike the operating and maintenance budget, the contingency is **not a recurring yearly expense**. In a typical year, you should not use up your entire contingency – if this happens consistently, then either your contingency is too small or your expense estimates are off.

For example, if your contingency is set at 10%, and you only only use 5%, then you still have the 5% unused portion to carry forward into the next fiscal year's contingency. Next year's fees only need to fund the **replacement of the portion that was used this year**.

Part III: Reserves

The purpose of reserves is to fund ongoing, but long-term, repairs and maintenance of the common property.

The operating and maintenance budget (along with the contingency) is designed to fund repairs and maintenance that happen **during the budget year**.

The reserves are to fund repairs and maintenance that are **more than yearly** – every two years, every five years, every 15 years, or every 20 years.

This includes items such as road paving and repairs, roof repairs, elevator maintenance, painting common property buildings, or pool furniture replacement. The reserve fund is to make sure that funds for these items are available as and when these expenses come up – without the need for special assessments.

Therefore, your budget must include not only the calculated reserve fund contribution for this year (income), but also the projected repair, maintenance, or replacement expenses for each item that needs doing in that year. The main point to remember is that the reserves usually have both contributions **and** planned spending occurring each year.

It's important to understand that the goal of your reserves is **not** to achieve a predetermined level of reserves, and then have them sit there for a rainy day – reserves aren't meant to be a financial cushion waiting for some unknown event.

If you aren't doing planned maintenance and refurbishment from your reserves in almost every year, then you're probably not maintaining your condo properly – it'll likely deteriorate, and property values will decrease.

As well as planned long-term maintenance, the reserves are also there to fund emergency repairs and maintenance. For example, a portion of your perimeter wall collapses, your water main springs a leak, or your septic tanks overflow.

As with condo legislation in the US and Canada, the Jalisco condo law **requires** a reserve fund (**Civil Code Article 1026**).

The law allows you to invest your reserves, but you must never invest in securities that mature beyond the current fiscal year. These investments must also let you withdraw the money at any time without significant delay or penalty (other than the loss of interest).

Years of experience in Canada and the US have shown that such legislation is necessary to protect condos from themselves. Left to their own devices, the natural tendency is to want the lowest fees possible, and condos have historically neglected, or even ignored, long-term maintenance.

The consequences down the road can be a run-down condo with lowered property values that suddenly needs huge special assessments – an extremely unfair situation.

After several years of unsuccessful experimenting with both no legally set out reserve level requirement, and a minimum percentage requirement, recent condo laws in most Canadian provinces and US states now require that reserve fund levels and contributions be set by a reserve study, and that this study be updated on a regular basis.

Unfortunately, México hasn't yet caught up to this. The condo law here only requires that a reserve fund be created and kept up – it doesn't set a minimum reserve fund level.

The philosophy of this law is the same as it originally was north of the border: condos vary so significantly in the amount and nature of their common property, that there's no "one size fits all" solution that can be put into the legislation (such as 20% of the operating expenses or 3 months of fees – none of these make sense, or work).

I can tell you that, based on the experience of thousands of condos north of the border over the last couple of decades, that:

- a properly-funded reserve fund is essential to the long-term financial health and property values of a condo; and

- the single best way to work out a proper reserve level is through a reserve study – a "dart board" approach is irresponsible, and a fixed percentage is meaningless.

If you want to operate your condo in a fiscally responsible way, I highly recommend that you adopt the more stringent reserve practices used up north.

Article 1006 of the condo law requires that you must spell out the basis of your reserve funding in your by-laws.

Part IV: Income

Once all the expenses have been estimated, you need to work out an income level (fees) that will support them.

If you have income from sources other than fees (such as invested reserve funds, retail or other rental space, or usage fees – these last for non-owners only!), then these must also be forecast into the months where they're expected.

You'll also need to bring your contingency back up by the amount used in the current year, and work out a suitable reserve contribution for the new fiscal year.

Once your condo budget has been prepared, and it accounts for all known deficits, all foreseeable operating expenses, an operating contingency, and proper reserve funding, then the income side of the equation is put into place to offset all these expenses, while taking into account other income.

The total expenses, plus any shortfall from the last year, less any expected other income (for example, interest on investment of the reserve funds) gives you the annual fees that you must assess the owners to support your budget.

Carry-Forwards: Surpluses and Shortfalls

When finalising your budget for the next fiscal year (generally less than two weeks before your annual assembly), you must make your best estimate of any expected surpluses or shortfalls at the end of the current fiscal year.

You might have a surplus if expected spending either doesn't happen, or if items come in under budget.

A shortfall can come about from operating expense overages, unexpected expenses, or owners not paying their fees.

If any of these look like they will happen, you need to start off the income side of your new budget with either a positive or negative carry-forward – effectively decreasing or increasing the fees needed for the next year.

Note that the above comments apply only to the operating portion of the budget. Your contingency balance (or shortfall) is always carried forward, and topped up each year as needed. The reserve balance (or shortfall) is also always carried forward each year, and added to by the amount needed to be collected in the next fiscal year according to the latest update of your reserve study.

Cash Flow Analysis

To correctly work out the quarterly or monthly fees, you must incorporate a cash flow analysis into your budget to adjust these fees to compensate for potential deficits caused by varying levels of expenses during the upcoming fiscal year. It's unlikely that just dividing your total needed income into four equal quarterly amounts will work.

There are many reasons why your expenses won't be evenly spread across your yearly budget. For example, some utilities could be bimonthly, some expenses could be one-shot or sporadic, or weekly employee or contractor expenses will increase in months with five weeks.

Another example: you have a number of budgeted repairs that, by their nature, must be finished before the rainy season; these will cause a heavier weighting of expenses in your first quarter.

Because of all these possibilities, evenly spread, equal fee payments will likely not properly fund your budget.

For example, your cash flow analysis might reveal that your first quarter assessment needs to be 25% higher than average, your second quarter can be 75% of average, your third quarter must be 15% higher than average, and your final quarter must then be 85% of average.

If you just charged an average assessment each quarter (the total funds needed for the year divided into four equal quarterly assessments) you'd find that you were running into deficit at various points during the year.

The condo legislation doesn't allow your condominium to run a deficit!

The moment you know this is happening, you must charge a special assessment to collect enough funds to fix this situation (**Article 1030**).

If you do this a few times in a year, you'll be very unpopular with your owners – especially if it was unnecessary, and resulted from not properly calculating the income needed to support varying expense levels for each portion of the year.

Getting Community Support for Your Budget

"Can a budget be developed so that it's easily approved at the annual assembly?" **You betcha!** … here's my recommended process:

- **Time your assembly**: ideally, your annual ordinary assembly should be in the last month of your current fiscal year (March). This lets the assembly approve an accurate budget that's based on almost complete historical data for the current year, plus the latest knowledge of upcoming expenses.

- **Start early**: because of the size of the task, you should start the budgeting process about three months before your annual ordinary assembly to allow adequate time (January).

- **Update your reserve study**: the reserve study from the last year should be updated to reflect:

  - the actual reserve spending during the last fiscal year;

  - any new knowledge about upcoming repairs or refurbishments;

  - any new knowledge about the usable life of any of the common assets; and

  - any new knowledge about yearly inflation rates.

- **Administrator develops an initial "bare bones" draft**: since your Administrator has managed the finances all year, this person is in the best position to prepare the initial draft budget for discussion and review by your Administrative Council. This will normally be a budget that your Administrator believes reflects the minimum level of operating expenses, contingency, and reserves needed for the coming fiscal year.

  Your Administrator's basic budget will be based on:

  - the experience of the current fiscal year, coupled with historical data;

  - conversations with the property management company (if you use one), other condos, and other industry professionals, as needed; and

  - estimates from contractors or engineers for known upcoming repairs.

- **Council examines this draft and amends and adopts a "proposed budget"**: your Council should then sit down with your Administrator at an open council meeting (a special meeting to deal only with this topic). Ideally, your Administrator will have sent all councillors the budget materials well before this meeting (a week is about right) so that they can prepare themselves (a homework assignment!).

  This should be a roll-up-your-shirt-sleeves session, during which your Council thoroughly examines the budget in detail. Owners should be encouraged to be at this meeting, and any owners there can be solicited for opinions, **but**:

  - don't let the meeting get out of control;
  - remember that the budget can't contain any items that are improvements – these must be approved at an extraordinary assembly (the means of paying for them will also be approved at this assembly); and
  - remember that the responsibility of your condo administration is to make sure that your condo is adequately funded – don't give in to vocal owners who want lower fees at the expense of proper maintenance.

  The proposed budget based on changes resulting from this council meeting should be a budget and fee proposal that a majority of your Councillors are in agreement with, and that's been approved by a minuted motion as the budget to be presented to the owners for review (and change, if needed). Therefore, it has your Council's "stamp of approval."

- **Seek community input before the assembly**: once your Council has approved and adopted the proposed budget, it should be sent to the community for their examination and comment.

- There must be a due date for comments well before the date of the assembly (I recommend the final council meeting). You should also post this budget on your condo web site.

    Invite owners to either submit their comments by email or in person at the council meeting.

- **<u>Update this to a final budget using the community feedback</u>**: owner comments and input will be considered and discussed at a council meeting for this purpose. This is often the final council meeting of the fiscal year, held within two weeks of the assembly.

    Send out the final community-vetted budget to all owners just before the assembly. Include all updated financial data. Assume that any owners still in arrears at this point will create an income shortfall to be carried into the new budget.

    The proposed fees supporting the budget should also be sent to the owners so they can see the impact on their unit. Use a spreadsheet showing the monthly or quarterly fees for each unit – these are proportional, based on each units condo rights.

Approval of the Budget and Fees

The budget and corresponding fees don't become official until they're approved at the annual ordinary assembly (**Article 1020**).

If you've done all the ground work above, you'll end up with a workable budget that's been thoroughly examined and approved by your administration, and understood and supported by the majority of owners – all of this before the date of the assembly.

Therefore, budget approval at the annual assembly should be almost a foregone conclusion. Ideally, this should go smoothly with little dissent or discussion, and no changes.

Will you have dissenters? Oh, yes ... human nature again!

You'll most likely receive negative comments at the budget meetings before the assembly, and even at the assembly itself. Be prepared – some of these people may be rude and abusive. This will be particularly true if you've raised the fees.

It's important that your administration stand its ground in the face of this. A condo administration has a fiduciary duty to make sure that your condo doesn't go into deficit, that all maintenance and repairs are done as needed, and that the reserves and property values are kept up.

You cannot compromise the financial health of the community to appease a few vocal individuals who are only looking out for their own self interests.

How Detailed Should Your Budget Be?

You need to develop a month-by-month budget with full line-item detail to make sure your predictions and assumptions are as accurate as possible. The higher the level of detail in your budget, the more likely that you've captured all the possible expenses.

You should also present this level of detail to the owners during the budgeting process and at the assembly where the budget will be approved.

The more they know, the more informed a decision they will be able to make. Always remember that you must be open and transparent, and nothing can ever be hidden from the owners.

This detail work is never wasted, since the detailed budget will form the basis for the monthly budget tracking reports for the Council, and the core of the condo's financial records for the year.

Financial Reports

Chapter
46

The condo legislation requires that the Administrator give a financial report to the Administrative Council once a month (**Article 1017**) – in fact, the law requires that your Council meet at least once a month to receive this report.

Your Administrator must also send out a quarterly report to the owners that gives a detailed accounting of your condo's finances (**Article 1012**). A financial report must also be presented at the annual ordinary assembly as part of the general report to the owners (**Article 1020**).

Monthly Financial Report

The monthly report to the Council is an important management tool that allows it to see if your condo is on track. It alerts your Council to any financial issues and problems as they come up (such as unexpected expenses, or delinquent owners).

To maximise its effectiveness as a management tool, I recommend that this report should contain two spreadsheets plus a text explanation, as follows:.

1. **The first spreadsheet** is a year-to-date (YTD) summary from the start of the fiscal year to the end of the month before the council meeting. For example, if this report is for a council meeting on August 20, then the report will be from April 1 to July 31.

    This summary should only list totals for each major budget category, and not show the line items within each. Being a summary, it only needs three columns of figures: Actual YTD, Budget YTD, and the Variance (difference between the two).

2. **The second spreadsheet** is the detailed report with the same major budget categories as the summary report, but expanded into all the individual line items. Like the budget, these are shown on a month-by-month basis for the entire year.

Therefore, it will have twelve columns, one for each month of the fiscal year. Three columns similar to the summary report should also appear: Total Projected, Total Budget, and the Variance.

> **Total projected**: is the total for each line item that shows the actual amounts spent YTD plus the projected amounts for the remainder of the year. This will change each month as actual data and new projected expenses are added.
>
> **Total budget**: is taken from the approved budget, and never changes.
>
> **Variance**: is the difference between the two (are we over or under the budget?).

This part of the report is based on the approved detailed budget you prepared for the assembly vote, and is one reason for the amount of detail in the budget (the others are accuracy and transparency).

This report shows actual month-by-month expenses and income for the year-to-date (with the same cut-off date as the summary report). The rest of the fiscal year is shown as a best-guess forecast as of the report date.

At first, the forecast for the rest of the year will be based entirely on the budget. Amounts will be replaced each month by any expected budget variances.

For example, unbudgeted expenses that are known to be coming up, budgeted expenses that are now expected to be higher or lower than budgeted, or budgeted expenses that have been moved to a different time period from the original budget.

3. **The text explanation** is a written summary report highlighting important budget and financial issues including:

- a brief explanation of any income variances from the budget;

- a list of delinquent owners, and the steps being taken to collect from them;

- a list of any people who are owed money by your condo – other than standard monthly expenses; for example, a contractor who's been paid a down payment, and is still owed an unpaid balance once the work is finished;

- any expense variations from budget, with a brief explanation;

- any expenses charged against the contingency or reserves, with a brief explanation; a summary of the contingency and reserve balances vs. budgeted; and

- a brief explanation of any budget variances that form the forecast portion of the report.

As well as being a powerful management tool for the Council, these monthly reports form the financial accounting records for the condo. They track your actual expenses over the course of the year, and compare these to the approved budget. Budget numbers being replaced by actual expenses, and unbudgeted items appear under the contingency and, possibly, the reserves.

A sample monthly financial report is included in your BONUS Pack.

Monthly Reports Include Approved Improvements

Although improvements weren't part of the budget approved at the annual ordinary assembly, any improvements that were later approved at an extraordinary assembly and added to a modified budget must now be included and tracked on these monthly financial reports.

Quarterly Financial Report

The legal requirements for the quarterly report are:

- an analysis of the quarter's expenses;
- accounting of income and overdue fees;
- list of debtors, explaining the debt;
- list of creditors, explaining the credit owed; and
- the cash balance.

This report **must** be sent out by your Administrator **in the first 15 days of April, July, October, and January (Article 1012).**

While the law only requires that it be given to any owner who asks for it, I urge you to automatically send it out to all owners (for openness and transparency).

If you're following my guidelines, the quarterly report can just be another monthly report. The only difference is that you should give the text portion of the report a different title. For example, "*Quarterly Report as of June 30, 20xx,*" instead of, "*Monthly Report for Council Meeting of August 19, 20xx.*".

Report to the Annual Ordinary Assembly

The first item on the Order of the Day at the annual ordinary assembly is the General Report.

Note that this is truly a general report, and isn't only a financial report (**Article 1020**). The law requires that it must also be an overview of the administrative highlights of the year (accomplishments or changes) – specifically, that it must be *"as much about property and services as it is about finances."*

That said, there is a financial part.

I recommend that the President/Chair of your Council deliver the first part of the report, and then your Administrator continues with the finances.

To prepare this **almost** final financial report of the fiscal year, your Administrator must update the last monthly report with as much actual income and expense data as can be known at the report cut-off date. This is usually the last council meeting (held within two weeks of the assembly), and it must agree with the final budget sent to the owners.

The end result will be a statement of the actual financial status of your condo just days before the assembly – usually less than two weeks before the end of the fiscal year. This is as accurate a picture as is possible for the assembly.

My recommendation for delinquencies, is to assume that any owners who are in arrears now will still be in arrears at the end of the fiscal year (in about two weeks).

Year-End Report

The true year-end report is the **first monthly report of the new fiscal year** (the report given to the Council in April). This is the first time that the actual data for the final month of the fiscal year (March) is available.

This report will cover the last fiscal year from April 1 through March 31, and will show only actual income and expenses – there are no more forecasts. This report is your financial statement for the last fiscal year.

Starting a New Fiscal Year With a Shortfall

This Year-End Report will also show your final carry-forwards for the operating budget, the contingency, and the reserves.

These exact numbers must be reflected in the next monthly report presented at the May council meeting for the period ending April 30 – the first true report of the new fiscal year.

While it's unlikely that anything significant will happen to your condo's financial situation in the last week or two of a fiscal year, it is possible. If it does happen, then this must be reported and dealt with.

If it's necessary to offset a shortfall from the previous year against the new year's contingency, you must do it. The purpose of the contingency is to absorb this sort of thing. This is preferable to a special assessment in the first month of the new year to make up the shortfall.

PART 16 – Fees and Assessments

All About Condo Fees

Chapter
47

While the section of the Jalisco condo law titled *"CAPITULO V – De Las Cuotas"* ("CHAPTER V – Fees") comprising **Civil Code Articles 1026 through 1030** directly regulates condo fees, the following Code Articles also impact fees: **1006, 1011, 1012, 1015,** and **1030**.

Code Article 1026 - The Key to Condo Fees

The most important article in the condo legislation about fees is **Article 1026**. This one article sets out three important concepts about condo fees in Jalisco:

- all owners are required to pay condo fees;

- condo fees are for **both** maintenance/operation of a condo **and** for the creation and safeguarding of a reserve fund; and

- fees must be paid **in proportion to the condo rights of each private unit.**

The Legal Requirement to Pay

This first item from **Article 1026** is extremely important.

This not only gives your condo administration the authority to collect fees, but **requires condo owners to pay them** – with the force of a state law.

It's important to realise that there are **no exceptions**. Even if, before the transfer, the developer made a private deal with an owner to waive a portion or all their fees. This isn't legal, and has no meaning once your condo is administered by the owners (they cannot continue this illegal practice).

This owner is legally obligated to pay full fees, and must privately seek recourse against the developer – the original arrangement is not binding on your condominium.

This is a much better situation than exists for older condos or fraccs that are governed by an association, instead of a condominium regime. For them, the only requirement to pay fees is in their association by-laws, and these aren't binding on nonmembers (such as owners who have opted-out of the association). Further, association by-laws aren't as easily enforceable in the courts as the requirements of a state law.

Ignorance of this law is no excuse. The act of buying a property in a condo regime obligates an owner to pay the condo fees.

There's a misconception amongst some condo owners that dissatisfaction with the Council or the level of maintenance being done (or not) is a basis for withholding payment of fees as a protest, or to "force the hand" of the administration. This isn't the case.

These owners are violating the law, and are subject to collection procedures. They must express their concerns through the appropriate channels by bringing them up at a council meeting.

If this gets them nowhere, and if they feel strongly enough, then they should run for Council the next year (perhaps with a group of like-minded owners). In extreme circumstances, they may be able to impeach the Council.

Owners have no grounds to object to fees. Both the budget and setting out of the fees were approved by a majority of owners at the annual ordinary assembly. The proper time to question poor maintenance is during the budgeting process, before the assembly is held.

Owners also can't object to special fees for improvements, since these would have approved by over 75% of all condo rights at an extraordinary assembly.

If you do object to an improvement, you must raise this at or before the assembly. If the improvement vote is passed, then the majority has spoken, and you are legally required to abide by this decision. Condos are all about the will of the majority.

The condo law requires your Administrator and Council to charge a special assessment when the budget is exceeded because of unforeseen expenses or emergency repairs that can't be covered by the collected fees. Your condo cannot legally operate in a deficit (**Article 1030**).

If an owner objects to such a special assessment, then the time to raise an objection is when it's charged, and not later on. Even if they do object, it's unlikely that the assessment will be overturned unless it can be proven to be discriminatory or improper.

A sample Request for Payment of Fees is included in your BONUS Pack.

Purpose of Condo Fees

Article 1026 also clearly sets out the purpose of condo fees.

They're to pay for the maintenance and operational expenses associated with the common property. Therefore, they fund the operation and maintenance budget. They must also be used to create and maintain the reserves.

There are no other legal purposes for which fees can be collected or used.

Even improvements (which must be voted on and approved at an extraordinary assembly) must have the funds to pay for them specially authorised at the assembly where they were approved.

The method for collecting these funds must also be defined and approved at the same assembly. Improvements are almost always funded by special fees, and aren't normally funded from the operating budget.

Fees Are Not for the Use of Facilities

Perhaps the single most important concept to grasp about fees is that condo fees **are not for the use of the common facilities or property.** Some owners believe that they pay fees to use the pool or the rec centre – **this is not so.**

Each owner owns a percentage of all the common property (including roads, street lights, rec centre, or pool). They got this ownership when they bought their unit (it's included in their legal title). They're paying condo fees to operate, maintain, and repair the common facilities and property that they co-own.

Code Article 1008 covers this by saying that any owner who doesn't use either his private property or some of the common property must still pay the fees.

For this reason, **use of common facilities and property cannot be withheld from an owner who's delinquent in paying fees**, nor can access to an owner's property be restricted. For more detail on this, see the next chapter.

Terminology: 'Fees' vs. 'Dues'

Ahhh … I can see your eyes starting to roll back into your head … again … *"What earthly difference can this make?"*

There's a significant difference between "fees" and "dues".

> <u>Dues</u> are normally associated with membership – in an association or club, for example. They are normally for unspecified benefits (such as a membership), and can be difficult to legally enforce – typically, the most drastic penalty for non-payment of dues is cancellation of membership.
>
> <u>Fees</u> are for a well set out purpose, and are legally collectible.

Your condominium collects fees, and not dues. This isn't as big an issue as most of the terminology concerns I've raised so far, but if you want to be correct…

Requirement for a Reserve Fund

Condos in Jalisco are required by the condo legislation to have a reserve fund (**Article 1026**).

Unfortunately, the condo law only requires that a reserve fund be created and kept up – it doesn't set a minimum reserve contribution or level. This is left to the individual condo to work out. In my opinion, this is a mistake.

I can tell you that while a simple fixed amount such as *"25% of the budget"* or *"three months fees"* is definitely better than nothing, it doesn't create a reserve level that allows long-term maintenance of common property elements.

For more information on working out a reserve level, **see Part 15 – "Condo Finances."**

Fees Must Be Paid Proportionally

For reasons that I've never been able to understand, this is often a controversial topic.

This always astounds me, since the law is crystal clear:

- Fixed fees (all units pay the same) are not permitted.

- A combination of fixed and proportional fees is not permitted.

- Fees based on income or ability to pay are not permitted.

- Fees based on what an owner feels they should pay are not permitted.

- Fees based on an owner's shoe size are not permitted.

- **Fees must be paid proportionally to a condo unit's ownership in the common property** (its condo rights). **Period**.

> I've even heard the argument that the requirement in the state condo legislation to pay fees proportionally is invalid because it violates the Mexican Constitution (a common argument used to refute many things).
>
> First, let's consider the "logic" behind this statement:
>
>> Do you really believe that the state legislature is in the habit of passing unconstitutional laws?
>>
>> Do you further believe that if they somehow did do this, this law would stay unchallenged and unchanged for over 15 years (it was passed in 1995)?
>
> Logic aside, what does the Constitution **actually** say?
>
>> **Article 27** (which defines and creates private property) also says that the Nation will at all times have the right to impose on private property rules for use that are dictated by the public interest.
>>
>> **Article 121 II** says that personal and real property will be governed by the law of the place where it's located (such as the state or municipality).

OK … there's **one** circumstance where you might get away with charging fixed fees (although it's still not correct):

> If all the rights in your condo are within, say, 1% of each other, then you might not have a problem charging a fixed fee. The variation on a $200 USD/month average fee would be $2 USD.
>
> This would most likely happen with condo apartments, if they're all about the same size.
>
> However, if you do opt for this, it's important that you be aware that this **isn't the correct procedure**, and, although unlikely, it could still be successfully challenged by one or more owners.

I've never understood the resistance to proportional fees that seems to exist in some condos in México. The concept of proportional fees isn't unique to Mexican condos – it's the method used to collect condo fees almost everywhere in the world.

Charging proportional fees is just a fee payment method – it's no more difficult to administer than any other. It is, however, fairer than any other.

Here's the reasoning behind proportional fees, and why this payment method is fair:

> Remember, a condominium regime is a form of property ownership – one where each owner owns a portion of the common property, as well as their private property.
>
> The percentage of common property that you co-own is based on your lot or apartment size, and is recorded in the title document to your property (your deed). Your ownership right in the common property cannot be separated from the ownership of your private property, nor can it be changed in any way. It's a legal fact set out when your condominium was created.

In most condos, these ownership rights vary – sometimes significantly. This is because many condos feature a variety of sizes and price ranges of units (whether houses or apartments). The developer builds this way to appeal to the marketplace.

The fundamental principle of co-ownership is that the more common property you own, the more you must pay towards its maintenance and operation.

> Assume that you live in *Condominio Vista del Basurero*, and that your condo rights equal 3.54%. This means that you own 3.54% of the roads, street lighting, entry gate, rec centre, and pool. Assume that your neighbour lives on a much bigger lot, and has condo rights equal to 7.34%.
>
> With proportional fees, your neighbour pays about twice as much as you do because he owns around twice as much of the common property.
>
> If, however, you were all paying a fixed fee, then you'd be paying more than you should, and you and all the smaller lots/apartments would be subsidising the fees of the larger lots/apartments.
>
> This is absolutely unfair (and illegal). What makes this even worse, is that often there are more smaller units than larger ones – all the little guys are carrying the fat cats!
>
> Not surprisingly the most vocal opponents to proportional fees are often those living in larger units.

This is also the reason why proportional voting is used in assemblies – the assembly is meeting to make decisions about the common property.

Since these ownership rights vary, the fairest way to make these decisions is by voting property rights – someone who owns more of the common property (and has a greater stake in it) is entitled to a greater voice in how that common property is administered.

As I've said before (it bears repeating), there are no "condo police" who'll come in and arrest your Administrative Council for charging fixed fees. A condo can likely do this for years (many have) with no consequences.

The consequences arise when an owner discovers that this contravenes the condo law, that they've been paying higher fees than they should for years, and goes to court.

The decision will be easy, since the law is clear, and the refund in overpaid fees plus possible interest and other punitive damages can be a big hit on a condo budget. If this happens, other owners might jump on the bandwagon, and a domino effect could start.

Your Administrator and, particularly, your Council have a duty of care to the owners to **not knowingly put your condominium in jeopardy**.

Besides, if you think about it, what's the objection to paying proportionally? I've yet to hear one that makes any sense. As we've seen, it's the fairest way to assess fees, is the method used in most other countries, and, more importantly, **it's the law**.

Due Date and Late Interest

Article 1028 requires owners to pay fees beforehand, and on a set date. There's no specific requirement in the condo law as to how often fees have to be paid – that's up to your condo, and must be set out in your by-laws.

Possibilities are: monthly, quarterly, biannually, or annually. I recommend quarterly fees as the best compromise between ease of payment for owners, administrative convenience, and cash-flow. **Article 1006** requires that the basis of payment for your condo fees (such as monthly or quarterly) must be in your by-laws.

If an owner is late in paying their fees, Article 1028 also requires them to pay a penalty in the form of a late interest charge.

This interest must be equal to the average of the current interest rate charged by the two largest credit institutions in México for an unsecured 30-day personal loan.

At the time of writing, these institutions were **Banamex** and **Bancomer**. Interests rates in México can be high, and this average rate can easily be in the range of 35% to 40% a year.

A statement of accounts must be prepared by your Administrator 90 days after the date of payment of the fees. This report must clearly identify your condo's debtors.

The condo law says that this document is legally enforceable (**Article 1029**) – it'll be used in any law suit to collect delinquent fees. If you charge quarterly fees, then this report and your Administrator's quarterly report (required by **Article 1012**) can be one in the same.

A late interest calculator (spreadsheet) is included in your BONUS Pack.

As well as this interest charge, it may be possible to add other late penalties. For more on penalties and sanctions, **see Part 17 – "By-laws and Regulations."**

Tenants Also Have a Responsibility

Article 1029 also says something interesting:

> occupants are jointly responsible along with the owners for the payment of fees and special assessments, and jointly share responsibility for damages.

This means that if an absentee owner rents their unit, or allows someone else to live there, and becomes delinquent in their fees, then the tenants may be held jointly responsible for payment.

As well, if tenants cause damage to the common property, then they may be jointly responsible to pay for repairs along with the owner.

This also applies to other kinds of occupants such as guests, or a mother-in-law living in an owner's unit – although it's damage to common property for which a guest would most likely be held jointly responsible.

Article 1033 allows the Administrator to evict problem tenants with the approval of the condo (this needs an extraordinary assembly). If the owners of the unit object, then the condo can force the sale of the unit.

Owner's Right to a Statement of Account

Article 1029a says that each owner has the right to be given a statement of their account.

This is standard accounting practice, and the owner accounts must be kept by your Administrator. Each statement must show: all requests by your condo to pay fees, all payments made by the owner, all interest and penalties added, and the balance owing.

Note that this Code article says nothing about when or how often statements must be prepared, so a reasonable interpretation would be on-demand. Therefore, if an owner requests a statement of account, then your Administrator must produce one.

That said, I recommend that as part of your fee collection policy (more on this in the next chapter), your Administrator should send a current statement along with each collection letter.

A sample Owner's Statement of Account is included in your BONUS Pack.

Declaration of No Fees Owed Letter on Sale of Unit

When a house or apartment in a condo is sold, a *notario* (Civil Law notary) must be used to transfer the title.

Article 1029a requires the *notario* to ask the seller to get a declaration letter from your condo Administrator saying that there are no unpaid fees owed to your condominium – this request often comes from the real estate agent.

This is your golden opportunity to collect delinquent fees from an owner.

While this is great in theory, and even though *notarios* are state-appointed and bound by state law, and real estate agents should follow up on this, they're both human and can overlook this requirement (there is no recourse).

I recommend that your Administrator be proactive and, if they becomes aware that a unit has sold, and if fees are owing, contact the buyer's real estate agent to make sure that this statement is given to the *notario* so that he can collect the fees from the sale of the unit and pay them to your condo.

A sample Confirmation of Fees Paid letter as well as a WORD template is included in your BONUS Pack.

Special Assessments

Article 1030 says that the financial obligations of a condo must be paid from the common funds (collected fees). If these funds are insufficient, then the excess must be paid by all owners in proportion to their condo rights.

Your Administrator and your Council together are legally obligated to maintain the common property (**Code Articles 1009, 1012** and **1017**). Emergency repairs to the common property must be carried out by your Administrator in a timely fashion (**Article 1009**).

As a consequence, the administration must pay all operating expenses, and carry out all necessary repairs and maintenance including unforeseen emergency repairs.

Sometimes the cost of doing this can exceed the money in the budget – this can happen if the budget or contingency aren't adequate, or if the cost of an emergency repair is too large to be covered by the contingency.

Another circumstance where your condo budget can run into deficit is if one or more owners become delinquent, and the contingency can't cover it.

At any point where your administration reasonably believes that your condo is about to go into deficit, then your administration must charge a special assessment to make up the shortfall. As with fees, a special assessment must also be paid proportionally.

Unlike special fees for optional improvements, an assessment isn't an option, and **the owners do not vote on it**.

There's no choice in the matter of charging an assessment if your condo can no longer cover its operating costs, and the owner's cannot vote on this. Your condo isn't allowed to run a deficit. Think about it! If you did put this to a vote, and it was defeated for some reason – your condo would be bankrupt.

In the case of bankruptcy, the administration of your condo can either be taken over by the municipality (who will likely sue every delinquent owner), or your condominium regime dissolved (**see Chapter 59 – "Dissolving a Condo Regime"**).

Administration Members Must Be Up-to-Date

Articles 1011 and **1015** require that your Administrator (if an owner) and your Councillors must be up-to-date in their condo fees to continue to serve.

If a councillor, for example, becomes more than 90 days delinquent, then they're automatically disqualified from office.

Administrator Collects Fees and Reports on Delinquencies

Article 1012 requires your Administrator to collect the fees and to give receipts to the owners. This also gives them this authority.

This same article requires your Administrator to produce a quarterly report that lists income and overdue fees, and contains details on debtors (explaining the origin of the debt) – delinquent owners must be listed here.

Some administrations feel that the names of delinquent owners are a private matter, and don't want to embarrass them.

There's nothing involving the administration of a condo that's private, and the law requires that these delinquencies form part of your condo records.

It's also vital that delinquencies be listed in the quarterly report. When the debt is over 90 days, the report becomes enforceable, and will be needed in any legal action against the owner to collect the debt.

In my opinion, a delinquent owner should feel embarrassed – owners who don't pay their condo fees are hurting the entire community.

Regardless of how an overdue owner may feel, the Administrator is required by law to include their delinquency in the quarterly report.

Collecting Overdue Fees

Chapter **48**

Condo regimes are in a much better legal position to collect overdue fees than are *fraccionamientos* or older condos – because these last two are run by homeowners associations.

As we've seen, the condo legislation legally binds the private property into a condo regime, requires owners to pay fees, and allows certain routine reports prepared by your Administrator to be enforceable, and to be used in support of a lawsuit.

Ability to Force an Owner to Sell

The teeth of the condo law are in **Article 1032**. This is a forced sale article, and gives your condo the power to bring any owner who repeatedly fails to pay their fees, or who unjustifiably causes conflicts with other owners, before a judge to be ordered to sell their property at public auction to the highest bidder.

This can also be done if the owner has tenants that are causing problems in the condo, and the owner refuses to evict them after the owners decided to carry out this action (**Article 1033**).

In essence, the condo legislation pledges each condo unit (lot or apartment) as security for the payment of fees without any action on the unit owner's part. The owner is liable for the payment of all fees and assessments for as long as they own the unit (then the new owner becomes liable).

Disposal of the owner's property is governed by rules covering auction sales in the *Código de Procedimientos Civiles del Estado* (Code of Civil Procedures of the State).

Before your Administrator can carry out such an action, it must be agreed to by more than half of the owners at an extraordinary assembly.

This Is An Expensive Proposition

This is clearly a drastic step – and it's expensive.

To carry out such a suit you'll need to protocolise and register the assembly minutes where this action was approved (typically, $3,000 to $5,000 pesos) plus the legal fees (likely $10,000 to $20,000 pesos or more). The legal fees depend partly on the amount to be collected.

While you're entitled to a judgement for costs, in practice this may not work out to be your actual costs. The costs for the assembly aren't recoverable, and you may only recover a percentage of your actual legal fees.

You might feel that spending money to send a message to the community that you're tough on delinquencies is worthwhile. Certainly, if this lessens or prevents other delinquencies, it might make long-term economic sense.

Failing this, I recommend that you don't consider taking a delinquent owner to court until the amount they owe is worthwhile – legally, you must wait at least 90 days anyway.

> For example, assume that your direct costs will be $20,000 pesos ($5,000 for the assembly minutes plus $15,000 in legal fees), and that you'll recover $5,000 of these legal fees.
>
> If you're willing to give up 30% to collect the debt (this is on a par with the commission a collection agency typically charges), then the unpaid balance should be **at least $65,000 pesos before you should take legal action.** Of this you'll probably recover about $45,000 – certainly much better than nothing.

You should speak to a couple of local *abogados* (lawyers) to get an idea as to what the legal fees might be in your area, and their sense of the percentage of your legal fees that will be recoverable.

You should also talk about the time-frame – a suit of this type can take eight months or more to resolve.

Based on these estimates, you'll be able to work out the delinquency threshold for your condo (don't forget to add the cost of protocolising the assembly minutes!).

Make sure that you add late penalties to the amounts owed (this is required by the condo law), and, if your by-laws allow, late payment sanctions. These all serve as "padding" to build the amount of the suit to a level that makes more financial sense. These penalties and sanctions are gravy that can offset some of the unrecovered legal costs – what you really need to collect are the unpaid fees.

Have A Collection Policy

Since this is such a drastic action, and carries significant expense, I recommend that before going to court, you first go through a series of collection procedures to try to collect the unpaid fees. The best way to do this is to create a collection policy.

Doing this will also lay the foundation for future legal action.

The keys to a successful collection policy:

- it must be applied consistently; and

- it must be applied equally to every delinquency no matter who's delinquent.

Outline of a Typical Collection Policy

Here are the typical milestones in a collection policy:

1. **<u>Reminder letter (1st notice)</u>**: 31 days after the fee or assessment is due, your Administrator should send out a reminder letter and a statement to each delinquent owner.

This letter should only be a polite reminder that the fees have not been received, and that the owner may have forgotten.

You must add and show late interest on the attached statement. I don't think that penalties or sanctions should apply at this stage, but if your by-laws require them, then these must be applied. Regardless of any sanctions allowed by your by-laws, the late interest **must** be applied – this is in the condo law.

2. **Second notice**: 61 days after the fee or assessment is due, your Administrator should send out a second notice letter and a statement to each delinquent owner.

    The second notice must contain the fact that a reminder notice was already sent, and when. **It's important to have a paper trail of collection attempts if you eventually sue the owner.**

    Add a guilt paragraph about how your condominium depends on fees to function and to keep up the common services, and that even one late owner can create problems for everyone.

    Finish with a paragraph inviting the owner to contact your Administrator with any questions or concerns, or to work out payment options. Give detailed contact info, and make it easy to get in touch – address, local telephone, email, and VOIP number.

    Don't forget to add more late interest along with any penalties or sanctions allowed by your by-laws. These amounts must appear on the statement.

3. **Third notice**: 91 days after the fee or assessment is due, your Administrator should send out a third notice letter and a statement to each delinquent owner.

    The third notice must contain the fact that a reminder notice and a second notice were already sent, and when.

Include a summary of any promises made by the owner and, if possible, when they were made.

> Speaking of payment promises, you'll be in a much stronger legal position if you get these in writing, signed by the delinquent owner.

Ramp up the guilt paragraph by saying that this owner (now you must make it more personal) is jeopardising the budget used to operate and maintain the common property such as roads, street lights, or septic tanks. Deliberately mention non-sexy portions of the common property, since it's possible that this owner believes that fees as for use of the pool or rec centre (which this owner might not use) – this might make them think twice.

Repeat the contact-me paragraph, and add an invitation for them to talk over the reasons they've not paid to see if something can be worked out (suggest a meeting).

Again, don't forget to add more late interest along with any penalties or sanctions allowed by your by-laws. These amounts must appear on the statement.

I believe this is when your by-laws should start adding sanctions. The reason is that, the condo legislation only recognises an owner as being delinquent when they are more than 90 days late. The debt is now enforceable by legal action.

4. **Final notice**: 121 days after the fee or assessment is due, your Administrator should send out a fourth notice letter and a statement to each delinquent owner.

   The final notice must contain the fact that a reminder notice, a second notice, and a third notice were already sent, and when.

Again, don't forget to include a summary of any promises made by the owner and, if possible, when they were made.

Cite the Civil Code, and mention the ultimate legal remedy (forced sale of their unit at public auction).

Now it's obvious that the person isn't responding, so you must now demand that they pay by a specific date (give them a week), or you'll turn the matter over to a collection agency or your *abogado* (lawyer) for collection.

Often, this will be enough to show that you're serious. The threat of legal action might cause the owner to pay.

Repeat the contact-me paragraph, and don't forget to update the statement with late interest charges along with any penalties or sanctions allowed by your by-laws.

A set of sample collection letters along with WORD templates for each is included in your BONUS Pack.

Make Sure You Know Who Owns the Unit

While this might seem obvious, you can only collect overdue fees from the title holder of the unit. **Don't assume you know who this is!**

There are many circumstances where the person living in the unit (and even the person who has paid fees in the past) is not the title holder. You can only sue the title holder (and the occupants, but only jointly **with** the title holder).

Often someone who owns more than one property, although they're the buyer of the property, will put the property in the name of a close relative for tax or other business reasons.

If your condo is on the coast in the Federal Restricted Zone, foreign owners will have bought their condo units through a *fideicomiso* (trust).

In a trust, **the title holder is the trustee**, and not the foreign buyer.

It's vital that these owners by trust get a power of attorney from the trustee (the financial institution). Without a power of attorney, they cannot exercise their rights in the condominium. This power must say that they're allowed to exercise their rights in all matters affecting their condo unit.

While the trust document gives them all rights of use and enjoyment of their property, this doesn't apply to condo rights. These are regulated by the condo legislation, and **only apply to the title holder**.

> If you're a long-term renter (a year or more) you should know that under the condo law, **you can be sued jointly with the owner of the unit** for unpaid condo fees. Many renters aren't aware of this!

Don't Underestimate the Personal Touch

As well as sending collection letters, establish a dialogue by speaking directly to your delinquent owners. The best time to start this is with the second notice (after 60 days).

Don't forget that they aren't legally in arrears until one of their missed payments passes the 90-day mark, so be careful what you say if you talk to them before this time limit. You can't threaten them with legal action yet – this is the persuasive stage.

Always keep any contact with an overdue owner professional and courteous. Your goal is to collect the fees, not to antagonise the debtor.

Don't be confrontational, angry, or aggressive – this accomplishes nothing.

Dealing With Mexican Owners on a Personal Level

When meeting with a Mexican owner to discuss non-payment of fees, it's important to understand some cultural differences.

In México, there are social conventions when talking about money. Start off the meeting with pleasantries – don't jump into the subject of their non-payment right away.

Always be courteous. Rude, threatening, or angry behaviour will get you nowhere – it usually makes matters worse. Treat them with respect, and you may get positive results. Always be polite and civil (DON'T raise your voice), even if it's gone as far as being turned over to your lawyer.

Keep a File on Each Overdue Owner

Put each collection notice and statement into a file, so you have a document trail of your collection efforts. This will be important if you need to take legal action.

Make notes for the file about each meeting, phone call, or other contact you have with this owner during the process. Record any promises or commitments they make. Make a brief record any conversations you have with your *notario* or *abogado*.

All new promises and discussions must be reported at the next council meeting, and recorded in the minutes.

The Council needs to be aware of everything that happens with an overdue owner, so they can make informed decisions as to what action to take.

Follow-up on Their Promises to Pay

If your overdue owner makes promises (such as, *"I'll pay you by the end of next month"*), keep track of these deadlines, confirm them to the owner in writing, and follow-up a day or two after they expire.

Record each promise and deadline in the file, report them all to the Council, and record them in the meeting minutes.

If promises are missed, the Council needs to decide whether to give the debtor more time, move to the next level in the collection cycle, or start legal action (only if the debt is older than 90 days!).

> Sometimes an owner will fall on hard financial times, or get themselves into a temporary cash crunch. It's important to show compassion and understanding in these circumstances – you're managing a community, not a corporation. However, there are those who might take advantage of this.
>
> If a delinquent owner comes to you with a tale of woe, carefully document and report it in the council minutes (there are no secrets in a condo – everything you and any owner does that relates to condo business must be public).
>
> Don't just leave it at that. Get them to commit to a date when they'll pay, or to a series of partial payments. Partial payments must be tied to a minimum or set amount, and there must be a final date to clear the debt. Once this has been worked out with the owner, confirm this agreement to the owner in writing. This letter needs to go into the condo records (and the debtor's file).
>
> If they fail to meet their promises, then you must move up to the next collection phase, including turning the matter over to your ***abogado*** (lawyer) if that's the next step (or the step that was delayed).
>
> The Council and Administrator must also be careful to apply leniency in collections consistently. The administration cannot be seen to be favouring one owner or a group of owners over the others.

When the Delinquent Owner is a Mortgagee

While not nearly as common in México as north of the border, mortgages are now available here.

If you know that a delinquent unit holder has a mortgage, it might put pressure on them if you copy the mortgage holder with your payment demands. **Do not do this until the owner is legally in arrears** (over 90 days delinquent).

If you're considering this, I recommend that you first talk to a *notario* about any possible unforeseen consequences of this course of action, including the rights of the mortgage holder if you take legal action.

Applying Partial Payments

If you receive partial payments from an owner, I recommend that they be applied to oldest debts before newer debts, and in this order:

- first apply them to the late interest;

- second apply them to any penalties or sanctions that have been applied (if permitted by your by-laws); and

- lastly apply them to the fees or assessments.

Consider a Collection Agency

Once you reach the Final Notice stage, you can talk to collection agencies to see if they're interested, and what they'd charge (30% is common). There are usually several in most major cities, and they'll be listed under *"Cobranzas"* (collections) in the yellow pages.

This might only work for an owner who's employed in México – a part-time resident or retiree may not be a good fit for collection.

In addition, a collection agency might not be interested if the amount owed is too low – this is where adding the late interest and any sanctions permitted by your by-laws is useful.

Time to Turn Things Over to a Lawyer (*Abogado*)

If you choose not to use a collection agency, or if this approach fails, as soon as possible after the expiry of the deadline in your final notice (or in the collection agency's last communication, if they got nowhere), turn the matter over to an *abogado* – but **not** to sue them for forced sale of property (just yet).

There are still some other choices before going to a forced sale:

1. **Lawyer-led mediation**: recent changes in Mexican state laws have created an effective mediation process designed expressly to avoid the cost and time involved in going to court. Any agreements reached during such lawyer-led mediation are as binding as a court order.

   I recommend that you find a local *abogado* **who has been trained and certified in this new state mediation process**.

   Your *abogado* will write and deliver a letter inviting the owner to come to an initial mediation session.

   This letter from the *abogado* alone might trigger a payment. If not, these *abogados* are skilled at reaching payment agreements.

   The cost for mediation is significantly lower than a lawsuit, and avoids the necessity of an extraordinary assembly.

2. **Judge-led arbitration**: if the delinquent owners refuse to engage in mediation, then your *abogado* may be able to go before a municipal judge to order them to appear for arbitration in front of the judge.

   If this can be done in your municipality, then the judge will give an order for them to appear.

   This action might be enough to scare someone into paying. If, however, they ignore this order, the judge may find against them by default, and issue an order for them to pay (it'll depend on the judge).

   While this process is more expensive than lawyer-led mediation, it's much faster and cheaper than your ultimate recourse, a forced sale lawsuit.

3. **Sue them for payment**: you can sue them for payment of the fees they owe without resorting to a forced sale. If you get a judgement (and you should), and for some reason they still refuse to pay, then you can still go ahead with your suit to force the sale of their property – armed with a judgement against them.

If lawyer-led mediation or judicial arbitration aren't available in your municipality (or they've failed), then you must now have your *abogado* write an intimidating letter to the delinquent owner citing the rules in the state law that could cause their unit to be sold at public auction to the highest bidder, and giving them a short deadline (72 hours is good) to come into the *abogado's* office to resolve the matter.

The cost of this letter can be anywhere from $500 to $1,000 pesos, and, if it gets results, is well worthwhile.

In many cases this final threat on an *abogado's* letterhead might get the message across that you're serious about collecting the money they owe you.

If not, you need to decide whether to sue them for the money owed, or go ahead with a suit for forced sale.

No More Threats - Time for Action

So ... you've turned the matter over to your lawyer, and you've both made your final threats and given final deadlines. **Do not drop back into an earlier point in the collection process**, under any circumstances.

Your debtor has already ignored all your collection efforts, and all your threats and deadlines. More threats and deadlines after giving them a "final" deadline will prove ineffective, and shows weakness.

You're clearly dealing with a debtor for whom drastic action needs to be taken. Keep your resolve – you must now take action, and be seen to take action.

Your intent is to not only resolve the issue with this owner, but to send a strong message to the rest of the owners that your condo takes fees and delinquencies seriously.

Since unpaid fees and assessments put a burden on all other owners, your administration has a legal responsibility to pursue collection of all delinquent accounts.

Your delinquent owner has clearly sent you a message that they have no intention of paying – likely ever.

These owners are deadbeats – they might not be able to afford to live in your condo. Perhaps they've fallen on economic hard times. While this is sad, it isn't your condo's problem.

By not paying their fees, these owners have become charity cases that the rest of the owners are forced to subsidise by paying their fees for them. This is not fair to those who do pay.

Now you must face the fact that this individual isn't going to pay, and you need to go directly to DEFCON 1 – either suing for the money owed, or calling an extraordinary assembly to vote on suing to sell their unit at public auction.

Often, when the owner is served the papers for the suit for money owed, they'll pay up. You've called their bluff, and it's obvious to them that you're serious. They have no legal defence. The act of buying a unit in a condominium regime obligates them to pay fees. Period. There are no exceptions or excuses.

If they're extraordinarily resistent to paying, the act of issuing a call for an assembly to approve the forced sale of their unit should cause them to finally pay up. It's foolish for them to continue, since the value of the fees owed is usually significantly less than the value of their property.

The good news is that by the time you've reached the point of either lawsuit, the level of fees owed plus penalties likely make the suit economically worthwhile.

What You Need to Go Ahead With Your Lawsuit

Normally, your Administrator is the one who must represent your condo in a lawsuit. This responsibility is given by the condo law (**Article 1012**), and may also have been granted by the assembly where your Administrator was appointed.

Your *abogado* (lawyer) will need the following:

1. ID of your condo's Administrator (your legal representative). For a Mexican citizen, this will be their national ID. For a foreigner, this will be a certified copy of their *no inmigrante rentista* or *inmigrante* visa (formerly called an FM3 or FM2).

2. Certified copy of the publicly registered minutes of the ordinary assembly where your Administrator was appointed and granted powers of representation.

3. Certified copy of your condo's publicly registered *escritura constitutiva* (establishing document).

4. If your by-laws have been changed since your condo was set up, then you'll need to have certified copies of the publicly registered minutes of the extraordinary assemblies where they were changed.

5. Full legal names of the owners of the unit. You'll also need the full legal names of any long-term occupants of the unit. I strongly recommend that you get a copy of the current title for the property – the owner may not be who you think it is.

6. Detailed statement of account showing all fees owed, all payments applied, and all interest and penalties charged.

7. Dates of each annual ordinary assembly where the budget and fees were approved that affect this particular owner.

These are the main things, there might also be other items that your *abogado* could ask for.

When the suit goes ahead, you'll also need as many supporting documents as you can gather.

These might include:

- Quarterly reports for the period of the delinquency, clearly listing the owner as being delinquent. These must be signed by both the Administrator and the Council President/Chair.

- Details of your attempts to collect, such as: notices sent; dates and notes from meetings; and any promises made by the owner to pay (including dates and details).

Your Suit Might Not Finish

You need to be prepared for the fact that if you do sue an owner, the suit might not follow through to the end.

The court process involves filing papers and interviews, and it can be several months (typically, at **least** eight months to a year) before a judge is ready to order the owner to pay the money owed, or to get a valuation on their unit and put it up for auction.

The owner might just pay their fees at some point along the way, and the suit will then end. While this can be frustrating, and you won't recover the legal fees you've spent so far, you'll still have reached two goals:

- you'll have collected some of the money (hopefully all the overdue fees); and

- you'll have sent a clear message to this owner and the whole community.

Publicising Your Debtors

I've heard people suggest posting public notices in the condo, and even taking out newspaper ads proclaiming the names of their delinquent owners to the world.

Presumably, this is to shame them into paying.

While issuing a report to the owners that lists these individuals isn't only legal, but required, going beyond this might enter the territory of libel. This is especially true if the delinquent owner has a local business, and such publicity could affect it.

Be aware that México has advanced libel laws, with real consequences – libel is taken seriously here. If you haven't yet gone to court, presented your evidence, and gotten a judge's ruling, you haven't yet legally established that they owe you the debt.

Before starting a public shame campaign, I highly advise you to talk it over first with an *abogado* (lawyer).

Publicly announcing that your condo has problems does nothing to enhance your property values. Would you want to buy a unit in a condo with a long list of debtors posted at the entrance, or which takes out ads shaming its overdue owners?

This tactic is really more about expressing the administration's or owners' frustrations, than actually collecting the debt.

Consider the fact that someone who's seriously delinquent in their condo fees, and who has resisted your attempts at collection and mediation, has no shame and can't be embarrassed. This action is unlikely to cause them to pay. It will, however, anger them.

One guiding rule you must always bear in mind when collecting from an overdue owner is that you must **always try to keep up an atmosphere of cooperation.**

No matter how late the owner is, or how frustrated you feel about the situation, nothing is ever gained by antagonising the debtor and causing them to "dig in their heels" – there's just no payoff. For anyone.

Also remember that this is one of your neighbours. Short of a forced sale, if they do eventually pay, they'll still be a member of your community. You'll have to live with them, and vice versa. The bad feelings that these actions can cause can be irreparable to a community.

The bottom line: be patient!

Go through the process in a legal and professional way. It can take a long time, it can be frustrating, but in the long-term it's the right approach, and is the most beneficial one for your community.

If you choose to ignore my advice, and decide to publicly shame your debtors, be **absolutely 110% sure that they're the title holder of the property** before you go ahead.

If they're not, you leave the condo wide open to a libel suit, since they don't legally owe you anything.

Do Not Withhold Services or Restrict Access to Property

This was mentioned in the last chapter, but bears repeating.

> **Condo fees are not for the use of the common facilities or property.**

Each unit owner also owns a percentage of all the common property (including roads, street lights, community centre, entry gate, or pool). This ownership is included in their legal title, and they're paying condo fees only for operation, maintenance, and repair of the common facilities and property.

Use of common facilities and property cannot be withheld from an owner who's late in paying fees, nor can access to an owner's property be restricted. This access is through common roads and gates that are co-owned by the delinquent owner.

Again, condo fees are only to cover the expenses of operating and maintaining the common property. They're not for its use or benefit – these are both inalienable rights of ownership, and can't be taken away.

"What about withholding common services?", you ask. *"A common service isn't property, and isn't co-owned by the delinquent owner. It's a service that's paid for by fees, and this owner isn't paying these fees. Right?"*

While this argument might hold technically (I would advise getting an opinion from an *abogado* before going ahead), it's almost impossible to withhold services selectively.

> For example, if you live in a gated condo, the security guard provides guard service for the entire condominium, and there's no practical way of withholding this service from one or two houses. It can also be argued that your administration has an obligation to protect owner's property.
>
> The pool maintenance contractor or common property gardener also can't withhold their services from, say, 6.31% of the pool or common garden areas.

Restricting Access to Water

There are some condominiums that have their own water supply (such as a well), instead of municipal water. All water belongs to the federal government, and your condo must have been given a concession from CONAGUA (*Comisión Nacional del Agua –* National Water Commission) to use and distribute it.

While it's common practice in *fraccs* to try to limit access to well water as an incentive for a delinquent owner to pay, **this may not work in a condominium.**

Unlike a *fracc*, in a condominium all owners own a portion of every common facility and area – this **may** include the well and the concession to the water. This isn't clear cut, and you'd be well advised to talk to a ***notario*** before trying to limit water access for a delinquent owner.

At a minimum, you must examine the ***escritura constitutiva*** (establishing document for your condo regime) along with the actual water concession agreement before any decision can be made.

PART 17 — By-laws and Regulations

Overview of Condo By-laws — Chapter 49

Your condo by-laws contain rules about the operation and administration of your condo. These add to those in the condo legislation.

Quick Facts About By-laws

- The first by-laws for your condominium are contained in the *escritura constitutiva* (publicly registered document that set up your condominium regime).

- The only legally binding version of your by-laws (or any subsequent changes) is the Spanish language version.

  While a translation can (and should) be given as a courtesy to your non-Spanish speaking residents, it's important to realise that whenever your translation and the original differ, the Spanish version always takes priority.

- Your by-laws only **add to** the condominium legislation. They cannot change, negate, override, or contradict the condo law.

- By-laws can only be changed by an extraordinary assembly.

Ranking of Regulations

Your condo is governed by the following, in order of priority (each item on this list takes priority over everything below it):

- federal, state, and municipal laws;

- the state condo legislation;

- your condo's by-laws; and

- other condo rules, regulations, and policies (including rules of order).

It's vital that no part of your by-laws contradicts either the condo legislation or any other laws. Any clauses that do so are **automatically invalid and unenforceable**.

Minimum By-law Requirements

Civil Code Article 1006 XI sets out the minimum contents for a condo's by-laws:

- Rights and obligations of the Owners, which must be proportional to the percentage of the common property ownership that belongs to each owner;

- Powers of the Administrator, the Council, and the government;

- Setting up of committees to help the Administrative Council; these committees can be financially independent;

- Setting out the basis of payment of condo fees, and the creation of the reserve funds;

- Setting out criteria for limiting business activities; this will be respected by the town council when authorising business licenses;

- Procedures for resolving disputes between owners;

- Circumstances and rules under which the by-laws can be changed; and

- Transformation and extinction of the condominium.

Suggestions for More By-law Items

Apart from these minimum needs, there are many other things that you might consider for inclusion in your by-laws.

Here's a list of some of the more common by-law items over and above those required by the law (not all may be applicable to your particular condo):

- administrative structure, including: the make-up of your Council and standing committees; Assistant Administrator or Operations Manager (if you have them);

- regulations about committees, including appointment of special committees;

- other records to be kept by your Administrator;

- ways resigning members of your Council or a committee can be replaced; ways a councillor or committee member can be removed;

- authority of your Council to make and change rules and policies (for example, usage rules for the meeting area, or pool rules); this section must severely limit the scope of such policies and rules; this cannot be a loop-hole where significant clauses can effectively be added to your by-laws by a Council in the guise of rules or policies, bypassing the approval of an extraordinary assembly;

- notifications (such as a notice to an owner of a by-law violation, or the intent of an owner to carry out emergency repairs on common property); use of email and your condo web site for notifications to owners (never rely on the web site alone);

- council and committee meetings (open meetings with advance notice and invitation to the community) and minutes (requirement for committee minutes, and distribution of minutes);

- rules of order for assemblies and meetings;

- use of proxies at assemblies;

- election procedures for assemblies;

- maintenance and appearance of private property;

- rules for rentals (be careful here, property owners in México have significant rights over the use and enjoyment of their private property – don't contradict these);

- duties and obligations of renters and tenants;

- retention of records;

- rules for selling a unit (open houses, signage, or access – don't be unreasonable or draconian);

- vehicles and parking on common property (you probably can't control vehicles in driveways of houses in a horizontal condo);

- satellite dishes;

- pets; don't try to eliminate them, but you can control their behaviour; for example, they must be on a leash when on common property;

- noise;

- flags, flagpoles, and signage; **be careful** – it's important for many to proudly display a Mexican flag during September;

- landscaping, paint colours, and architectural standards; and

- sanctions for by-law violations.

Changing Your By-laws

The condo law requires that your by-laws be created even before construction starts on your condo's buildings.

Overview of Condo By-laws

These first by-laws are in the document that set up your condominium regime.

After living with your by-laws for a few years, however, you may feel that they need changes, additions, or, in extreme cases, rewriting.

Your by-laws can only be changed by approval of the owners at an extraordinary assembly.

Article 1006 requires that the procedures for changing your by-laws must be in your by-laws.

Getting Community Support for By-law Changes

I recommend that you follow an open process similar to the one I described for getting support on a new budget (**see Chapter 45 – "Your Condo Budget"**):

- Announce to the community that you're planning to make changes to your by-laws. Hold special council or committee meetings to do this, and invite the community to each one or to send in comments and suggestions.

- When this process is finished, send out a document listing all the proposed changes in summary form. It might contain several entries like, *"Change the wording of Article 32 from, "xxx" to "yyy"."* Send this to all owners before the day of the assembly, along with a copy of the current by-laws for comparison. Also post it on your condo web site.

- At the assembly, a motion must be made to adopt all the changes contained in the document (which will be attached to the assembly minutes).

- If there's any last minute dissent (there shouldn't be if your process was public and encouraged input and participation), it can come out during discussion of the motion. There may or may not be changes needed as a result. It's not wise to try to make by-law changes at an assembly, where the full impact of the change can't be properly thought out.

When you make these decisions openly, and you involve the community in the process, you wind up with by-laws that work for the majority, and are easy to pass at the assembly.

Republish the Full By-laws

I urge that after getting the approval to change your by-laws, you republish the new version in Spanish. You can also have an English translation for foreign residents. Send these to all owners, and give them to new owners when they move in.

It's just too confusing to send out a copy of the old by-laws plus the change summary.

Clearly mark these new by-laws with the revision date, along with the date of the extraordinary assembly where they were approved.

Don't Forget to Publicly Register Your By-laws

The minutes of the extraordinary assembly where you changed your by-laws must be publicly registered. If you only made a few changes, then these must contain a list clearly explaining these changes. If the changes were extensive, this must include the complete text of your by-laws.

Be sure to budget for the cost of protocolising and registering your by-laws (if the changes are significant, the cost can be much higher than is typical for an extraordinary assembly), as well as the translation costs.

Pay Attention to the Order of Your Assemblies

If you're holding your Annual Ordinary Assembly on the same day as an extraordinary assembly (this saves money), you must be careful.

If you're voting to change by-laws that affect the make-up of your Council, or that affect anything that could happen at an ordinary assembly (such as disallowing nominations from the floor), then you must hold the extraordinary assembly to change your by-laws **first** (**before** the ordinary assembly) so that the changes are in effect for the ordinary assembly (assuming they pass).

By-law Language Must Not Be Vague

Your by-laws are a legally binding extension of the condominium legislation, and apply specifically to your condo.

Since your by-laws are a legal document, proper terminology, consistency of language, and form of language are all important. It's especially important to use the same terms as in the condo law.

Here are some guidelines:

- Avoid vague language, or language that's open to interpretation. Spell out the particular qualities you want.

    For example, avoid vague adjectives such as *"appropriate"* or *"suitable"* that can be widely interpreted (and, therefore, argued).

    > *"Put trash in an **appropriate** container"* is better worded as *"Put trash in a covered garbage container"* since one person's idea of what an ***appropriate container*** can be quite different from someone else's.

- Each by-law clause must be a clear directive to the owners, and the use of *"must"* (preferred) or *"shall"* (out of date) is needed.

Avoid using soft language like *"will," "may,"* or *"should"* – none of these terms are enforceable.

> "All dogs *will* be on a leash," or "All dogs *should* be on a leash," aren't enforceable requirements. "All dogs *must* be on a leash," is a clear and enforceable instruction.

"Will" can be used to state a fact, but not to give an instruction.

> For example, "No proxy form *will* be accepted unless…" is a fact, and not an instruction.

- If you name something one way when it's first mentioned, call it the same throughout the document – consistency is very important.

  > For example, don't call the Council *"the Council," "the Administrative Council,"* and *"the Board"* in the same document – pick one, and stick to it.

When By-laws Aren't Authored in Spanish

If your condo consists largely of foreigners, you can decide to write changes to your by-laws (or completely rewrite them) in English for convenience.

This is fine during the writing process, and even for the vote to approve the changes at an extraordinary assembly (unless you have Mexican owners who ask for these in Spanish).

Once approved and adopted, however, your newly changed by-laws **must** be translated into Spanish before they can be publicly registered.

You must publicly register your by-laws for them to be enforceable (and for these changes to replace the last version of your by-laws).

Terms Must Agree With the Condo Legislation

There are some important terms defined in the condominium legislation. You must be careful to refer to these in your by-laws using **exactly the same term as the condo law**, or confusion or disputes might arise.

Inaccuracies in these terms are most often created when foreigners write their by-law changes in English, and then have them translated into Spanish.

Here's a list of some of these predefined terms in English, followed by the correct Spanish translation:

- <u>**Administrator**</u> – *administrador*: this is the correct legal term. Don't use *"gerente* (Manager)" or *"tesorero* (Treasurer)."

- <u>**Administrative Council**</u> – *consejo de administración*: while you can call this a *"Board"* or a *"Board of Directors"* in English if you wish (although I wish you wouldn't), please make sure that the Spanish by-laws use the correct legal term.

- <u>**assembly**</u> – *asamblea*: when referring to a "meeting" of all condo owners to make decisions, appoint a new Council, or approve a new budget, you **must** use the word *"asamblea"* (assembly). The reasons are detailed in **Chapter 22 – "The Condo Assembly."**

    If you decide to use the word *"meeting"* in your English documents (and I strongly discourage this), then please make sure that your Spanish by-laws say *"asamblea"* and not *"reunión"* or *"junta."*

    By the way, the two types of assemblies are *ordinaria* (ordinary) and *extraordinaria* (extraordinary) – avoid terms like *"regular"* and *"especial* (special)" in either Spanish or English

If you're referring to council or committee meetings, then the term *"meeting"* is perfectly accurate, and this should be translated as *"reunión"*.

- **by-laws** – *reglamentos* (actually means *"regulations or rules"*): watch out for the tendency of some translators to translate *"by-laws"* into Spanish as *"estatutos* (statutes)" – this term applies to associations, but *"reglamentos"* must be used for condominiums.

- **common property** – *bienes comunes*: sometimes translated into Spanish as *"propiedad comunal"*. While this is a correct translation, *"bienes comunes"* is a term defined in the condo law, and must be used for consistency with the legislation.

- **condominium regime** – *regimen del condominio*: sometimes inaccurately translated into English as *"condominium system"* or *"condominium concept"* – these are all terms from north of the border that, while similar in meaning, aren't legally accurate in México.

- **councillor** – *consejero*: again, you can use *"members of the Board," "Directors,"* or *"Officers"* in English, but you must make sure that the Spanish by-laws use the correct legal term.

- **easement** – *servidumbre*

- **establishing document** – *escritura constitutiva:* this is the publicly registered document that set up your condo regime. Sorry, I know this is a bit cumbersome, but there's no short English translation, since there's just no similar word or concept.

    You can safely use *"establishing document"* in English, but, if you do, you must verify that this gets translated as *"escritura constitutiva"* and not something like, **"documento establecedor."**

Another choice, since there's no direct translation, is to just use *escritura constitutiva* in the English text as well. This is my preference.

Note that this term is also sometimes inaccurately translated into English as *"deed," "establishing deed," "founding deed"* or (worst of all) *"constitution."*

- **fee – *cuota***: although perfectly correct in English, the word *"assessment"* can be mistranslated into Spanish because its meaning in Spanish is an evaluation or appraisal (*tasación, valoración,* or *evaluación*). Under no circumstances ever use the word *"dues"* in English.

- **owners** or **condo owners** – *condóminos* (actually means *"title holders in a condominium"*): often inaccurately translated into Spanish as *proprietario* or *dueño*. Yes, these both mean property owners, but *condómino* is specific to **condominiums** and specifically refers to the registered title holder.

- **unit** or **private unit** – *unidad privativa*: a unit of private property that's typically either an apartment or a lot. Sometimes translated as *"unidad privada"*, but *"unidad privativa"* agrees with the legislation.

Check your Spanish version to make sure these translation inaccuracies don't creep in.

From a legal perspective, it doesn't matter what terminology you use in the English version of your by-laws, since they have no legal validity. Bad terminology, however, can creep into the legal Spanish version by inexact English terms being translated literally. Besides, why not be legally accurate in both languages?

It's important, therefore, that you have someone verify that all the terms on the above list are correctly translated in the Spanish document before it's approved and registered.

You can also give this list to your translator – telling them which Spanish term to use when translating your various English terms.

Be Reasonable

It's important to have a balance between looking out for the good of the community and unreasonably limiting owner activity.

Your by-laws must protect the goals of the community, make sure that your condo operates and functions smoothly, and property values are kept up.

In fact, the enforceability of your by-laws depends on this – unreasonable rules and regulations may not be enforceable, particularly if they violate legal rights.

Enforcement of By-laws

"What's the point of having by-laws if they aren't enforced?" Excellent question!

First, it's important to realise that it's the obligation of your condo's administration to enforce your by-laws. Further, each owner has a right to have your by-laws enforced by sending a complaint about a violation to your Council.

It's a fact of life that there are two categories of owners in a condo:

- the vast majority of your owners are responsible community members who are naturally inclined to "do the right thing" – these people aren't normally a problem; but

- a minority of owners either don't pay fees, disregard the rules when they don't suit their own purposes, or both.

What can be done about this last group?

They're an annoyance to the rest of the community who follow the rules, and a nuisance for your administration – who must deal with complaints about them on a regular basis.

I've already dealt with the collection of delinquent fees in **Chapter 48 – "Collecting Overdue Fees."** But what about those people who pay their fees, but just refuse to follow the rules?

Good news and bad news – while the condo legislation gives you a legal remedy (**Article 1032**), it's pretty extreme.

It's the same remedy you have with a delinquent owner – forced sale of their condo unit.

You can (with the approval of an extraordinary assembly) call them before a judge to order their unit sold at public auction to the highest bidder – effectively getting rid of them, and replacing them with a new owner.

There are two significant problems with this remedy:

- this is a rather extreme measure to take against an owner who, say, repeatedly fails to leash their dog or parks where they shouldn't; and
- this can cost a few thousand **dollars**.

Before the majority of the community would approve such an extreme and expensive measure, these people would have to be the *"neighbours from hell."*

While people who break the rules on a regular basis are frustrating and annoying, the majority of them just don't meet this characterization, nor does their behaviour generally warrant such an extreme reaction.

You must keep in mind that it's vital to strike a balance between a smooth running community, and a police state where you're infringing on owners' rights and freedoms.

To this end, you should neither set unreasonable rules, nor should your enforcement methods be either sporadic or draconian.

Therefore, before taking the extreme measure given by the condo law, I recommend that you follow the processes I've outlined in **Part 20 – "Resolving Disputes and Conflicts."**

Problems With Non-Owner Tenants

Article 1033 of the condo law gives you some relief if tenants are causing problems in the condo (for example, an absentee owner rents their unit).

After getting permission at an extraordinary assembly, the Administrator can ask the owner to evict the tenants. If the owner refuses, then the condo can proceed against the owner as outlined earlier in this chapter.

Financial Penalties and Sanctions

"Well and good," you say. *"But what if the complaint process still doesn't solve the problem? What if the owner ignores the Council's rulings?"*

While this lack of compromise is unusual, I believe that the final stage you should consider after council involvement, and before a lawsuit, is the use of sanctions.

These are financial penalties levied by your condo for repeat violations of your by-laws. In many Mexican states, such sanctions are built into the condo legislation. This is, unfortunately, not the case in Jalisco.

One solution is to include them in your by-laws.

Sanctions are in the form of fines. These must be specific, and your by-laws must explicitly set out the circumstances when they can be used, and the amount of the fine (generally a range to allow them to escalate for repeated offenses).

Fines in México are commonly based on the **general minimum wage in use in the Federal District**. For example, here are some of the sanctions listed in the condo law for the Federal District (at the time of writing, the minimum daily wage averaged about 58 pesos):

- for violations that affect the tranquillity or comfort of neighbours: 10 to 100 days minimum wage;

- for violations that affect the operation or functioning of the condo, without affecting its security: 50 to 200 days minimum wage;

- for violations that damage condo property, or that put the condo's security at risk: 50 to 300 days minimum wage; and

- for failure to pay fees and assessments on time: no greater than 100 days minimum wage; this is over and above the interest charges.

This concept of using a variable rate in a piece of legislation as a basis for penalties or financial limits, rather than a fixed amount, is common for Mexican laws. This is because the rate is based on inflation, and is updated on a regular basis. This saves having to keep track and update fixed amounts in hundreds of pieces of legislation.

You should be aware that it's possible that these sanctions may be difficult to legally enforce with a lawsuit – the condo legislation in Mexican states that allow sanctions also has clauses forcing the courts to uphold them (your by-laws can't do this).

In spite of the fact that there's no law forcing the courts to uphold your sanctions, it can be argued that if they form part of your condo's by-laws, if they were properly passed at an extraordinary assembly, and if the minutes containing them were publicly registered, then they're legally binding on each owner.

Sanctions don't contradict any other provision of the condo law. Whether they're in contradiction of any other state law, I honestly don't know. If they are, then they are not enforceable in court.

That said, the mere fact that sanctions exist in your by-laws can be a deterrent, without having to ever put them to a legal challenge.

Having sanctions in your by-laws can be further reinforced by making sure that all new owners are given copies of your by-laws when they buy a unit (or, better yet, before).

Note that ignorance of the by-laws by a new buyer is never an excuse. It's assumed that all owners in a condo are aware of the rules governing the condo. This applies both to the condo law and to the particular condo's by-laws. In addition, your by-laws are a matter of public record.

The other advantage of sanctions is that they add value to the amount you're seeking from the owner if you need to go as far as taking legal action. This might serve to help offset some of the legal fees – you will not usually recover your full legal expenses.

They can also be used as a bargaining chip: *"we will lessen or waive your sanctions if you…"*.

It's important to note that all such fines must be clearly spelled out in your by-laws, and can never be arbitrarily charged.

Your by-laws must clearly set out the amount of the sanction (in multiples of the minimum wage, as a percentage of a fee or assessment, etc.).

If a lower and upper limit are set out for some sanctions, then your by-laws must spell out who decides the final amount (generally your Council), along with a brief description of the process (usually a hearing followed by deliberation).

Special Considerations for By-laws

Chapter **50**

There are a few common issues with condo by-laws that are particularly thorny, and merit their own chapter.

Paint Colours and Architectural Standards

The condo law gives authority to your Administrative Council to approve all changes to an owner's unit (**Article 1010**).

That said, most condos will temper this in their by-laws to only include work that's visible from the common property outside the unit, that directly affects a neighbour, or that impacts the common property. This prevents the decoration of your bedroom from being under Council control – an unreasonable use of authority, and one which may not be legally enforceable.

Once phrased in this way, this rule then has minimal impact on condo apartments (very few changes or decoration can be seen from outside the unit) – unless the owner tries to hang things out of windows, or modifies or installs things on balconies. A significant amount of the "outside" of an apartment unit is common property or may be "limited use" property (such as a balcony or ground-floor patio).

It can, however, still have a huge impact on horizontal condos consisting of individual houses and lots.

It's important, however, to draw a line between things that make a community look "junky" (negatively affecting property values), and becoming the upholders of elegance and style – the "good taste police."

Legitimate concerns are such things as visible satellite dishes, infrastructure, or clothes hung out to dry.

It's also important to realise that whatever your architectural standards say, the approval process for an owner's application for construction must be fair, and the rules must always be consistently applied.

You must never turn down a construction request without a detailed reason, and such reasons must never be arbitrary (*"We don't like the look of it."*).

In apartment or townhouse construction, it's vital to keep a consistent design for siding, roofs, windows, doors, and many other architectural elements. This is because the nature of these projects is such that multiple units occupy a single building structure. Architectural consistency is pretty much essential.

Individual lots and houses are very different, however. In this type of community, variation should be encouraged rather than stifled.

Nothing looks more uninviting to a prospective buyer (and this is what property value is all about) than row on row of almost identical houses (remember the song, *"Little boxes made of ticky-tacky … and they all look just the same"*).

It is unlikely that your condo developer used the same design for every house – so you are starting off with some variety and divergence. A neighbourhood becomes interesting when personalities emerge – not every one uses the identical columns to support car port and terraza roofs, window details vary, or some roofs styles vary slightly.

Arguably, the most contentious issue is paint colour. One person's beautiful blue might be the ugliest colour another individual has ever seen.

Special Considerations for By-laws 451

Again, this can be straightforward for apartments (most visible items that can be painted are common property), but more difficult for a horizontal condo – each house is an owner's private property, including the exterior walls.

Unfortunately, all such aesthetic issues are purely a matter of taste. Who should get to determine what is acceptable and what is not? An arbitrary group of individuals such as your Council or a committee? Why?

What guarantees that this group of people have the best taste in the community? How is good/bad taste even measured?

What happens when this group changes, and different people with different tastes make the decisions – over time, any aesthetic consistency goes out the window anyway.

"OK...OK...we'll solve the problem of personal taste on the Council or the Architectural Committee by just saying in our by-laws what colours are acceptable or not!"

Good luck! Unless you say that every house must be painted the same specific colour (please don't), written rules for colour just don't work. How do you describe acceptable vs. unacceptable shades in words? What exactly does too bright or too dark mean?

The real problem is that you can't legislate taste, and you're doomed to failure if you try.

For a condo consisting of lots and houses, the architectural standards in your by-laws should avoid aesthetics, and concentrate on practical issues such as (not exhaustive):

- lots cannot be subdivided;

- house numbers must appear on each unit (don't try to set out the style or type of house number);
- descriptions of, and requirement for, easements for access to common property elements and infrastructure;
- maximum height of houses or structures; this is important to prevent someone adding another story or building a monster house or addition that destroys the view from their neighbours mirador;
- maximum heights for walls, fences, and hedges around a property; an abnormally high wall can look out of proportion, and dominate a street;
- requirement to keep tall trees trimmed to prevent them from obscuring the view from their neighbours house;
- construction or foliage cannot overhang the property line;
- locations of infrastructure elements so that they are hidden from view from the street or common areas; this should include roof elements such as satellite dishes and solar heating systems; this prevents the community from looking "cluttered" and "junky;"
- hours for construction;
- construction rules such as: not blocking the street or neighbours access, cleaning up debris on a daily basis, storage of construction materials, or repair of damage to the common property; and
- conduct of contractor's workers.

No Pets or Kids

While communities restricted to seniors only, or nonsmokers, or people without pets may be legally enforceable in the US and Canada, they are not in México. Even north of the border, restricting a condo to senior adults only (no children) usually requires government registration and approval.

In México, however, such restrictions violate basic rights given by the Mexican Constitution. If such restrictions are in your by-laws, they might act as a deterrent to some buyers, but you must be aware that they aren't likely to be legally enforceable.

If a young family buys a house in your "seniors-only" condo, or someone with three dogs and two cats moves into your "pet-free" development, there's almost nothing you can do about it.

I can assure you that trying to enforce a ban on children in México won't likely get you very far. The bigger issue you may face might be the fact that some owners may feel they were misled if they bought their unit on the understanding that they were moving into a "seniors-only" complex, and now a young family has moved next door.

By the way, you can have by-law rules that control pets (such as requiring them to be on a leash when on common property), and not to bark or disturb the tranquillity of your condo – these are supported by provisions in the condo law. Outright banning of pets, however, likely cannot be done.

Don't Get in a Flap Over Flags

Many condos north of the border have flag rules, and these are almost always contentious. You have to balance the goal of keeping the community from looking "junky" with the legal right of someone to express their feelings about their country (or adopted country).

You should be aware that the law isn't on your side here. **Article 32** of the *"Ley del Escudo, la Bandera e Himno Nacionales"* (Law of the Coat of Arms, Flag, and National Anthem) gives individuals the right to fly the Mexican flag on their cars, **in their places of residence**, or at work. In all cases, the flag can be of any size.

Apart from permanent flags, you can expect owners to fly the Mexican flag during *el mes de la patria* (independence celebrations covering all of September). As well, the flag might also appear around February 24 (Flag Day) and November 20 (Anniversary of the Mexican Revolution).

It's insensitive and rude to flaunt allegiance to one country while living in another – it's both bad manners and bad civics. While you might consider an outright ban on foreign flags, it might be wise to check with a *notario* first. It's possible that foreign owners have this right under the right of free expression (I haven't researched this).

Be careful about disposing of Mexican flags. **Article 54a** of the flag law says that you can only destroy a copy of the Mexican flag by incineration, and it must be in a respectful and solemn act.

Noise Problems

Noise in a condo comes in all forms: leaf blowers, barking dogs, loud home theatres, or parties.

In condo apartments, the most common source of noise is the unit above.

The condo law says that each neighbour must try to make use of their unit without affecting the tranquillity of the other owners (**Article 1008**).

If an owner complains about another owner being noisy and disturbing them, then your Council **must deal with this complaint** in the same way as with a by-law violation (**see Chapter 56 – "Dealing With Complaints"** for more information).

Because of this, you shouldn't need any specific by-law clauses. You can cover yourself by saying something like, *"Noise that disturbs an owner will be investigated by the Council to decide if it violates the owner's right to quiet enjoyment of their property."*

Avoid Unnecessary Restrictions

It's easy to get caught up in writing concisely worded by-law clauses, and not realise that you're imposing an arbitrary or unnecessary restriction on the owners that might come back to bite you.

Here are some examples:

- **Standing committees**: when you define a standing committee in your by-laws, you **force its creation and staffing every year**. Be sure that this makes sense.

    This is fine if the committee has a continuing role in the administration of your condo. The reason you want to define a standing committee is to make sure that it always exists, and that it doesn't come and go at the whim of future Councils.

If any committee has one special task that has a finite end (such as a committee to rewrite your by-laws), then it's better to create a special committee, and not define one in your by-laws.

- **Number of councillors or members of a committee**: if your by-laws say, for example, that your Council must consist of five members. If one of them resigns and can't be replaced right away, then your Council can no longer legally function. Any decisions made by it while only consisting of four members have no validity, and can be ignored or challenged by any owner.

  A better approach is to set a minimum number (generally three). This way you make sure that you have a Council or committee that can function, but you're not restricting it. If you want to prevent too large a Council, you can also set a maximum.

  In this case, you might have a **goal** of five councillors, and you can beat the bushes for this number of volunteers before your annual ordinary assembly. If (and this is unusual) you have even more people champing at the bit to volunteer to serve as a councillor, then you should seriously consider expanding your Council beyond your goal. Unless you have so many volunteers that your Council would be unworkable (say, more than 12), I recommend that you never discourage people from serving.

  In any event, by setting a minimum workable number, you're free to expand and contract your Council to any number you see fit, and, if changes happen during the year, any number above the minimum still gives you a legal Council.

- **Quorum for council and committee meetings**: in my opinion, there's no reason to put a quorum requirement in your by-laws – standard rules of order already define this. If you must do this, then I caution you against putting in a specific number.

  If you follow my advice above, and set only a **minimum** number of councillors or committee members, then you actually can't set out a specific number for a quorum.

  Normal meeting rules say that a quorum is *"a majority of the members,"* and this will normally work well without needing to be changed.

  The exception is if your Council is large and difficult to gather for a meeting. For example, a 12-member Council would need seven councillors for a quorum. If some of these councillors are part-timers, then this might be difficult to get.

  In this case, you're better off defining the quorum in the Terms of Reference for the committee or your Council (and not in your by-laws) as *"the number decided at the first council meeting after the appointment of the Council by a vote of whatever number of councillors attend."*

  Then, at the first council meeting after the ordinary assembly where they were appointed, the Council decides on a reasonable number for quorum based on its size and make-up (hopefully after informal discussion with all the new councillors). In our example above, they could set the quorum at four. This decision must be recorded first meeting minutes of this Council to become valid.

- **Any list of specific items**: for example, a list of expenses that are covered by your condo fees.

While this might seem innocuous, you can inadvertently paint yourself into a corner. For example, if a by-law clause says that *"Condominium fees are to cover the following expenses:"* and then lists five or six types of expenses, then technically you're prevented from paying for anything **that is not on this list**!

I absolutely guarantee that no matter how carefully you've thought about your list, something will crop up in the future that's not on it.

Look at your list and decide if it's necessary – does having the list in your by-laws actually benefit your condo?

If you must have this list, then always add a catch-all as the last item, for example, *"Any other expenses for the operation, repair, or maintenance of the condominium."*

Another option is to add something like the following to the preamble to the list, *"consisting of, but not limited to, the following expenses:"*.

- **Things that aren't reasonable or violate people's rights**: a few real-world examples, to give you an idea of what to watch out for:

    - This appears innocent at first glance,

        "When a change of ownership of a private unit is finalised, the Administrator must provide a letter to the owner or to his notario certifying that there are no outstanding condominium fees."

        The problem is that this puts the onus on your Administrator. How is your Administrator to know when a sale has been finalised? Sometimes private sales aren't even advertised.

Special Considerations for By-laws

By changing it to, *"...the Administrator must provide **on request** a letter to the owner..."* it becomes a reasonable directive.

- Take a look at this one:

    "The word "resident" will be taken to include owners of private units, their guests, or their renters ... Residents must ensure that any contractors or employees adhere to these regulations."

    While this may seem OK at first glance, it actually makes your visiting guests responsible for the behaviour of contractors and condo employees – not reasonable.

    As well, it makes everyone responsible for everyone else's contractor and the contractor's employees (although the employee relationship is rather vague as worded here). If someone on the other side of your condo hires a contractor to renovate their property, this clause makes you or your renter responsible for controlling this contractor – again, not reasonable.

    This should have been written something like this, *"... **Owners and renters** must make sure that any contractors **that they have hired** or **the contractor's** employees adhere to these regulations."* This is now both clear and reasonable.

- Here's another example:

    "Domesticated animals are permitted as pets, but exotic pets and farm animals are not permitted in the condominium."

    Both the words *"domesticated"* and (especially) *"exotic"* are open to individual interpretation.

Which category do ferrets, de-scented skunks, pot-bellied pigs, or llamas fall under? Who makes this decision? Is there an appeal process? Is this even legal?

It's much better to have your by-law article directly address the problem that you're trying to solve, by saying something like, *"Animals that bother other residents or that damage common or private property are prohibited."*

With this clause, you don't have to analyse an animal to see if it falls into an arbitrary pet category – if you receive complaints about it being bothersome or causing damage, then you can investigate the complaints, and, if they're valid, ask the owner to control the animal or get rid of it.

- Try not to be overbearing in the authority granted to your administration. I've seen clauses regarding "For Sale" signs that state that:

  - *the sign must meet certain minimum standards of aesthetics* – this may be reasonable, but is questionable;

  - *"For Sale" signs may only be placed on an owner's private property* – good and reasonable rule;

  - *"Open House" signs may only be placed outside the main gate and on condominium property* – nothing wrong here;

  - *All such signage placement is subject to approval by the Council* – uh oh, now we're overreaching our authority.

  Your Council doesn't have the authority to say where on an owner's private property they can put their "For Sale" sign. Can you imagine a councillor telling the owner to, *"move it two feet to the left, and up a bit."* Unreasonable.

- **Paying your Administrator**: even if you only envision ever having a volunteer owner as Administrator, don't include a by-law clause that prevents you from paying your Administrator.

  This decision **must** be left up to the assembly that appoints the Administrator based on current circumstances (which will always change).

  If you run out of people willing to volunteer, you may not be able to hire anyone because of your by-laws. Your condo can no longer operate. You'd be forced to call an emergency extraordinary assembly (with all the associated delays and expenses) to repeal this by-law clause before you can hire an Administrator.

- **Watch out for clauses that aren't restrictive enough**: the condo law requires that any restrictions on business activity be in your by-laws (**Article 1006**), but be careful not to be too restrictive. For example: *"No resident may conduct business within the condominium."*

  This might seem fine until you realise that if someone allows another person, **who is not a resident of your condominium**, to operate a business from their unit (a beauty salon, for example) then they're not in violation of this by-law clause. The resident isn't conducting business.

  Better wording would be, *"No **business may be carried out** in the condominium."*

  The intent of disallowing business activity is to avoid disruption to the community. You may not necessarily want to stop businesses that have no impact on your condo.

For example, if an owner has an online business, there are no customers coming and going or parking in your condo. Neighbours would be unaware of this business.

Therefore, even better wording would be, *"No **business that disturbs the tranquillity of the condominium may be carried out** in the condominium."*

Now the problem can be investigated and ruled on by your Council when (or if) they get a complaint. They have some leeway in dealing with this – common sense can be applied. If your by-laws ban business activity outright, they have no choice.

PART 18 – The Transfer From the Developer

Overview of the Transfer

Chapter 51

The transfer of the administration of a condo from the developer to the owners is not covered in the condo legislation. This section of my book has little to do with the condo law, and everything to do with practical advice.

It's about understanding the situation of a new condo that's still being administered by the developer, and enabling you to prepare and pro-actively work towards the inevitable transfer to the owners.

Developers - Law vs. Reality

While the comments in these two chapters don't apply to all developers, you can avoid a great deal of frustration if you have an understanding of how certain developers work in the real world.

Don't be shocked if your developer seems surprised at some of the requirements of the condo law if you point them out – including the requirement to hold annual assemblies with protocolised and registered minutes during his administration.

It's possible for a successful developer to have little or no knowledge of the condo legislation, in spite of the fact that he builds and sells them for a living. It's also possible to find that he's contravening multiple rules in the condo law while administering your condo. Remember, he's in the business of selling homes, not administering condominiums.

What is the Transfer?

According to the condo legislation (**Article 1011**), the developer appoints the first Administrator (often himself or an employee). The developer also sets up the first Administrative Council, which may consist only of one person (himself or an employee). These will be named in the *escritura constitutiva* (registered establishing document) that set up your condominium regime.

According to the condo law, the developer must start holding annual ordinary assemblies to appoint a new Administrator and Council for each following fiscal year.

Since most condos aren't built, nor the majority of units sold, in a single year, this could happen once or even twice, with the developer continuing his administration by controlling the majority of votes at the assembly (if he bothers to hold one).

There will come a time, when he'll have to hold an assembly, and he'll have sold enough units that the administration will be transferred to the owners.

It's important to realise that this "transfer" is not some kind of special operation or process, and that there's no transfer document, certificate, or letter involved.

All it means is that an ordinary assembly is held where an Administrator is appointed by the owners (rather than the developer) and a Council (Board) is elected by the owners, consisting of owners. Together, they start administering your condominium. The developer is now no longer directly involved in administration, and just becomes another owner – often an owner of multiple units.

When Does the Transfer Take Place?

Since the developer starts off owning all the units, his voting block at an assembly is large at first – this voting block decreases as he sells the units. Therefore, he can, for a time, control the appointment of the Administrator and the Council – allowing himself to stay in control of your condo administration.

At some point (often when construction on units is almost finished and most of the units are sold), the developer will decide that it's time to transfer the administration of your condo to the owners at the next ordinary assembly.

Some developers want to keep control of the administration of a condo as long as possible while still selling units – sometimes well after the construction is finished.

One reason is that they might be subsidising the condo fees to keep them artificially low to attract buyers. This isn't necessarily a bad thing for you either, as long as you're realistic, and are prepared for a reality-check when you prepare your first budget (fees **will** go up).

Unlike some jurisdictions north of the border, the condo legislation doesn't contain any time limits for the transfer other than after the initial year. The actual timing depends on the number of units not owned by the developer, and the wish of those owners to take control.

If the developer doesn't start the transfer voluntarily, the community might have enough votes to force the issue at the next ordinary assembly – although it may not be in your interest to do this too soon. You definitely should wait until all the construction is finished, you've inspected all common property construction, and you've made all your preparations for the transfer.

This differs slightly from standard practice north of the border, where a condo board normally has a legal standing to make claims against the developer. In México, you'll often be more successful in getting things finished and fixed while the developer is still in control, but wants to move on.

The date of the ordinary assembly where an Administrator and Council are first appointed by the owners, is the date of the transfer.

You should try to have the developer agree to pay for the translation, protocolisation, and registration of the minutes of this assembly.

Getting Ready for the Transfer

Well before the date of the ordinary assembly where the transfer will take place, you should start to get all your ducks in a row.

I recommend a preparation period of at least four to six months, where the owners work with the developer before the transfer – there are many issues to consider during this transition period.

The transfer will most usually happen at an annual ordinary assembly rather than a specially-called ordinary assembly – therefore, in January, February, or March of a given year.

Your first step should be to set up an informal meeting with all available owners to explain the situation, the process, and the need for a transition team. If some owners aren't present, then they should be informed and updated by email – copies of meeting notes should be sent to them.

At this meeting, you should appoint a transition team that's, ideally, made up of owners who'll be there during the entire transition period – I recommend a minimum of three.

This team is an informal committee to represent the owners in negotiations with the developer to try to make sure the transition and transfer go as smoothly as possible.

Hopefully, you're already considering who your Administrator will be, and who'll serve on your first Administrative Council (Board) after the transfer. I highly recommend that your transition team be made up of some or all of these people.

If you're considering hiring or contracting an Administrator, now might be a good time to get them involved – at a minimum, keep them in the loop.

You may also wish to set up an informal budget for the team, since you'll need to make copies of documents, you might need translations, you will likely need to hire construction experts or inspectors, and you might need to seek legal advice. I recommend that you use a *notario* (Civil Law notary) for legal advice on these matters, rather than an *abogado* (lawyer) – a *notario* has the needed specialised knowledge.

I suggest a budget of $8,000 to $10,000 pesos minimum.

Try your best to get the developer to fund these expenses. If he refuses, then you can consider voluntary contributions from the owners.

If you don't feel that owner donations are fair, you can make the contributions a conditional loan. The loan amount is put in the new condo budget to be approved at the same assembly as the transfer as a one-time expense. If approved by the owners at the assembly (it's very unlikely to be defeated), the money will be repaid to those who contributed (keep records of who contributed what).

What Does the Transition Team Do?

The transition team should:

- verify that your condominium regime has been legally set up, and gather all documents associated with this for your condo records;
- verify that your condo records are accurate, complete, and up to date (don't be surprised if they're almost nonexistent);

- examine the operating expenses, and prepare the first owner-operated budget;

- verify that all unpaid expenses have been paid by the developer before the transfer; and

- verify the integrity of the common property construction, and make sure that all needed repairs are done before the transfer.

Meetings With The Developer

When meetings are held with the developer (and there will likely be several), meeting notes must be taken (like informal minutes) that detail your transition team's understanding of what was discussed, and what was agreed to by both parties. Documenting agreements is vital as you move through the transition period towards the transfer itself.

These meeting notes should be printed, signed by the leader of your transition team, and a copy hand-delivered to the developer **as soon as possible after each meeting**.

In my experience, Mexican businessmen will almost always respond to written requests, agreements, and deadlines, and infrequently to verbal ones. By doing this, you're documenting the developer's commitments, as well as your own.

You're also showing the developer that you're serious and professional.

Distribute copies of these notes to the transition team and the other owners. Be sure to use these for follow-up at subsequent meetings. It's important to keep focused on finishing all your tasks.

Be prepared to not get everything you want. Always prioritise your issues, and be prepared to give away lesser issues as bargaining chips to get more important issues dealt with.

Preparing for the Transfer

Chapter 52

Once your transition team is in place, it's time to get started preparing for the transition. There are many things to organise. You'll need at least four to six months before the ordinary assembly for your team to get everything they need from the developer.

Again, the comments in this and the last chapter don't apply to all developers, but are representative of how some developers work.

Get a Copy of the *Escritura Constitutiva*

Article 1026 of the Jalisco condo legislation outlines the steps and requirements for the developer to set up the *régimen de condominio* (condominium regime):

- he must have free title to the land where your condo is to be built;

- he must ask for and get authorisation from the municipality where the property is located; and

- the process must be formalised in an *escritura constitutiva* (publicly registered founding document).

This *escritura constitutiva* must be registered in the local *registro público de la propiedad* (Public Registry of Property), and is an **essential document for your condo records**.

Your team must request an official copy of this document. Don't take "no" for an answer, and pursue this like a dog with a bone. If you're getting nowhere with the developer, go to the property registry yourself and get a copy. If the registry office doesn't have one, be **very** concerned.

You need to examine this document to make sure that a *régimen de condominio* has been set up – these words will appear near the beginning of the document.

You should then verify that the *escritura constitutiva* contains the following legal requirements:

- a history of the property and its title;

- the location, dimensions, and boundaries of the overall property;

- any required concessions for: water rights (if your condo has its own water supply, instead of municipal water), beaches, estuaries, and islands; these are all part of the national public domain, and need specific permission from federal authorities; these don't apply to all condos;

- a general description of the common buildings and infrastructure, and the quality of materials that are used in their construction;

- a general description of municipal services, if any;

- a separate description of each condo unit (apartment or lot), detailing its numeric designation, location, dimensions, boundaries, grade of materials used, services to which it has a right, as well as its percentage ownership of the common property;

- a description of the common property or areas, showing: location, dimensions, boundaries, and parts that make them up; infrastructure; and equipment and furnishings belonging to them, and, when possible, their brand names and quantities;

- the allotment of the common areas vs. the private, their use and purpose;

- the classification of your condominium according to its characteristics of operation and use of the common property – for example, a simple horizontal condo for residential use;

- proof of having gotten authorisation to set up your condominium regime, as well as any opinions, authorisations, or licenses applicable to town-planning and the municipality; these are most commonly attached to the end of the *escritura*;

- information about construction licenses and permits; if the construction was already finished at the time of the application, the occupancy certificate must have been issued; again, these are usually attached to the end of the *escritura*;

- if the units are being sold in an unfinished form, so that each owner will finish or customise their unit, then this fact must be pointed out in all the certifications issued by the municipal authorities;

- proof of any guarantees (almost always in the form of a bond) given to the municipality to guarantee the quality and completion of the work;

- your condo's by-laws;

- the way the owners will pay the fees established in **Article 1026** of the condo law (such as monthly or quarterly); and

- zoning plans of your condominium, and general construction plans for the common property and of the units.

You may want to hire a *notario* to review these with you.

Plans and Drawings Are Important

As you can see, the developer must submit plans and drawings of all the infrastructure elements of your condo during the application process. These might include such systems as: electrical, telephone, intercom, cable TV, security, water supply, and sewage systems.

The drawings that the developer submitted to the municipality are preliminary plans needed to get building permits, and **must be stamped and initialled by the municipality**.

He must also submit plans showing: the overall dimensions and boundaries of the entire condo; the location, dimensions, and boundaries of the common property; and the dimensions of each lot or apartment – note that these are not normally complete floor plans of the units.

You definitely should have copies of these plans and drawings for your condo records. Your transition team should try to get the developer to give you a set of these as full-size architectural drawings (to scale).

The developer should also have "as built" plans that are these permit drawings updated from what was **expected** to be built to what was **actually** built. These are important to have, and, again, your transition team should hound the developer for these.

As time goes on, these plans and drawings will prove invaluable when problems come up with your condo infrastructure – especially with buried elements.

Try to Get the Minimum Condo Records

Article 1012 VI requires the Administrator to keep some minimum records for your condo: a book containing the minutes of all assemblies; a book containing the minutes of all council (board) meetings; and detailed financial accounts showing all income and expenses. Before the transfer, these records should have been kept by the developer (but may not have been).

- <u>**Assembly and council minutes**</u>: if, during the developer's administration, there were any changes made to by-laws, lot layouts, or anything else contained in the *escritura constitutiva*, or if any decisions were made directly affecting the operation of your condominium, then the minutes of the assemblies or council meetings where these decisions were made:

    - need to exist; and

    - if an assembly, need to be publicly registered.

    If these assembly minutes aren't registered, then they didn't legally happen, and none of these changes or decisions are enforceable or binding – something you may need to fix, depending on their nature and importance.

    Ideally, there should also be registered minutes of every annual ordinary assembly for each year after the development was created. These should name the Administrator and Council (often only two people from the development company).

    Note that this only applies **after** the first year, the first Administrator will be named in the *escritura constitutiva*.

If these meetings weren't held, or if the minutes weren't registered, then the Administrator and Council (usually the developer) technically had no authority to represent your condo or to legally enter into contracts.

The developer may not be forthcoming with these (he may not have them), but, with a little effort, he can still create these documents, and can still have them protocolised and registered before the transfer (insist that this be done at his cost). This will make sure that your condo records are accurate when you start out.

- **Financial statements**: this is where the wheels usually come off. Some developers just won't have this information.

    However, to prepare your first condo budget and work out real-world fees (yes, they'll likely go up!), you need to get a good handle on typical expenses for your condo.

    If you don't do this, you'll most likely run into deficit at some point during your first year, and will have to charge a special assessment to make up your budget short-fall. This doesn't generally go down well with the owners.

    Remember, even if the developer was charging fixed fees, you **must** change to proportional fees when you take over.

    I strongly advise that your future Administrator work with the developer to create a list of typical expenses for your condo, and to try to assign reasonable values to these based on the developer's experience. Such things as: security, common property gardeners and maids, pool maintenance, building maintenance, garbage collection, utilities, gas, supplies (cleaning, garden, or pool chemicals), or general repair allowance. **See Chapter 45 – "Your Condo Budget."**

A condo's first owner-administered budget could wind up as a "seat-of-your-pants" budget – because often the initial figures are not based on accurate records. If this is the case, you must incorporate a healthy contingency to try to avoid a deficit and special assessment. Remember, any excess in this contingency will be carried forward into the next fiscal year, and can reduce the fees needed in that year if the contingency can then be reduced.

As a rule-of-thumb, try to get as many documents and written information from the developer as you possibly can.

Sometimes There's a Lack of Accounting

As I've mentioned, you'll often find that there's a lack of any real accounting of your condo expenses that were paid out over the period of administration by the developer.

This is just the nature of the beast.

You have to understand that a developer's priority is to sell units. To this end, some developers will set artificially low condo fees that are not based on a budget or actual expenses. This is to make the units more attractive for sale.

This will often be a fixed fee (the same for every unit). The developer will do this in spite of what the law says and, most likely, what the condo's own by-laws say. This is just much, much easier for the developer to deal with, and it makes selling simpler.

The developer may collect these fees, and deposit them directly into the development company account. He'll also pay all condo expenses from this account.

This is often not the only use of this company account. It can also be used to fund construction or wages.

As a result, the developer won't necessarily have a separate accounting of condo expenses vs. income, and there may not be a condo budget as such.

In other words, all operating expenses are just paid as they arise, whatever they may be. The attractively low fees that make the units appealing to buyers may have no relationship to generating the income needed to cover actual expenses.

The other consequence of this practice is that fees will inevitably rise once you assume control of the administration, and you must create a budget that realistically covers your real-world expenses.

While this isn't unusual (nor is it unique to condos in México), it always seems to take people by surprise.

Make an Inventory of Assets

Your transition team should ask for a list of all the common property assets. For example, if you have a community pool area, this list would show all the patio furniture, umbrellas, pool heater, gas tank, etc.

This list should include details such as manufacturer and date of purchase or installation. This last, even if approximate, will be a big help in determining the useful life left for these assets when you carry out your first reserve study to set out your reserve funding plan over the long-term.

If the developer looks at you like you're crazy when you ask for this, and tells you that no such inventory exists, politely point out that the Administrator (at this point, likely him) is required to have such a list by **Civil Code Article 1007.**

Since it's unlikely that this list already exists, he should be willing to work with your team to create one, help fill in the blanks about the age of items, and, get you the approximate value of them when they were new. This will also be a big help in working out a reserve plan.

If all else fails, take an inventory yourself, and have the developer sign it. You'll need this for your initial condo records.

Have your team examine the condition of each of these items to see if they need repair or replacement – now is the time to negotiate this.

Your Condo By-laws

Each owner should have been given a copy of your by-laws by the developer when they bought their unit. Often, as a courtesy, the developer will also give out an English translation.

Bear in mind that an English translation of your by-laws has no legal force (only the original Spanish version is legally binding), and that this translation may not be high quality. As a result, the translated by-laws may not be accurate (or even understandable).

If owners don't have a copy of your by-laws (and they should), or if your English translation is poor, you can extract the Spanish version from the *escritura constitutiva* and, if you wish, have it translated into English **for informational purposes only** (I recommend that any translation of a Spanish legal document explicitly say this).

It can sometimes be a challenge to find a translator whose work results in an intelligible document.

I suggest that you extract some difficult Spanish passages (if you already have a poor translation, these would be the most incomprehensible paragraphs) and use this as an "audition" of several proposed translators – see which one produces the most understandable result.

Don't be afraid to keep on at your translator until any passages that seem garbled become clear.

The relatively small cost of this effort will be well worth it if the community has a copy of your by-laws that they can understand.

Fix Construction Issues Before the Transfer

It's important to make sure that you have all the problems with the common property fixed by the developer **before** the transfer. You need to identify as many common property construction problems as possible, and have them fixed before you take over the administration of your condo.

Before the transfer, the developer is usually still fully responsible for covering all the expenses of your condo, will normally be responsible for your condo buildings and constructions up to the transfer, and should still make repairs.

This is especially true when it's the developer who wants the transfer to happen – all the units are finished, the majority are sold, and now he just wants to move on.

That said, the developer's responsibilities don't end at the time of transfer. Typically, a developer's warranty period on common areas is one year, and it should start from the date of the assembly where the transfer took place. Be sure that your transition team negotiates a warranty (if you can get more than a year, great!), that it starts from the date of transfer, and that it's in writing (a signed letter will do).

Preparing for the Transfer **481**

Although the developer's warranty period will normally start with the transfer, it's sometimes easier to get repairs and changes done before this (when the developer is motivated) than it is under the warranty.

If you're planning to have a resident serve as an Operations Manager, or a number of them form an Operations Committee, then one or more of these people should be involved in looking into these construction issues.

You might find that some owners will approach the transition team with construction issues affecting their units. Unfortunately, the transition team can only be concerned with problems affecting the common property.

Individual owners must deal directly with the developer for issues with their private units. The transition team must stay out of these issues to keep up its credibility and its focus with the developer.

Inspect the Common Property Buildings and Structures

You should seriously consider hiring an independent home inspector or engineer (independent from the developer) to examine the common property buildings and structures, just as you would when purchasing a home.

This inspector may uncover problems that your well-meaning (but likely inexperienced) transition team could easily miss, such as: *salitre* and drainage problems, wood rot and termites, or structural, electrical, or pool problems.

Construction Problems: Gated Community Perimeter Wall

If your condo is a gated community, you should hire an engineer or reputable contractor to inspect your perimeter wall to look at its construction quality and integrity.

Be sure to get access to the neighbouring property to inspect the back of the wall.

Look in particular at: drainage, potential *salitre* issues, foundations, anchoring of *castillos* (vertical reinforced supports) into the foundation, expansion joints (or lack of them), and how well the top of the wall is sealed against the entry of rain water.

Get any needed repairs done by the developer, and, if there were significant problems, consider getting the finished work inspected again.

Replacement of a relatively small portion of your wall out of warranty, if it collapsed, could cost your condo more than $8,000 USD.

Construction Problems: *Salitre*

In both items above I mentioned *salitre*. This can be a significant problem when traditional masonry construction (bricks, mortar, and concrete) is used – this construction is common in México.

Salitre shows up as a white stain on the surface of bricks or concrete. This white powder is the result of salts in the bricks, concrete, and mortar being dissolved in water, and then carried to the surface. They evaporate, leaving behind a residue of dried salts.

When this masonry construction is inside a painted wall (again, common in México), these water-borne salts penetrate the outer layer of "plaster" (actually concrete) covering the bricks, and will lift the paint – this can be seen as a blistering or bubbling. Portions can flake off, exposing the white powdery *salitre* underneath. It sometimes appears as a white residue on the paint itself.

It can also appear on clay floor tiles – slowly disintegrating them.

If it's prevalent in a concrete slab floor, then it can even cause ceramic tiles to lift away from the sub-floor.

It's also possible for *salitre* to become a structural issue if the underlying water problem has created concentrated and long-term exposure.

One of the main structural parts in typical Mexican construction are *castillos* (metal rebar towers that reinforce vertical concrete columns embedded in a wall). Water with a high concentration of salts can, over the long-term, corrode the metal in the *castillo*, weakening the structure.

To compound the problem, these salts are there in the first place because they were added to the concrete to give it strength. As they're leached out by the water, the concrete itself is further weakened.

These salts are common in Mexican masonry because masons use *cal* (lime) to make the mortar easier to work with, and to increase its strength when set – this is the source of the *salitre*.

The trigger that causes *salitre* to form is water. It can come from a leaking internal water source such as a water pipe, but it's most often caused by rain or ground water.

Salitre in a wall will either be caused by rain water soaking into the top surface (masonry perimeter walls need something to seal the top) or rain and ground water wicking up from below.

Another cause is a leak in a roof – the *salitre* will then usually appear on the ceiling.

- <u>***Salitre* on walls of common property buildings**</u>: in a condo apartment complex, this is a huge task since it might involve the exterior of multiple apartments or even buildings.

On building walls, *salitre* can be caused by a leak from above – these can be tricky to find, and you'll likely need a qualified home inspector, engineer, or contractor. In particular, make sure that none of the wall's interior masonry is exposed to the elements.

Water might also be entering the wall at its base, and this can often be lessened by creating proper drainage to carry rain water away from the the building.

If the water is wicking up from below, it might be because of a leaking water pipe, or the floor slab or base of the wall being in direct contact with the soil. Solutions range from a special paint-on sealer (applied to the outside foundation walls) to excavating and changing the construction (not nice!).

- **_Salitre_ on ceilings from roof leaks**: leaks in roofs can be especially challenging, since the point where the water enters can be some distance from the visible *salitre* below.

    Flat roofs are especially prone to *salitre*-causing leaks.

    Flat roofs must be slightly sloped towards roof drains that will completely carry away rain water. Under no circumstances must water be allowed to pool on the roof – test this on a dry day by hosing down the roof (or throwing buckets of water), and observing what happens. It must all run off through drains. If not, you either need more drains or extra concrete to slope the roof towards the existing drains.

    Flat roofs must also be sealed. There are a number of products available ranging from a paint-like waterproof sealer to membranes – the best long-term solution is layers of membrane that have been professionally applied.

In the case of vertical condos (apartments), if the roof construction is prone to leaks, these problems can affect one or more of the topmost units.

Some apartment buildings aren't prone to *salitre* because they aren't traditional masonry construction, but roof leaks can still create damage.

- <u>*Salitre* on a perimeter wall</u>: *salitre* can be caused by water getting in at the top of your wall. Make sure there's nothing porous on the top surface such as brick (decorative or structural). If decorative tiles or bricks have been used, make sure that they're sealed with a skim coat of concrete on top to prevent water soaking through and between them (these are often porous). A sealer can also be added to this concrete coating.

Salitre at the bottom of your perimeter wall can be caused by a poorly built foundation, the foundation being at or below ground (often on the other side where the ground level can be higher), or poor drainage on the property behind your wall.

Dealing With *Salitre*

The first step in cleaning up a *salitre* problem is to completely remove the deposited salts from the affected surface. If the surface was painted, the loose and flaking paint must be thoroughly scraped away (use a putty knife and wire brush).

The exposed surface must then be washed with water, and allowed to dry. Then thoroughly scrub with a brush using a 50% muriatic acid solution. Repeat the acid wash three times, allowing a day between each application.

After the masonry has completely dried, a sealer must be applied and allowed to dry for a day.

Apply filler as needed to even out the area. Then apply a good quality primer (alkyd is best), followed by two coats of quality paint.

If this is all you do, **then the problem might come back**. Since you can't do anything about the presence of the salts in the mortar, concrete, and even the bricks, to "cure" a *salitre* problem you must solve the underlying water problem.

Construction Problems: Drainage

Salitre and other problems caused by poor drainage can be especially bad if the property on the other side of your perimeter wall is undeveloped, and is uphill from you.

Undeveloped land may not be walled. If it's uphill, during the rainy season (June through September in most of Jalisco) heavy rain water will run downhill, and will pool against the back of your wall.

During a heavy downpour, look at what's happening on the other side of your wall. If water is running down and pooling against, or flowing along, the base of your wall you'll likely have problems.

If this is the case, contact the owner of the property, explain the situation, and get permission to excavate a drainage ditch system on the property to divert heavy rain water away from your walls until they develop the property, and have their own drainage.

This will prove to be a worthwhile investment.

A drainage ditch system might cost you in the order of $1,000 to $1,500 USD to build. Replacing a 15m (50 ft) section of wall that's collapsed because its foundation was eroded by inadequately drained rain water can cost five to ten times as much.

Developed land is normally completely walled, and drainage is normally taken care of once construction begins.

If, however, in spite of the property behind your wall being developed, you observe water running down and pooling against, or flowing along, the back of your wall, alert the property owner – they should take corrective measures. At a minimum they should allow you to add protection for your wall on their property.

If you discover these problems before the transfer, try to get the developer to either make the necessary changes, or help you talk with the owner of the other property.

Construction Problems: Mould

Water problems may also be accompanied by mould that grows because of the underlying dampness. Be careful, these moulds can be dangerous if the spores are inhaled (especially if the mould is black in colour).

Carefully (never scrape or scratch dried mould) clean it with bleach – leaving the bleach to soak in for about 15 minutes.

Construction Problems: Wood Rot

If you have roofs on the common property that are supported by wooden support columns, **inspect these very, very carefully.**

While the look of these structures can be an attractive selling feature, they can be prone to both wood rot and termites. Especially if the bottoms of the columns (below ground) have been directly embedded into soil.

Collapsed car port

Supported by four wooden columns – about five years old. Mainly wood rot caused by water with some termite damage. Collapsed without warning, each of the four support columns sheared off at ground level.

Wood rot is caused by water wicking up into the base of the columns from below ground, as well as rain water pooling around the column base – usually until the puddle evaporates. The first sign of this is a dark stain at the base of the column, and a hollow sound when it's tapped.

Construction Problems: Termites

Termites come from underground – their nests, like ants, are in the earth below. They'll eat their way up through a wooden column, and will continue into any wooden beams supported by the column – entering the beam at the point of contact with the column. They eat cellulose, and much prefer dead wood to living trees.

You can spot evidence of termites if you look for little piles of fine sawdust, or if you see "tracks" along the outside of the wood.

Preparing for the Transfer   489

These tracks are usually lighter in colour than the wood, and are either random and meandering, or follow and fill a crack in the wood.

These tracks on the surface of a column or beam are tunnels that the little critters make from a sort of mud (you really don't want to know what it's made of). They use these to move from one part of their interior construction project (or destruction project) to another while avoiding sunlight, heat, and dry air.

Termites need moisture, and so water-damaged wood is even more attractive to them. Therefore, wooden columns are a double whammy that can have damage from both causes.

Wood support column that held up a roof over a community terraza

There is wood rot from water damage at the bottom (top of photo), plus extensive internal termite damage.

It was removed just in time – collapse was imminent.

It split open like this on removal.

It was originally a solid round log, about 30cm (12") in diameter. The inside was eaten to the point that it had lost all structural integrity.

It was about six years old.

A termite can look a lot like an ant, but has wings and a two-section body (winged ants have a three-section body). Although termites may look like ants, they are not closely related. Like ants, they have a social structure, with work divided amongst different types of termites.

If you break open a surface track (it's actually a hollow tube), you might see small white maggot-like bugs inside – these are also termites.

The termites' aim is to eat all the wood inside a wood column or beam until only a thin outer shell is left. Unfortunately, since these are weight-bearing structures, they'll collapse long before the termites reach their goal of wood domination.

The structural integrity of this sort of wooden support construction might only last five years at most. **You need to take this seriously**!

If these wooden support columns and beams are holding up a roof structure that has wood rafter beams and *tejas* (clay roof tiles), the weight they are supporting is huge. If this roof collapses, there could be serious damage, injury, or possibly even a death.

If you have any of these wooden columns or beams, I recommend that you hire an engineer to inspect them. If there's obvious water damage or evidence of termites, then press your developer to replace them with reinforced concrete columns and metal main support beams.

For a complete and permanent fix you should also consider replacing any smaller wooden rafter beams with metal 'C'-channels, and the wood strapping supporting the *tejas* with welded rectangular metal tubing. These can be faux-finished to resemble wood.

If the developer won't do this, plan for this work to be done sooner than later in your reserve funding plan.

Termites can also get into door frames, because they touch the floor at the bottom. They're also very attracted to cardboard.

Construction Problems: Septic Systems

If your condominium has a septic system (rather than being connected to a municipal sewer system), then you should hire an engineer or a reputable contractor to examine this system to make sure that it's properly sized to handle a full compliment of residents (all units sold, occupied, and flushing).

For example, a 30-house condo will need a much bigger septic system than a 10-house condo.

There are ways of calculating the size of the tanks needed based on the number of units. It might surprise you to learn that not all developers make (or know about) these calculations.

Despite popular belief, septic system needs routine maintenance in the form of pumping. How often you need to do this depends on: whether the tanks are large enough for the community; if drain water from sinks, showers, and laundry is flushing out the bacteria that's breaking down the sludge; if there are garbage disposals being used; and if residents are flushing bleach, anti-bacterial soap, and toilet-tank cleaners that destroy your friendly bacteria.

If any of these things are preventing the system from breaking down the sludge, it can backup. This is a messy and smelly experience, needs an emergency pump out, and could damage the absorption area (a vital part of the septic system).

For a detailed description of septic tanks, see my other book, *"Practical Guide to Buying Property in México."* A chapter in this book is dedicated to septic tanks, and features: how they work, proper sizing, maintenance, and a list of Dos & Don'ts for the community.

I recommend that you try to negotiate to have the developer pump out the septic tanks just before the transfer. This will let you hire an expert to make measurements to work out how often pumping needs to be done, and allows you to budget for it in future.

If it looks like your tanks will need to be pumped often, I recommend that you have access hatches built for regular inspection and pumping. You can then monitor the condition of your tanks over time to work out exactly when they need pumping.

Try to convince the developer to install these hatches. They'll more than pay for themselves if they prevent a backup.

Knowing how often you need to bring in a pumper truck to empty the tanks is a budget issue. Your budget or reserve study must reflect this – for example, pumped every year (a budget item) vs. every three years (a reserve item).

Your Goal is a Zero-Sum Transfer

Your financial goal for your transfer is to make sure that you inherit a condominium for which all debts associated with the developer's administration are paid, and all you're dealing with are future expenses.

Continuity of Common Property Services

The common property usually needs a number of contractors (or employees) to maintain and operate it. It's important that there are no gaps in these services after the transfer.

If the developer has entered into any contracts (especially for maintenance or service work), then your transition team must try to get copies of these for your condo records.

This is especially important if you plan to continue with any of these contractors after the transfer. If you don't, you need to know what's involved in cancelling their services.

- **Security guards**: if your condo has security guards, and if the developer has been using his own staff for security, you'll need to find a security company to whom you can contract this service.

    You want to have this contractor in place so that there's no gap in security after the transfer. If the developer is already using a security company, then you can just continue to use them if you're satisfied with their service. Don't forget to change the contract into your condo's name, and put the amount of the contract into your condo budget.

    Hiring your own guards as employees can be costly. For instance, you'll have to register with *Hacienda* (the tax department) to get a tax number, and make regular filings and payments.

    You'll also need to pay IMSS (social security) as well as a number of other employee deductions, and you'll need to provide training, uniforms, security equipment, and replacement guards when they're sick or away.

    For more information on employees, **see Chapter 44 – "Contract Workers vs. Employees"**.

If you decide to hire a security company, then all you need is a contract. They'll look after training, discipline, equipment, and organising the shifts and replacing guards who are sick or away. The security company's 24 hour emergency number can be posted to allow residents to contact the company directly if there are any problems.

As with all other expenses, have your transition team make sure that the developer pays all unpaid charges for this service up to the date of the transfer.

- **Pool maintenance**: if you have a community pool, you need to look into replacing the developer's staff with a contractor, or continuing with an existing maintenance contract – don't forget to change it into your condo's name. Add the amount of this contract to your condo budget, and make sure that the contractor is paid up to the transfer date.

- **General staff**: the comments above also apply to gardeners, maids, maintenance men, office staff, and other general workers.

- **Property management company**: you may be considering hiring a property management company to assist your Administrator.

    They do this by letting you use their bank account, collecting fees and issuing receipts, paying the condo expenses on your behalf, and keeping track of owner accounts.

    You'll need to start the search so that this company can be brought on board to start right after the transfer.

    Before the transfer, the developer is administering your condo, and doing all these things.

For more information on the use of a property management company, **see Chapter 12 – "Lessening the Burden on a Volunteer Administrator"**.

Make Sure Utilities Are Paid Up

It's essential that you verify that all the utility bills have been paid before the transfer. Have your transition team check this, and don't take the developer's word. Get receipts, and go to the utility office. At the same time you can work out the average cost of these for your budget.

If you don't do this, your condo might be on the hook for what could be a large amount of money in back charges. This can have a serious impact on your first condo budget.

If you've decided to appoint a volunteer resident Administrator (as opposed to hiring an employee or contracting the position), then they should be given the responsibility of looking into the payment of utilities.

- **Telephone**: there can be one or more telephone lines associated with the common property (such as in a guard house, a meeting facility, or an administration office).

    Your future Administrator or a member of your transition team should visit the telephone company's office a week or two before the transfer to see whether there's any amount owing.

    The bill should be paid by the developer up to the date of the transfer.

    I've seen a situation where a condo was stuck with three months of unpaid phone bills that included long distance charges and calls to cell phones (in México, the caller pays when a call is placed to a cell phone number).

You also need to check to see if you need a new contract. Often the old contract will be in the name of the development company (for example, "*Desarrollo Vista del Basurero S.A. de C.V.*"), and it needs to be changed to your condo ("*Condominio Vista del Basurero*").

- **Electricity**: your team should visit the local CFE (*Comisión Federal de Electricidad*) office to see if there's any amount owing – you can easily be left with an unpaid bill going back months.

  Note that CFE bills typically cover a two month period, and are usually sent out in each even-numbered month.

  Again, check to see if you need a new contract (most likely). There's usually a small charge for this.

- **Water**: if your condo is on municipal water (you don't have your own well), then you also need to make sure that you don't get stiffed here.

  Back charges for water can be much more significant than telephone or electricity, and it's vital that you make sure that all these are taken care of before the transfer.

  The way it's often **supposed** to work is this:

  > At first, the developer is responsible for paying for all water. During construction, this should be minimal.

  > As soon as water is functional on the common property, the developer should report this fact to the water utility.

For example, if you have a common pool, and the water is connected and operational **even though the pool is still under construction**, then the date of this working connection is the date that water was available for use on the common property.

From that point on, the developer is responsible for paying the common property water bill. This will be based on a formula that looks at the percentage of the common property that's garden (these need watering – roads don't), and there will be a big bump if you have a pool.

The developer is also responsible for paying the water bills on finished, but unsold, units.

As each unit is sold, the developer is supposed to let the water utility know about the date of the sale and the percentage rights of the common property belonging to the unit.

From that point on, the new owner is responsible for the water bill for his unit **plus their percentage of the common property water bill**.

The developer continues to pay for unsold units and the unsold percentage of the common property water, which will gradually decrease until all units are sold.

As you can see, this needs a lot of organisation, record keeping, and communication with the water utility. It'll probably come as no surprise then, that a lot of this often falls between the cracks – especially when the developer is concentrating on finishing the condo.

In some cases, you might find that the water utility is unaware of some combination of the following:

- the date when the common property water had a working connection;
- the dates when each individual unit was sold; and
- the percentage rights of each individual unit.

This can be quite a mess, and, when finally straightened out, can result in a large unpaid water bill (several thousands of pesos isn't uncommon). You want to be sure that this is sorted, and any unpaid balance is paid by the developer, before the transfer.

You'll also likely need to set up new contracts with the water utility.

You should also be aware that this process might trigger some back charges for water for some owners as well. If this happens, they might try to get compensation from the developer – this is easier to do **before** the transfer. However, **don't involve the transition team in this**.

An alternative arrangement is for each unit to pay their own water bill, and the condo to pay the water for the common property only. There are pros and cons with both approaches. Also, your local water utility may only offer one choice.

The water utility will probably send around a team to check the common property and some of the units.

Some local water utilities base their charges on a formula (rather than a meter) involving: area of garden, whether a pool exists, number of bedrooms, and number of bathrooms. Not all of these apply to any given unit or the common property.

If you believe that this formula model will result in an overcharge for your situation, then you can ask that they install a water meter.

You'll then be charged based on actual usage, rather than the formula. There will be a charge for the meter and its installation (likely around $1,000 pesos).

- **LP gas**: there could be a propane tank belonging to the common areas – for example, if you have a communal BBQ or a heated Jacuzzi.

  Your transition team should try to get the developer to fill this tank just before the transfer. Failing this, you need to know its present level, how often it usually needs to be filled, and the typical cost of a fill (you should be able to get this information from the developer). You'll need this information for your first budget.

- **Misc. outside utilities**: there may be other utilities providing services to your condo – for example, a local cable TV provider.

  These bills should be paid by the developer up to the date of the transfer. You also need to check to see if you need a new contract.

Make Sure There Are Reserve Funds

The condo legislation requires that your condominium has reserve funds (**Article 1026**). There's no set level, and, without a reserve study, it's impossible to properly work out the amount needed for your particular condo.

After negotiating all the construction repairs, the payment of unpaid contracts, utilities, and other bills, have your transition team try to negotiate a transfer of cash equal to a reasonable starting reserve balance. Gently remind the developer that this is a legal requirement.

Check your by-laws to see if a specific reserve level has been set out. If not, and since it's extremely unlikely that the developer will have carried out a Reserve Study, use 25% of your estimated total yearly condo expenses as a reasonable starting point. If you don't have a handle on the expected yearly expenses (and you should by now), use four month's total condo fees (this is higher than 25% because the existing fees are likely too low).

Your First Owner-Administration

As soon as your first owner-based Council is appointed at an ordinary assembly, and an Administrator of the owners' choosing has been appointed, the transfer has taken place.

Unlike some legislation north of the border, there's no requirement for the developer to be represented on the Council. If there are unsold units, you can choose to do this as a courtesy and a means of working cooperatively, but there is no legal requirement.

Jalisco Condo Manual **501**

PART 19 – Effective Communications

Communications from Owners

Chapter 53

This section of my book is a bit of a departure in that none of these procedures is mandated by the condo legislation. It's been my experience, however, that one of the biggest sources of owner dissatisfaction in a condo is **poor communication**. This chapter and the next contain recommendations that will help you avoid these problems.

The fundamental philosophy of this chapter is:

> *When your Administrative Council or Administrator receives a communication from an owner, it must be responded to and dealt with quickly. Once the issue has been resolved, the resolution of the problem must be communicated right away to the owner.*

I strongly recommend that you appoint one person on your Council to be responsible for communications, and that all communications be funnelled through this individual.

Written Communications

If a communication is received from an owner in writing by email or letter, then the person receiving the communication must forward it right away to the President/Chair, Secretary, or whomever your Council has appointed as being responsible for communications (assuming this person hasn't already received a copy). They should not reply to the owner themselves – they should hear only one voice from your administration.

The communications person must then do the following:

1. Confirm receipt of the letter right away to the owner who sent it, and assure them that the Council will look into their concerns as soon as possible.

This response should be sent to the owner in the same format as it was received (email or letter). A copy must also be forwarded to all councillors and to your Administrator along with a copy of the owner's original email or letter.

2. Keep the owner updated on the status of the issue. For example, you might say, *"... your concern was discussed at last week's council meeting, and the Administrator is doing some research. He's expected to have a report in about two weeks ..."*.

3. Let the owner know what the final resolution of the issue is; if this impacts the community as a whole, or is of general interest, send an email to all owners.

Verbal Communications

Avoid verbal communications – they're untraceable!

If an owner's issue is brought up in conversation, and if the issue can't be resolved in this conversation, then the person receiving the call or speaking with the owner must ask this owner to send their comments/questions to the Council and your Administrator in writing.

If they're unwilling to do this, then the member of the administration who was a party to this conversation must document the issue and send it right away in writing to the President, Secretary, or your Council's appointed communications person (assuming they weren't the one who received the call), and send a copy to the owner.

> Be careful about deciding whether a verbal communication from an owner "has merit" before passing it on.
>
> An issue that might seem insignificant to you, is always important to the person bringing it up. Most people don't raise an issue unless they feel it has some importance, so be careful about dismissing an owner's concerns.
>
> Remember, **the owners are the supreme authority in your condominium**, and every owner has a right to bring an issue before your Council.

The communications person must then do the following:

1. Confirm receipt of the owner's issue right away **in writing** (email is generally used), and assure them that the Council will look into it as soon as possible. This response should contain a brief summary of the current understanding of the owner's issues.

2. Send a copy of the response along with the original submission to all councillors and your Administrator.

3. As with a written communication, keep the owner updated on the status of the issue, and let them know the final outcome. Again, if it impacts the community, or is of general interest, send an email to all owners.

Internal Communications

Chapter
54

Communication problems aren't confined to communications to and from owners. Many condos also suffer from poor internal communication amongst the Administrative Council, Administrator, and the committees.

It's important that each member of your condo administration follows one simple rule:

> *When a Councillor (or your Administrator) receives a communication from another member of your administration, if it's only been sent to some of the administration, and it concerns the condo, they must forward it right away to the rest of the administration (including your Administrator).*

A similar procedure should be followed by committee members for communications amongst themselves.

It's vital to avoid side conversations inside your administration or a committee on issues that involve condo or committee business, but which don't include all the members of the administration or the committee.

Since most internal communication these days is typically by email, it's easy to create a group in your email program that contains all councillors plus your Administrator, or all members of your committee. This way no one can be accidentally left off the email distribution.

You should also take advantage of an important feature of email. Each response on a subject should keep the email message chain by including the previous emails in the body of the reply. This message chain must be sent to the entire administration or committee by **always** using "Reply To All" rather than "Reply" or "Reply To Sender Only".

When replying to an email, your reply must always be sent to at least the group of people who received the email to which you're replying, unless there's a necessary reason not to.

If a person replying to an email notices that one or more members are missing from the email distribution, then they must add them at once.

Remember that administering a condo is both a public and cooperative process. There's no reason for individual members of your administration to be discussing issues that affect your condominium without including the entire administration (your Administrator and all councillors) in the conversation.

This is also true for committees – any discussion related to a committee's work must include all committee members.

It's imperative that you avoid forming cliques or "inner circles" – this is neither effective nor ethical condo administration.

Tips for Effective Communications

Chapter 55

This chapter contains recommendations for simple techniques you can use to enhance communications between your administration and the community to help foster a stronger sense of community and inclusion.

You can use this material to develop your own communications plan.

Send Out Council Meeting Minutes

Email the minutes of each council meeting to all owners shortly after the meeting, and post them on your condo web site. Include all the attachments.

This complies with **Code Article 1017 V** that says your Administrative Council must carry out its administration under observance by the owners. It's a simple way of letting owners (particularly absentee owners) know what's happening, and what actions your Council is taking. For more details **see Chapter 15 – "What Are the Duties of the Council?"** and **Chapter 17 – "Your Council Must Always be Open and Transparent."**

Send Out Council Decisions and Condo Policies

Once your Council has made a decision on an issue affecting the community, or if a policy has been created or changed, let the owners know by sending out a copy of the policy or notice of the decision and posting it on your condo web site.

Don't rely on the council minutes for this! Most owners won't pick up on a policy change that's buried in the council minutes.

Send Out Quarterly Financial Reports

The condo law only requires that the administrator give a quarterly financial report to any owner **who asks for it**.

I strongly urge you, however, to be proactive and inclusive by emailing the quarterly financial reports to all owners when they're ready. You should also post them on your condo's web site.

Send Out Committee Status Reports

Either the Council or each committee chair must send out a brief status report about each committee's work – if they've changed or created policies, or if they've started or finished a project. If work on a project is under way, and it's a long-term project, then just report on the status periodically so that people know that something is happening, and they don't feel "out of the loop."

Publish a Condo Directory (Contact Sheet)

Have someone volunteer to create and keep up a directory-style contact list for your condominium, and to send it to all owners. This should also be posted on your condo web site.

By making one person responsible, it's much more likely to be kept up to date than if the responsibility is unclear (in my experience when it's left that "someone should update the contact list," "someone" seldom gets much of anything done).

It should contain:

- names of each owner, and names of tenants if applicable (it definitely should include long-term tenants);
- the telephone number and email for each owner and tenant;
- emergency contact information; and
- important phone numbers such as the security guards, ambulance, police, or fire.

It must be updated and re-sent shortly after any significant changes (owners or tenants change, phone numbers or emails change, or emergency contacts change). If no changes have been made for, say, three months, then send it out again anyway.

Consider a Condo Newsletter

Consider producing a regular monthly or quarterly newsletter, but **only do this if you have the volunteers and resources to keep it up**.

If only one issue is ever produced, or if it's sent out randomly and sporadically, then you're probably better off **not** doing a newsletter.

Have a Condo Web Site

A web site is arguably the most powerful communications and administrative tool that you can use, and it solves a wide range of communications issues.

It allows all members of the community a way of instantly accessing:

- latest news on events and condo activities;
- schedule information for common area facilities such as a party room or BBQ area; it's even possible to let them book the facility using the web site;
- latest versions of condo policies, rules, instructions, and by-laws; no one can say they have an old version, and you don't have to keep track of who has what;
- council and committee minutes and news;
- latest financial information and reports, including budgets and fees;

- current contact directory, list of councillors, and committee lists; and
- latest and past newsletters.

Create a Welcome Pack

A few days after a new owner or tenant moves in, a Council representative or a member of a Welcome Committee should introduce themselves, welcome the new resident to your condo, and present them with a welcome pack.

This pack should include, at a minimum:

- a welcome letter from the President/Chair of your Council;
- a guide outlining important concepts of life in a condo, particularly the ins and outs of assemblies; don't assume that new owners know anything about condominium living; a sample *"Condo FAQ for New Owners"* is included in your BONUS Pack;
- a copy of the current by-laws (the legal Spanish by-laws plus a good English translation – this last must be clearly marked *"for information only"*) along with any other condo rules and policies;
- information on condo procedures; for example, the gate is always locked during certain hours, or there's a communal mail drop at the security office;
- the latest budget, including the fees (owners only);
- the latest condo contact sheet;
- a list showing who your Councillors are as well as each committee and its membership;

- copies of council and assembly minutes for the current year to date (owners only);
- copies of Quarterly Financial Reports for the current year to date (owners only);
- copies of the current year's newsletters (if any):
- login instructions for your condo web site (if any); and
- consider a small welcome gift (cookies, a plant, etc.)

If your condo has a web site, then much of this pack might seem unnecessary. It's always a good idea, however, to officially welcome new owners or tenants in person, and to give them hard copies of some of these documents.

Be sure to show them the web site, and how it works – including helping them with logging in for the first time.

PART 20 – Resolving Disputes and Conflicts

Dealing With Complaints

Chapter **56**

It's a fact of life in a condo that complaints will arise. Complaints fall under a number of categories, which are discussed in this chapter along with recommended techniques for dealing with them.

Complaints About Your Condo's Administration

It's impossible to please everyone, and you'll inevitably hear from those whom your actions have displeased. Unfortunately, there are as many different forms and types of these complaints as there are issues that come up in your condo.

I'll cover two broad categories of complaint style, along with some tips for dealing with them:

- **Complaints couched in an abusive or insulting tone**: some people seem to become incensed over an issue, even a seemingly small one, and choose to deal with it in a way similar to "road rage."

    You may receive a written communication that doesn't just lay out the complaint, but goes as far as insulting or attacking your Administrator, your Council, or individual councillors. Sometimes the language can be abusive or even profane.

    Worse, one of these individuals might show up at a council meeting, and berate the Council in person.

    While these are clearly people with immature emotional responses, they're members of the community and they must be dealt with.

    The first step is to get them to tone down their destructive emotional outbursts and rhetoric, and deal with the issues in a rational way.

Your reaction **must** be calm and professional. While this is an easy thing to say, it's definitely not so easy to do.

You have to let this person own the anger and emotion, and not take it on yourself. If you have a personality that naturally reacts when attacked, this could take some work to bring about – the results will be worthwhile, however.

If the complaint arrived in writing, wait until the next day to respond – both you and the complainer will be cooler and more rational.

If the person is present at the council meeting, you may need to raise your voice at first to gain control of the situation. This is fine, but don't catch their anger – it can be contagious.

Your response to this person should be short, polite, and professional. **Do not engage them!**

Tell them that the Administrative Council doesn't respond to abusive, insulting, or demeaning behaviour (choose a suitable adjective), and the Council isn't prepared to talk about their concerns until they rephrase their issue without the offensive language.

It can't hurt to remind this person that you're all unpaid volunteers doing your best at a difficult job. You're not perfect, and you're willing to fix any mistakes you've made. However, insults and abuse are unacceptable, and as long as they continue, the issue will be ignored.

Stop there! Don't deal with or engage this individual any further until they change their attitude.

Hopefully, their next step will be to resend their complaint in a rational and calmer way, and then it can be dealt with like any other.

If they persist with an abusive attitude, **refuse to respond further**. They'll usually change their tactics when they discover that their approach isn't getting them anywhere.

- **Reasonable complaints about the Council's actions or inactions**: these are complaints that are couched in rational terms without abuse. They spell out the owner's problem – or try to.

The first step is to make sure that you understand the issue, and that you have all the facts. Carefully examine and investigate the owner's complaint, and don't be afraid to ask the owner for more information. Be certain that the "facts" are accurate and true.

It's important to follow the rules I've already set out for dealing with owner communications (**see Chapter 53 – "Communications from Owners"**): respond to the complaint, tell them how you plan to go ahead, keep them up to date on the progress, and let them know the result.

If the topic is to be discussed at a council meeting, let them know this, and give them the opportunity to be there. The important thing is to **deal with complaints as soon as possible** – no one likes to be ignored.

Always deal with these issues in a calm and professional way. Their nature can range from critical to bordering on petty. It doesn't matter. The issue is important to the owner who brought it up, and it must be dealt with reasonably. **Never dismiss an owner's concerns as trivial or unimportant.**

Complaints About an Owner

Owners will often complain to the Council about a perceived "violation" of your by-laws by another owner. **It is important that these complaints be received in writing** – or else your Council shouldn't act on them. Your Council must then see if:

1. <u>**The parties have tried to resolve this between themselves**</u>: they must have done this and failed before your Council should consider the complaint.

2. <u>**A by-law or rule preventing the other owner's actions exists**</u>: you would be surprised at how often an owner assumes that there's a rule forbidding something, when there isn't. Sometimes the administration makes a similar wrong assumption. **Don't assume** – check your by-laws and rules.

3. <u>**The violation actually took place**</u>: don't be caught off-guard by human nature – an owner can be convinced that their neighbour's cat is ruining their garden, when it can turn out to be a stray or a racoon. Always investigate, and insist on reasonable proof before accusing anyone of anything.

It's wise to have a procedure for responding to by-law and rule infractions. Here are some important strategies:

- The single most important guideline is to apply the rules fairly, equitably, and consistently. The rules must apply to the entire community, and everyone who breaks them must be sanctioned equally (including friends of councillors and, especially, councillors themselves).

- If there's been a reported violation of the rules, then your Administrative Council **must** act, and they must act as soon as possible.

If any individual isn't following the rules, it affects the entire condominium.

Your Council must not be seen as being lax in enforcement.

- Once your Council decides to deal with a violation, then they must send a notice to the violator right away. This notice must include the specifics of the violation, and must cite the specific by-law or rule that's being violated.

The notice of violation must also contain the expected corrective action – this could range from stopping a particular behaviour, to removing an offensive item, to repairing damage.

If there are any penalties or sanctions that are being charged, or that may be charged if the violation is repeated (these penalties **must** exist in the by-laws), then these must also be spelled out.

> While penalties and sanctions are a valuable compliance tool, they should be carefully considered.
>
> Except for serious infractions, penalties and sanctions should be reserved for at least the second repeat of the offense.
>
> Many times an owner will violate a rule or by-law through ignorance. In this case, they're usually more than happy to fix the problem, and won't repeat their actions.

The violation notice should finish with an invitation from the Council to the owner to schedule a hearing if they feel that they shouldn't comply. This hearing can be either a special or regular council meeting.

If the violation involves a renter, then the owner of the unit must also be notified.

A sample Notice of By-law Violation is included in your BONUS Pack.

- If a hearing is held, then the first step is to announce the facts as the Council sees them – a repetition of the violation notice.

  The owner must then be allowed to present a defence.

  Councillors can then engage in a question and answer session to get more information, and discover the owner's point of view.

  The Council must then discuss the matter and make a ruling. The result must be documented in writing and sent to the violating owner. Informing the violator verbally at the hearing isn't enough.

> If the complaint turns out not to be a violation of your by-laws, but just a dispute between neighbours, then your Council is required to mediate between the two parties (**Article 1031**).
>
> I've given you detailed procedures for mediating disputes in the next chapter on **"Dispute Resolution."**

- Whatever the process and ultimate result, the owner who made the complaint must receive a confirmation that the complaint is being investigated, and be told of your Council's actions, progress, and the result.

By-law Violations Discovered by the Administration

Sometimes a violation of the rules is uncovered by a member of your administration, rather than through an owner complaint.

Dealing With Complaints

Each member of the administration has a duty to report significant violations of your condo's by-laws and rules to your Council on discovering them.

While no one likes to be a whistle-blower or feel they're acting like the "condo police," it's both your duty and obligation to the community.

Once your Administrator or a councillor has reported a rule violation to your Council, then the Council must go ahead in the same way as if the violation were reported by an owner.

Dispute Resolution

Chapter 57

Disputes arise between neighbours living anywhere. In condos, however, they can sometimes take on another dimension.

Mediation Is Better Than Court

For condos in most countries, mediation is the preferred method of dispute resolution, and should be used instead of lengthy and costly court cases.

This is also true in México.

Your Council Must Arbitrate Owner Disputes

Code Article 1031 says that disputes between owners must be dealt with by your Administrative Council using arbitration. If this fails, the owners can then use the courts.

This isn't uncommon in condos north of the border as well, and is usually called **IDR** (Internal Dispute Resolution). It's effective, and can help avoid a simple issue escalating into the Hatfields and McCoys.

Article 1006 requires that your dispute resolution procedures must be in your by-laws.

Four-Stage Resolution Process

I recommend that you add two more stages of dispute resolution to your by-laws than those contained in the condo law. You'll end up with a four-tier dispute resolution system:

1. Before asking the Council to arbitrate, require the owners to talk to each other and try to reach an agreement between themselves.

While this might seem obvious, you'd be amazed at how many people don't want to talk to their neighbour, and equally amazed at how often this is all it takes to resolve a situation.

2. If the owners fail to reach an agreement between themselves, then your Council is legally required to mediate.

3. If Council arbitration fails, encourage the owners to seek **ADR** (Alternative Dispute Resolution) using an *abogado* (Mexican lawyer) licensed to do this. Although this seems like a duplication of effort, your Council (well-meaning though they may be) aren't professionally trained mediators.

   The agreements reached with the abogado are legally binding.

4. If all this fails, then the two owners can choose to go to court.

Council-Led Mediation (Internal Resolution)

Unless you have a retired mediator on your Council, councillors aren't usually trained mediators.

The single most important mistake to avoid, is to try to mediate by committee. Mediation is only effective with a single mediator.

Have your Council appoint the councillor who's most able to stay calm, and allow this person to mediate alone. There's also nothing preventing your Council from appointing someone who isn't on the Council to mediate (this must be in the minutes of a council meeting).

In either case, make sure that this person has no personal interest in the dispute or with the parties involved.

If they like, the rest of the Council can observe – **but they must keep silent, and not interfere with the process.**

Internal Resolution: Overview

Since most volunteer councillors have likely never carried out a mediation session before, I'll go over the basics step-by-step.

Entire books have been written on the finer points of mediation, so this chapter isn't intended as a complete course on the subject!

Internal Resolution: Step 1 - Gather Information

Before you can start mediating a dispute between two parties, you must have a clear understanding of exactly what the dispute is, and what the positions of each party are. Each party must have expressed their feelings about the issues – **and these expressions of feelings must have been heard by the other party**.

1. <u>**Interview both parties together**</u>: always interview the two parties together. Separate interviews are time-consuming, each party is more likely to distort or exaggerate the issues if the other party isn't present, and the mediator can be more easily swayed by persuasive tactics.

    As well, if you interview the two parties separately, they can get the impression that you're going to decide what action will be taken (this is **not** the goal of mediation). However, talking to the parties in each other's presence allows them to solve their own problems through guided discussion (**this** is mediation).

    During your interviews, it's important to draw out the details of exactly how each of them views the problem – there'll be two quite different perspectives. If either party feels that they've not been able to tell their story fully, they'll become frustrated and likely won't follow the resolution plan.

2. **Don't provoke either party**: avoid questions that might provoke either party – your goal is to find out how each party sees the conflict. Say something like, *"Tell me, in your own words, what happened,"* then just listen and make notes. Don't make any comments – these might only serve to add fuel to the fire.

3. **Keep the situation under control**: when one party listens to the other tell their side of the story, it's human nature for them to start to feel angry again. This can also apply to the party who's telling their story.

   Angry people tend to forget their manners, and are likely to interrupt to "correct" the other's version of events.

   If this happens, you must be prepared to control the situation by using any of the following techniques:

   - **Set out the ground rules at the beginning**: start by introducing yourself (if they don't both know you), give an overview of the process, and then say firmly something like, *"For this to work, I expect you both to follow my instructions."* Next, lay down the basic ground rules by saying something like,

     > *"I'm going to start by getting some information about how each of you sees your problem. I'll do this by talking to you one at a time. I'll start with XXXs view of the situation, and then I'll ask YYY how he sees it. Here are the ground rules. PAUSE When one of you is speaking, the other must not interrupt. Don't speak to each other, only to me – just like on Judge Judy!"*

     Both parties now know that if they interrupt or argue, they'll be breaking your rules.

You're now ready to have each party tell you their side of the story. While one is talking, the other must be listening in silence. This is important, because if you allow the parties to talk to each other, they'll most likely start arguing – things will then get out of hand quickly. Again, think "Judge Judy."

- **Create a physical barrier**: always sit between the two parties so that if they do start to argue, you can just lean forward to block their view of each another – this simple action will redirect their statements to you.

- **Use nonthreatening gestures**: avoid shaking or pointing your finger – this is aggressive, and can antagonise either or both parties.

  If you want to encourage one party to talk to you, hold your hand palm upward, fingers pointing toward the person, and bend your fingers towards you a few times (like a "come to me" gesture).

  If you want to stop a party who's interrupting, hold your hand palm down, fingers pointing towards the interrupter, and move your hand up and down a few times (like a "tone it down" gesture). Try to do this without breaking eye contact with the party who is supposed to be speaking. If need be, face the interrupter, and use the palm-down gesture along with a brief restatement of the ground rules.

- **Make sure you have room to intensify your authority**: if you start out with a strong show of authority (for example, by raising your voice), you have nowhere to go – it can be difficult to back down.

Instead, start with a gentle, but firm, manner and gradually increase the intensity of your voice, words, and gestures as the situation warrants it.

4. **Keep both parties on topic**: if one party gets sidetracked from giving their perspective on the problem (such as by repeating other people's opinions or views), get them back on topic by interrupting them, and saying something like, "*We're not interested in XXXs views. What's the problem as you see it?*" You can also interrupt by summarising what they've already said about how they see the problem.

   Sometimes the parties can have many unresolved conflicts. Your job is to try to keep the focus on just one problem – the most current one. If you can get a successful result in this one area, it might encourage the parties to work towards resolving their other problems.

5. **Focus on the situation as it is right now**: try to keep a here-and-now focus, and avoid accounts of earlier conflicts. You can try saying something like, "*That's water under the bridge. What's done is done. What's the situation right now?*"

6. **Stay impartial**: it's vital that you don't comment on the problem, or offer your opinions. This could lead one or both parties to feel cornered, judged, or that they're on the wrong side of favouritism. When one party feels backed into a corner by both the other party and yourself, they will likely become defensive.

   Don't even **appear** to agree with either party. The moment you do this, you're implicitly disagreeing with the other – you've just chosen sides. That said, you should fully expect both parties to try to get you to agree with them – just be careful to avoid falling into this trap.

You must also avoid offering any reassurance or sympathy to either party. As innocent as these actions may seem, they can be interpreted as a vote of confidence for one party's position over the other.

Your effectiveness as a mediator depends on your absolute impartiality.

7. **<u>Never make a judgement or carry out an "investigation"</u>**: here's where we diverge from the "Judge Judy" model – a mediator isn't a judge. Nor are you a detective trying to figure out which story is "true."

   The important thing to remember is that **it isn't necessary to discover the truth of the situation to resolve the conflict**. However, it's crucial for each party to hear how the other party perceives the problem.

   When making decisions, people always act based on their perceptions – right or wrong. When you question or express judgemental opinions about someone's story, you're contradicting their perception of the dispute. Once people feel judged, they start to edit out the parts of their story that they believe might make them look bad. They'll also start to exaggerate aspects they believe will make them look good. This is counter-productive to the goal of mediation.

8. **<u>Get specific information</u>**: the more you narrow the problem down to specifics, the better. The risk of reaching a wrong solution can be minimised by focusing only on facts: *"What did XXX do?", "What did he say?", "When and where did this happen?"*

9. **Accept each party's perception of the situation**: this is an essential point. While your interview questions do have the goal of clarifying the problem, and of gathering information, you must **never** question the validity of a party's perceptions. It's essential that perceptions be brought out so that each party hears how the other see the problem.

10. **Encourage both parties to express their feelings**: sometimes in an effort to avoid looking immature or petty, one or both parties may try to cover up their feelings. As a result, they might not succeed in fully describing their issues.

    When someone's feelings are ignored, the problem solving process can suffer. Even if the original problem appears to have been resolved, frustration or resentment can affect future interactions between the parties.

11. **Summarise often**: it's an important part of the process that both parties hear how the other side views the problem. When you think you understand their story, summarise what they've said by saying something like, "OK ... *my understanding of the issues as you see them, is...*".

    Once the first party agrees with your summary, you can start to interview the next party. You may need to repeat this step before you can move on to the next party.

    Make sure that you've summarised both stories, and that they both agree with your summarisation, before starting Step 2.

Internal Resolution: Step 2 - Get Specific Suggestions

After you've summarized both party's stories, turn to one of them and ask for a suggested solution by saying something like, "*How do you suggest we solve this?*"

Don't be discouraged if this is met with something like, *"I don't see a solution."* Ask once more for a suggestion, perhaps a bit more firmly. If you still don't get some sort of suggestion after two or three tries, turn to the other party and repeat the question.

1. **Don't offer suggestions yourself**: it's natural for the parties to try to shift responsibility to you by asking for your suggestion. Ignore this, and firmly repeat your invitation for a suggestion from one of them.

    The moment you offer a suggestion, you become responsible for solving the problem – this isn't the role of a mediator. People are much more likely to follow through on their own suggestion than on one which has been set out by a third-party.

2. **Draw out concrete suggestions**: find out what specific change is needed to resolve the issue. Suggestions such as *"I want her to stop annoying me!"* aren't workable because this is far too vague.

    Only a specific change can be turned into an agreement. When specifics are used, both parties know **exactly** what each has agreed to do. This also puts pressure on them, because a party who doesn't follow through looks bad.

3. **Don't analyse the suggestions**: occasionally one or both parties might offer a nonsensical or extreme suggestion. Just as in brainstorming, accept these suggestions, and ignore that they might be unreasonable.

    If you comment on the validity of the suggestion, you destroy your impartiality and lessen the chances of a successful mediation. Leave evaluation of a ridiculous suggestion to the other party, who just won't agree to it.

Once you get a specific suggestion from one party, propose it to the other party. Edit the suggestion by eliminating insulting or judgmental language from it before repeating it to the other party.

For example, *"Tell the jerk to get off his ass and clean up the s**t in front of his house!"*, should be restated to the other party as *"Bob suggests that you clean up the mess in front of your house. What do you think of that?"*

If the suggestion is rejected, ask for a different suggestion from the party who rejected it, *"Then what do you suggest instead?"* Once you get this suggestion, take it back to the first party and get their opinion.

Continue this back-and-forth until the parties arrive at an agreement.

Internal Resolution: Step 3 - Get an Agreement

Mediation must end with a clear statement specifying what each party has agreed to do.

Summarise the resolution to the problem, and get a final agreement from both parties.

Put this in writing as an agreement. Have both parties and yourself sign it. A signed written agreement is much more likely to be followed than a verbal one.

Internal Resolution: Step 4 - Follow-Up

Your job as mediator does not end with the signed agreement!

1. **Have follow-up sessions**: if you carry out one or more follow-up sessions, you're more likely to succeed. This is because the parties will then have to account for any of the ways they didn't keep to the agreement.

These follow-up meetings can also give both parties an opportunity to renegotiate the agreement if it turns out to be unworkable.

2. **Reward small changes in behaviour**: during your follow-up, look for ways where either party is living up to the agreement, and specifically reinforce these in a positive way.

   Remember that it's difficult for people to change. It's important to help them by giving positive reinforcement of any change – no matter how small it might seem.

Lawyer-Led Mediation (External Resolution)

Recent changes in Mexican state laws have created an effective mediation process designed specifically to avoid the cost and time involved in going to court.

- As of 2006, 22 Mexican states have created mediation laws, built mediation centres, and trained mediators (normally an *abogado*) in most municipalities.

- Because this is court-annexed mediation, agreements reached have the weight of court orders, and are enforceable under Mexican law. The state of Jalisco has now adopted this strategy.

I recommend that you find a local *abogado* who's been trained and certified in this new state mediation process.

Most of them will give an initial consultation with both parties (usually half an hour to an hour) to assess the situation, get an overview of both sides, and present a plan to continue.

The subsequent mediation session will then hammer out a legally binding agreement at a significantly cheaper cost than a lawsuit.

Dealing With People

Chapter 58

When you live in a condo, you have to deal with your neighbours much more than if you lived in a single-family house or a non-condo apartment. This is especially true if you're part of your condo's administration.

It's All About Attitude

Yes, some people are difficult by nature. That said, this can be magnified by your attitude in dealing with them. You can't control how they behave, but you **can** control your own actions and reactions.

What Are Difficult People?

What exactly makes a person *"difficult"*? Is it really their actions, or is it just that they disagree with you?

It's hard work to overcome human nature, but that may be the best way to get along with others.

It's important to differentiate between genuinely *"difficult people,"* and those who are just detail-oriented, hard-working, inquisitive, or strong-willed. It can be a fine line, and these people shouldn't be discouraged.

As I've said earlier, there are some people who have an abusive or combative personality. This is a different matter entirely, and this behaviour must not be tolerated. I've given you tips on how to deal with this in **Chapter 56 – "Dealing With Complaints."**

Once this type of person realises that they're not getting anywhere, and they adopt a new attitude (maybe still not ideal, but no longer abusive), then you must listen to them and you must treat them the way you would anyone else – they've turned a page, and now you must too.

When you work with others in a condominium setting, whether they're owners or members of your administration, it's important to try to resist the urge (this is a human need) to label them (*"disgruntled," "grouchy," "slow on the uptake,"* or *"trouble maker"*).

Once you mentally label someone, this label will cause you to treat them differently. As a result, you'll tend to prejudge everything they say, or, worse, tune them out completely, and you could easily miss the real point of their argument – perhaps a valid and important one.

If, in spite of your feelings about this person, you try to listen and give them the benefit of the doubt, you might find that they have something to contribute.

The bottom line is that you need to always try to treat everyone equally, fairly, and respectfully.

This is particularly true when dealing with *"demanding"* owners. In condos, inconsistent treatment of owners (particularly enforcement of by-laws) is one of the number one causes of owner dissatisfaction – along with poor communications.

Even if someone is a genuinely difficult individual, they must be treated consistently.

The Administration's Perceptions of Owners

Some councillors fear dealing directly with owners because they feel that most owners who speak out only do so to voice a complaint. As a result, they may become defensive or tune out owners' comments at a council meeting.

The first thing that all councillors must realise is that the condo legislation requires council meetings be open to the owners.

Since owners must be invited to your meetings, you need to accept their being there as a fact of life. Treat this as a positive, and develop techniques for dealing with them.

As a councillor, you need to adopt the attitude that:

- there are, and always will be, legitimate problems in your condo;
- you're not perfect, you make mistakes, and you may have caused the problem;
- it's your job to look into and solve these problems; and
- problem solving can be a positive (and fun) activity, if you choose to make it so.

If you listen carefully to an owner who's bringing up an issue, you may find that they're not just complaining, but that they may be suggesting a solution (constructive criticism). If they don't volunteer one, you should **always** ask them what they suggest you do to resolve the matter. This simple technique can give useful input into the Council's discussions surrounding the issue.

Then, even if you cannot resolve the owner's issue, by having listened, recognized their issue, and responded (even if it was only to say that there's nothing you can do – **and why**), the owner will at least feel that they've been heard, and that the Administrative Council is responsive.

If it's clear that your Council or Administrator has made a mistake, own up to it, apologise, and try to fix it. Don't try to cover it up, or pretend it never happened – think how you react when politicians and governments do this. **Don't lie under any circumstances!**

Although allowing owners to come to council meetings is a legal requirement, there's no need to view it as some sort of burden.

If you think about it, the presence of owners at council and committee meetings has many positive benefits for both the administration and the community:

- it gives the owners an opportunity to meet, become familiar with, and address their Administrative Council;

- when an owner is allowed to air their complaint, it has the effect of nipping it in the bud before it grows into a bigger, and bigger issue;

- it might introduce the Council to a new problem or issue they didn't know existed;

- it presents the Council with the opportunity to hear new viewpoints; it's easy to get bogged down in one way of looking at an issue – a fresh voice can often break a log jam;

- it lets the Council know what the owners' concerns are, what they're thinking, and what kind of issues, rumours, or misconceptions might be circulating amongst the owners; and

- it's an opportunity for the Council to meet and assess the owners who actively participate for future recruitment (such as to the next Council or a committee).

The Owners' Perceptions of the Administration

Perception works both ways.

If a group of owners forms to promote a cause, and one or more of this group has labelled any or all your Councillors or your Administrator as being unreasonable, difficult, arrogant, or incompetent, then the others in the group may take on these beliefs.

This can happen even though they have no personal experience with the administration, or **even if there's no basis** for the label.

These preconceived opinions can range from simple misperceptions, to deliberate misinformation. They can prevent this group and your Council from working together effectively.

This can be amplified, and become much more serious, if one or more group members circulate these opinions publicly to all owners.

The reasons for someone doing this can range from innocently repeating misinformation (without trying to verify it), all the way to malicious intent – generally to further a personal agenda.

These perceptions can be difficult to change – it's human nature to want to believe the *"oppressed little guy"* over the *"evil power structure."*

If this seems to be going on, then your Council should meet with the group to talk about and repair their differences for the good of your condo. This must not turn into a battle. The goal must be to turn around faulty impressions, and to find common ground to work together to solve whatever issue the group has.

The best way to keep this from happening in the first place is to make sure that you always carry out your condo's business in an open and consultative way, with good and frequent communications to the owners.

Character Assassination

Unfortunately, the dark side of being part of a condo administration is when people turn ugly. Passions can run high in a condo, and some owners might resort to "dirty tricks" to have their agendas carried out.

The worst of these tactics is when misinformation is circulated deliberately. When it's aimed at one individual, it's called *"character assassination."*

It can be devastating for the person under attack, and is almost impossible to defend against. It can result in not only a loss of reputation, but also alienation from the community – or, more correctly, alienation of the individual by the community.

The larger and more political your condo is, and the more contentious its issues are, the more likely this is to happen.

It usually follows this pattern:

- one person communicates with all or a large group of owners;
- this communication starts with deliberate misinformation, and then continues to build seemingly reasonable complaints or accusations against the targeted individual based on the untrue premise;
- a few more people jump on the bandwagon, and repeat the founding lie, reinforcing it in everyone else's mind – if a lie is repeated often enough, it becomes the truth.

The misinformation is usually some combination of: double talk (language deliberately constructed to distort its actual meaning), rumour, innuendo (a remark that suggests something bad without directly saying it), or outright fabrication.

This technique can be highly effective when used to carry out the goal of either tarnishing the reputation of an individual, or to tarnish a claim or proposal that the targeted person is making (generally to further the attacker's personal agenda), or both.

This last goal is the most common, and it works well. If people believe that the target of the attack is offensive in some way, then they can be more easily convinced to view with suspicion, or outright objection, a proposition that the target is trying to present to the community.

Think of political attack ads – while unpopular, these are used more and more often because they really work.

Defending against a single baseless accusation is usually just a matter of publicly denying the allegation by presenting the facts – **this does not work with character assassination.**

There are two elements at play that make this tactic almost impossible to defend against:

1. the accusation is coming from more than one source (the attacker **plus** their supporters) – greatly enhancing the credibility of the attack in the minds of others; and

2. the attacker and their supporters are not interested in facts – they can easily answer anything offered in defence with more made up "evidence".

The person under attack winds up getting in deeper and deeper, and the more "evidence" that's circulated by the attackers, the more other people are convinced that the accusations must be true.

The majority of the community at large (whom the group is trying to influence) won't make any effort to verify these "facts," and is predisposed by human nature to believe the group over the individual.

The only defence sadly, is no defence – the person under attack must **let the matter drop**, without trying to deny the accusations in public. They must make absolutely no response.

This is as difficult and frustrating as it sounds (it's human nature to want to defend yourself when attacked), but, by not responding, any further disastrous public communications should stop because the dialogue isn't being kept up.

Remember, it's impossible to win a public debate with a group of people who are willing to make things up. If they're given the opportunity to continue their attacks, they'll simply make the person under attack look worse and worse.

The type of person who uses tactics like this is usually passionate to an extreme about their agenda.

There may be nothing you can do to prevent this. Just be aware that it can happen, and hope it doesn't happen to you.

If it happens to a member of your administration, then the rest of the administration must publicly back up the person being subjected to this – and do this right away.

If you see a series of public emails being sent out in your condo, and they have the earmarks of character assassination, don't blindly buy into them. Do some basic fact checking (it's usually not difficult – the perpetrators are counting on no one doing this). At an absolute minimum, you should **talk to the person under attack to see what their side of the story is.**

Don't Wash Your Dirty Linen in Public

No condo anywhere in the world runs smoothly, without problems or conflict. It's also human nature to complain to whoever is handy to listen.

It's important, however, for all owners (and especially members of your administration) to avoid complaining about internal condo problems to people outside of your condo.

In expat communities, gossip and rumours tend to spread like wildfire – often being embellished along the way.

Unfortunately, if the reputation of your condo becomes tarnished in the greater community, property values can suffer. Real estate agents may pass this "information" on to clients looking to buy, or, worse, might avoid showing apartments or houses in your condo.

All condo owners owe it to themselves and their neighbours to think before they speak! Remember, loose lips lower property values.

PART 21 – Dissolution of the Condo

Dissolving a Condo Regime

Chapter 59

Article 1034 of the condo law says that if disaster strikes (such as a major earthquake or tidal wave, a plane or meteor crashes into the complex, or a neighbourhood kid gets a chemistry set), and if the buildings making up your condominium are at least 75% destroyed (based on their current value), then any owner can ask that the common property be divided according to the general rules of co-ownership contained in the Civil Code.

These rules are in a different part of the Code (**Articles 961** through **1000**) from the condo legislation.

If the destruction isn't as serious as outlined above, then reconstruction can be decided by an extraordinary assembly.

If a resolution is passed to reconstruct the condo, then owners who are in the minority of this vote at the assembly are obligated to either contribute towards the reconstruction in proportion to their ownership rights, or to sell their rights to those in the majority.

The selling price will be based on an evaluation of the unit by an expert appraiser – this price can vary significantly from market real estate prices (often much lower).

These rules also apply if your condo becomes bankrupt, or if the buildings became unusable for some reason (for example, they become structurally unsound, and are condemned).

Article 1006 requires that procedures for the dissolution of your condominium regime must be in your by-laws.

FREE BONUS PACK!

Receive a FREE pack of sample documents & templates for your use – just by registering your book online!

Register your book purchase to claim your **FREE** collection of <u>over 50</u> sample documents & Word and Excel templates **worth $29.95** – more than 140 jam-packed pages – useful documents that you can adapt for use in your condominium.

Your instant download will contain the following proven sample documents and templates:

- assembly call notice samples & templates
- sample assembly materials
- proxy form sample & template
- voting spreadsheet & scrutineer instructions
- guide: *"Owner's Guide to Condo Assemblies"*
- guide: *"How to Chair a Condo Assembly"*
- sample assembly scripts
- assembly minutes samples & templates
- council & committee meeting notice, agenda, & minutes
- annual condo budget
- monthly Administrator's report
- notice of by-law violation
- collection letters with templates
- request for construction/renovation
- FAQ sheet for new residents
- and more . . .

Simply go to
registermybook.jaliscocondos.org
and fill in your book registration details –
your **FREE BONUS PACK** will then
be available as an **instant download**!

Appendix A - More Resources

JaliscoCondos.org Web Site

JaliscoCondos.org is committed to giving you the most comprehensive and accurate information about running a condo in the Mexican state of Jalisco.

To this end, our web site will evolve over time into an innovative online resource.

Here's our implementation plan:

> **Phase 1**: give you information on hard-copy books and downloadable ebooks and reports about Mexican condos that can be bought online – some reports and other resources will be free. New content will be continually added, and you can opt to be notified by email when this happens.
>
> **Phase 2**: subscription-based in-depth video training modules covering each main topic will be added over time. Each major topic will be broken into sections, with reviews and quizzes to help you assess your online learning. You can access these any time to suit your schedule, as long as your subscription is current.
>
> **Phase 3**: hosting and design services for condo web sites. A condo web site is arguably the most efficient and effective communication tool available to a condo administration. You'll be able to pick a condo site template, and have a customised web site specifically designed to suit the needs of a condo set up and running in a few days. Maintenance and content addition can be done by one or more members of your community, with no special knowledge of web site design or programming needed. All this for a small one-time setup fee, plus a modest annual hosting fee.

"AT LAST ...
THE DEFINITIVE REFERENCE"

Jalisco Condo Law In English

State law has regulated condos in Jalisco since 1995, and is binding on both the condo administration and all owners.

Would it surprise you to learn that many condos don't follow the Jalisco condo laws?

This should concern you, because it exposes your condo to potential consequences down the road that could result in *financial costs or decreased property values*.

Unfortunately, many condos:

- do not correctly collect condo fees
- do not hold proper owners meetings
- do not carry out proper votes at these meetings
- have an incorrect administrative structure

Compliance with state condo laws doesn't always happen in Mexican condos run by foreigners. **The administration of these condos is often unaware of the details of the condo legislation** – in some cases, it's unaware of the very existence of the law.

Appendix A - More Resources

If you're an owner, or if you're part of a condo administration, you need to know what the law says and what the proper procedures are.

If you're considering buying into a condo, you need the knowledge to find out if the condo is being run properly before you buy into potential trouble.

A major part of the problem is that the condo legislation is written in Spanish, and there's no high-quality translation designed for use by foreigner-run condo administrations.

This book contains the complete text of the Jalisco condo law translated into English. It's presented in a unique side-by-side format, with both Spanish and English synchronised paragraph by paragraph.

As well as a high quality translation, there are in-line comments and notes to help clarify certain passages and issues. *It also contains translations of other related legislation relevant to condo operation and administration.*

As well as the condo law, this book also contains English translations of the codes and laws regulating: co-ownership of property, the Public Registry of Property, Powers of Attorney, Sanctions, Civil Associations, and a few excerpts from sections of the law that apply to the day-to-day operation of a condo.

This is the perfect companion book to the "**Jalisco Condo Manual.**"

For more information visit **www.jaliscocondos.org**

"A MUST-BUY FOR ANY FOREIGNER LIVING IN MEXICO"

Practical Guide to Buying Property in México
legal system, property purchase, & handy advice

México uses **a civil law system** – a significantly different concept from the legal systems used in most of the US and Canada (these are based on common law).

If you're a foreigner living in México, it's important for you to have a basic understanding of the legal system.

If you're a foreigner considering buying property in México, you need to be aware of how procedures differ from what you're used to, and how to avoid potential pitfalls.

The first section of the book gives you an overview of the Mexican government and legal system in nontechnical terms – designed to be easily understood.

The second part focuses on buying property in México. It gives you a detailed explanation of the laws regulating foreign ownership of property, along with the process of buying and closing on a property.

There's also a ***BONUS Section*** with tips on how to choose a real-estate agent, and advice on practical stuff such as utilities, taxes, fees, insurance – including an entire chapter on septic systems.

YOU'LL LEARN ABOUT:

- The concept of civil law and the structure of Mexican law and government
- The court system, including typical court procedures
- The difference between abogados, notarios, and corredores
- Mexican contracts and dispute resolution
- Types of land and property ownership, including foreign ownership
- The *Calvo clause*, *Ejido land*, the *Maritime Zone*, and the *Restricted zone*
- Buying property by trust, direct deed, or corporate title
- Who's involved in a real-estate transaction, along with their roles and duties
- The process of closing and registering title (including title insurance and taxes)
- Carrying out your own due diligence

For more information visit **www.jaliscocondos.org**

Upcoming Books from JaliscoCondos.org

(Coming Soon)

How to Prepare & Track a Condo Budget - a step-by-step tutorial

> An accurate budget is vital to the year-to-year management of your condominium.
>
> A budget that covers all regular expenses, gives you enough of a contingency for unknown expenses, and sets out planned reserve contributions and expenditures is the mark of a competent condo administration.
>
> This tutorial guides you step-by-step through the preparation of a sound budget, as well as showing you how to track the actual expenses vs. the budget throughout the year.
>
> This tracking process forms the basis for the Administrator's monthly reports to the Council, and the quarterly reports to the community. As well, it gives you experience-based data for your next years' budget.

How to Carry Out Your Own Condo Reserve Study

> Condo reserve funds aren't only a legal requirement, they're also the corner-stone of proper financial management.
>
> Dart-board approaches based on a percentage of condo fees or some arbitrary number of months of expenses just don't work.
>
> Proper reserve fund management is based on the planned funding and scheduling of repairs and maintenance of the condo assets over their life. A reserve study both expects these expenses, and plans for them to happen.

The end result is proper maintenance of the common property (resulting in higher property values), along with the ability to pay for major replacements and refurbishments without the need for unpopular special assessments.

This book shows you step-by-step how to carry out and update your own condo reserve study, and come up with a reserve funding plan and maintenance schedule for your condo assets.

How To Write Effective Condo By-Laws

While the state condo legislation gives the frame-work and structure for a condominium and its management, these need to be added to with by-laws that suit the specific needs of your individual condo.

Condo by-laws often suffer from common problems such as: contradicting the condo law, or being unenforceable; being vague and open to interpretation; contradicting themselves; overlooking important issues; or being overzealous and controlling.

This book will give you in-depth information, plus effective tips based on experience. Together, these will allow you to come up with a set of reasonable, enforceable by-laws that'll significantly help your condo administration to run smoothly, as well as give you a practical set of rules for the community.

Appendix B - Language Conventions

Spanish Terms

When I first introduce a Spanish concept, term, or name, I'll show it in Spanish ***highlighted in bold italics***, followed by the English translation in parentheses.

Later uses of the term will also be ***highlighted in bold italics***, but might no longer have the English translation.

Gender Neutral Terms

To avoid clumsy constructions such as *"his/her"* I've used the plural form. For example, rather than, *"...your Administrator or **his/her** assistant..."* I've used, *"...your Administrator or **their** assistant...".*

Language and Spelling Used in this Book

This book is written in International English – rather than American English.

International English uses spellings adopted by nearly all English-speaking nations in the world **with the exception of the U.S. and its various territories**. These spellings, in many cases, differ from spellings used in the U.S.

For example:

> **labour** and **neighbour** rather than **labor** or **neighbor**,
>
> **centre** and **theatre** rather than **center** or **theater**, or
>
> **authorise** rather than **authorize**.

My reasons for adopting this language usage for my book are as follows:

1. this book is intended for an international English-speaking audience from such diverse regions as: Canada, the U.S., México, the U.K., Ireland, and Australia;

2. this book deals with issues specifically about living in México;

3. our company isn't in the U.S.; and

4. lastly, but not least, I am a Canadian.

Index

A

abogado (Mexican lawyer) *161, 187, 351, 369, 410, 414, 418, 419, 420, 421, 423, 425, 427, 469, 526, 535*

A.C. (civil association)
See *associations*

ad hoc committees
See *committees: special committees (ad hoc committees)*

administrador
See *Administrator*

Administrative Council (Board)
See *Council (Board)*

Administrator *65–68, 69–76, 77–80, 81–84*
appointment of *65–68*
  first Administrator *65*
  minutes of assembly must be registered *65*
  next Administrators *65*
  term *65*
Council (can't be on) *50, 107*
definition of 'Administrator' *49*
duties of *69–76, 77–80*
  common property (maintains) *71*
  delinquencies (reports on) *406*
  duties must be in by-laws *432*
  fees (collects) *406*
  records (maintains official) *77–80*
  reports (produces financial) *385–390*
  represents condo for lawsuits *69*
  responsibility (cannot delegate) *73*
  responsible to owners & Council *69*
lessening burden on volunteer *81–84*
  Assistant Administrator *81, 107, 433*
  Maintenance Manager or Committee *82, 129*
  sample management agreement *84*
management company (splitting work with) *82–84, 349, 494*
  sample management agreement *84*
  sample payment authorisation *84*
powers (granting to) *60, 67, 156–157, 190*
relationship with committees *126*
relationship with Council *50–51, 98–100*
removal
  forced removal
    fees must be up-to-date (if an owner) *406*
  impeachment by owners *95*
  removal by ordinary assembly *67*
  resignation *67*
responsibility (legal) *53–62*
salary *51*
  foreigners need a work permit *51, 74*
  hiring an outside administrator *75*
  paying an owner-administrator *74*
talk to before buying *18*
who should be your administrator? *73–74*

agenda
council meeting *166–169*
definition of 'agenda' *153*
terminology: 'order of the day' vs. 'agenda' *153–154*
'agenda' not used for an assembly *153*

AGM (Annual General Meeting)
See assemblies (condo owner meetings): Annual Ordinary Assembly

aguinaldo (Christmas bonus) *353, 368*

aljibe (water cistern) *370*

amparo *100, 157*
definition of 'amparo' *100*

Anniversary of the Mexican Revolution *454*

Annual Ordinary Assembly
See assemblies (condo owner meetings): Annual Ordinary Assembly

apellido paterno & materno (family name) *269*

arbitration
See also disputes
at assembly (trained abogado) *161, 187*
for collection of overdue fees *420*
labour boards *350*

architectural standards
See rules of construction (architectural standards)

Archivos expandibles (expandible archives) *326*

asociación civil (civil association)
See associations

asociaciones de colonos (homeowners associations)
See associations

assemblea (assembly)
See assemblies (condo owner meetings)

assemblies (condo owner meetings) *149–162*
See also meetings (council, committee, & misc.)
advance notice of *153*
Annual Ordinary Assembly *65, 66, 91, 93, 98, 121, 123, 134, 139, 192, 292, 308, 309, 388, 437*
authority (ultimate) *149*
call notice for *72, 116, 150–153, 154, 155, 186, 198, 289, 304*
definition of 'call notice' *150–153*
must be in Spanish *151*
must include the Order of the Day *152*
template (call notice) *153*
chairing an *160–161, 249–258*
See also rules of order: chairing a meeting or assembly
sample chairing guide *191, 246, 257*
script (using) *160, 191*
Chair (presidente de la asamblea) *160, 187, 200*
definition of 'assembly' *49*
efficient assembly (holding an) *162*
extraordinary assembly *195–206*
advance notice of *195*

dissolving the condo *197–198*
forcing an owner to sell *197*
frequency (no minimum) *195*
improvements *196–197*
minutes of *205–206*
passing resolutions at *198–200*
quorum (there is none) *198*
second call (there is none) *198*
subjects that can be discussed at *195–196*
typical meeting plan for *200–205*
'notario-friendly' assembly *159–160*
notice (lack of adequate) *156*
order of the day *95, 152, 153–154, 155, 159, 160, 161, 162, 186, 188, 191, 198, 201, 219, 242, 243, 244, 245, 249, 255, 289, 291, 292, 369, 388*
   definition of 'order of the day' *154*
   must be followed *154*
   must be included in call notice *152*
   terminology: 'order of the day' vs. 'agenda' *153*
ordinary assembly *181–194*
   advance notice of *181*
   frequency (at least once a year) *181*
   minutes of *191–193*
   passing resolutions at *186–187*
   quorum *183–184, 188, 283–284*
   second call *185*
   subjects than can be discussed at *181–182*
   typical meeting plan for *187–191*
powers (granting at) *156–157*
recording of *161*
resolutions are binding *155*

rules of order for *241–246*

   See also rules of order

sample "Owners' Guide to Assemblies" *150, 191, 240*
Secretary of *187, 200*
terminology: 'assembly' vs. 'meeting' *149–150*
types of assemblies *150*

assessments

   See fees

associations
   civil associations (A.C.) *5, 7, 12*
   condo associations *8, 14, 394*
   homeowners associations *4, 5, 13, 49, 89, 317, 409*
   condo law eliminates owner associations *6–7, 13*

B

bank account

   See finances (of condo): bank account

bidding (open) *113*

bienes comunes

   See common property

Board (of Directors)

   See Council (Board)

budget (operating) *365–384*
   approval of budget & fees *383*
      getting community support *380–383*
   definition of 'budget' *366*
   detail (how much) *384*
   examine before buying *16*
   fiscal year of condo *365–366*
   income *378*

operating & maintenance expenses   367–371
 committees   371
 improvements not included   372
 insurance   371
 'Misc.' account (don't have)   371
 misc. expenses (itemised)   371
 payroll expenses   367
 repairs & maintenance   370
 services (common property)   368
 services (professional)   368
 supplies   370
 utilities   369
 web site   371
reserves   374–377, 375–378
 are required by law   41, 376, 377, 393, 395, 397, 499
 balance carried forward   379
 Council (Board) must verify   100
 definition of 'reserves'   375
 examine before buying   17
 expenditures against   376
 investment of   376
 monthly financial report (must be included in)   70, 387
 property values (reserves protect)   17, 60, 376, 377, 384
 reserve funding must be in by-laws   432
 reserve study   377, 379, 381, 491, 492, 499
  first reserve study   478
 special assessments (help avoid)   17, 60
 transferred from developer   499
 sample budget   371
 structure of a condo budget   366
 surpluses & shortfalls   378
  cash flow analysis   379
by-laws   431–448, 449–462
 be reasonable   442
 changing of   39, 434
  community support for changes (getting)   435–436
  order of assemblies   437
  procedures must be in by-laws   432
  public registration required   436
  republish full by-laws   436
 enforcement of   442–444
  non-owner tenants   444
 examine before buying   18
 language   437–438
  must be in Spanish   438
  terms must agree with condo law   439–442
 overview   431
 penalties & sanctions   444–447
  wait until second or repeat offense   521
 restrictions (avoid unnecessary)   455–462
 rules & regulations
  architectural rules   449–452
  business activity   42, 101, 461
   limitation of business activities must be in by-laws   432
  flag rules   454
  minimum legal requirement   432
   more suggested articles   432–434
  noise   454
  paint colours   449–452
  restricting pets & kids   453
 sample notice of violation   522
 Spanish (must be in)   438
 violations discovered by administration   522

C

cal (lime)   483
castillos   482, 483
CFE (electrical utility)   496

chairing (assembly or meeting)
 See rules of order: chairing a meeting or assembly
character assassination *541–544*
civil association (A.C. or asociación civil)
 See associations
Civil Code (of the State of Jalisco) *9, 10*
 See also condo law
 'Jalisco Condo Law in English' (book) *10, 61, 554*
civil law system *3, 156, 556*
 'Practical Guide to Buying Property in México' (book) *556*
 'Understanding Mexican Law' *10*
cobranzas (collection agencies)
 See fees: collecting overdue fees
Código de Procedimientos Civiles del Estado (Code of Civil Procedures of the State) *72, 409*
Código Fiscal de la Federación (Federal Tax Code) *346*
collection agencies
 See fees: collecting overdue fees
Comisión Federal de Electricidad
 See CFE (electrical utility)
Comisión Nacional del Agua
 See CONAGUA
comité de vigilancia (Oversight Committee)
 not used in Jalisco *87*

comités
 See committees
committees *121–124, 125–128, 129–138, 139–146*
 advantages of *125*
 Chair of *142*
 common committees *129–138*
  Communications Committee *134*
  Construction Committee *131*
   Rules of Construction *98*
   sample forms *131*
  Events Committee *136*
  Financial Audit Committee *134*
  Maintenance Committee (or Manager) *82, 129*
  Nominating Committee *137*
  Rules & By-laws committee *132*
  Security Committee *133*
  Welcoming Committee *135*
 councillors shouldn't be on committees *127*
 ex officio members of *144*
 mandate of *139*
 practices for (recommended) *139–146*
  set out a clear mandate *139*
 quorum *143, 457*
 relationship with Administrator & Council *126*
 relationship with owners *125*
 reports *143, 510*
 special committees (ad hoc committees) *122–124, 137*
  creation of *141*
 standing committees *121–122, 455*
  committee rules must be in by-laws *432*
  don't call for a fixed number of members *456*
 voting *143*

common property *3, 26, 36, 71, 100*
  changes to *44*
  co-ownership of *3, 20, 23, 46*
    assembly votes in proportion to *59, 186, 198, 245, 400*
    condo rights *25, 36, 184, 281–282, 396, 399, 426*
    contribution towards restoration based on *198*
    definition of 'co-ownership' *30–31*
    dissolving condo in proportion to *549*
    fees paid in proportion to *37, 59, 383, 393, 405*
    law governing *31*
    owners rights & obligations proportional to *432*
    quorum for ordinary assembly based on *183*
  definition of 'common property' *29–30*
  exclusive use *20*
  improvements to
    approved at extraordinary assembly (required) *19, 45, 49, 100, 195, 196–197, 382*
      register the assembly minutes *206*
      voting on *202, 295*
    bids (getting) *113*
    budget (not included in) *372, 382*
      included in monthly report *388*
    Council (Board) cannot authorise *101*
    inform owners of progress *114*
    special fees *19, 195, 196, 197, 295, 382, 395, 396*
    supervision & monitoring of (required) *45, 72, 100*
      can be by committee *122–124*
    work not allowed *45*

  maintenance of *4, 44*
    administration required to carry out *38, 53, 71–72, 100, 382, 384, 405*
    fees (can't withhold for lack of) *394*
    Maintenance Manager (or Committee) *82, 126, 129–130*
    management company *82–84*
    paying for
      by fees *41, 345, 366, 367–371, 393, 396, 400*
      by special assessment *405–406*
      whether used or not *37, 396*
    property values (affects) *16, 18, 60*
    provision of access for *36*
    reserves (planned long-term maintenance) *17, 376*
    transfer (continuity after) *492–495*
  non-use of *37*
  repairs to *18, 367, 370, 374, 376*
    administration required to carry out *38, 53, 71, 100, 384*
    bids (getting) *113*
    damage from construction *452*
    paying for
      by owners & renters *403, 521*
      by special assessment *17, 395, 405*
      whether used or not *37, 396*
    provision of access for *36*
    transfer (during) *479, 480–481*
    urgent / emergency *44, 71, 163, 170, 196, 405, 433*

communications *503–506, 507–508, 509–514*
  from your owners
    complaints
      See disputes
    don't dismiss owners' concerns *505*

in writing *503–504*
verbal (avoid) *504*
rules of order (communicating to owners) *240*
Spanish (documents in) *115–117*
to your owners *114–115*
  consider a newsletter *511*
  have a web site *511*
  publish a directory *510*
  send out committee reports *510*
  send out council minutes *509*
  send out decisions & policies *509*
  send out quarterly reports *509*
  welcome pack *512*
within administration *507–508*
  include all members *507*

complaints
See disputes

CONAGUA *11, 427*

condo
See condominium

condo associations
See associations

condo law *23–32*
avoiding law (cannot even with owner agreement) *58–60*
consequences of not following *55–57*
  assemblies & by-laws may not be valid *57*
'Jalisco Condo Law in English' (book) *10, 61, 554*
just follow the law *60*
specific articles (references to)
  961 to 1000 (co-ownership) *31, 59, 549*
  1001 (definition of condo) *23*

1001 to 1038 (entire condo law) *13, 23*
1002 to 1005 (types of condos) *26*
1006 (condo regime & by-laws) *24, 38, 42, 59, 73, 101, 121, 378, 393, 402, 432, 435, 461, 525, 549*
1007 (common property) *29, 69, 478*
1008 (rights of owners) *35, 396, 455*
1009 to 1010a (responsibilities of owners) *41, 43, 59, 69, 97, 122, 131, 149, 372, 405, 449*
1011 to 1013a (Administrator) *49, 65, 75, 149, 191, 406, 465*
1012 (duties of Administrator) *51, 69, 77, 97, 122, 123, 150, 172, 323, 325, 326, 329, 339, 365, 385, 388, 393, 402, 405, 406, 422, 475*
1014 to 1018 (Administrative Council) *50, 91, 149, 191, 393, 406*
1016 (paying councillors) *51*
1017 (duties of Council) *50, 69, 97, 99, 111, 163, 164, 334, 385, 405, 509*
1019 to 1025 (assemblies) *149*
1019 (ultimate authority) *49, 149*
1020 (ordinary assembly) *41, 91, 122, 181, 311, 365, 366, 383, 385, 389*
1021 (extraordinary assembly) *195*
1022 (calling an assembly) *95, 150*
1023 (quorum & voting) *183, 188, 265, 366*
1024 (assembly Chair) *187, 304*
1025 (call notice) *153*

1026 (payment & reserves) *25, 41, 56, 59, 149, 376, 393, 395, 397, 471, 473, 499*
1026 to 1030 (fees) *393*
1028 (late interest) *401*
1029 & 1029a (owners' accounts) *69, 91, 97, 105, 402, 403, 404*
1030 (no deficit) *59, 380, 393, 395, 405*
1031 (owner disputes) *97, 522*
1032 (forced sale) *69, 149, 196, 200, 291, 409, 443*
1033 (evicting non-owners) *69, 403, 409, 444*
1034 (dissolution) *59, 149, 549*
translation (get a quality one) *61*
where is the condo law? *23*

condo meetings
<u>See</u> *assemblies (condo owner meetings)*

condominium
administration (body)
<u>See also</u> *Administrator*; <u>See also</u> *Council (Board)*
carry out duties under observance by the owners *97*
ex officio members of committees *144*
four-part structure *49–50*
relationship between Administrator & Council *50*
benefits of ownership *4*
buying tips *15–22*
classifications of *26*
compound *26*
duplex *28*
horizontal *27*
most common *29*
municipal services condo *28*
nonresidential *27*
residential *27*
simple *26*
vertical *27*
creation of *24–26*
definition of 'condominium' *3*
differences from a fraccionamiento *11–14*
duplexes *28*
municipal services condominiums *28*
public vs. private *28*
regime (legal entity) *7*
creation *24–26*
dissolution *549*
residential vs. nonresidential *27, 42*
limitation of business activities must be in by-laws *432*

condóminos (owners)
<u>See</u> *owners (of condo units)*

Condo President (doesn't exist) *105*

condo rights
<u>See</u> *common property: co-ownership of*

conflict of interest *171–172*

consejo de administración (Administrative Council)
<u>See</u> *Council (Board)*

constitution (of condo)
<u>See</u> *escritura constitutiva (founding document)*

Constitution (of México)
property ownership *398*

contingency
<u>See</u> *budget (operating): contingency*

co-ownership (of property)

See common property: co-ownership of

Council (Board) 87–90, 91–96, 97–104, 105–110, 111–118
- appointment of 91–96
  - minutes of assembly must be registered 91
  - term 91
- authority (overstepping) 101–102
- councillors (members of Council)
  - committees (shouldn't be on) 127
  - don't call for a fixed number 109, 456
  - odd number not necessary 108
  - removal of
    - *automatic* 93, 406
    - *recall* 94
    - *resignation* 92
  - salaries 51
    - *foreigners need a work permit* 51
  - term 91
- definition of 'Council' 50
- duties of 97–104
  - act for the owners 97
  - carry out duties under observance by the owners 97, 111–118
  - duties must be in by-laws 432
  - maintain common property 100
  - work with the Administrator 98
- ex officio members of committees 144
- granting of powers to 60, 67, 93, 106, 156–157, 190, 308
- impeachment of (by owners) 95
- legal responsibility of 53–62
  - carry out duties under observance of the owners 97, 111–118
- makeup of the Council 105–110
  - Administrator can't be on Council 107
  - Chair/President 105
  - Council Secretary 107
  - recommended makeup 108
  - Treasurer (not used) 106
  - Vice-President 106
- open & transparent (required) 111–118
  - bidding must be open 113
    - *sample Scope of Work* 113
  - closed meetings not permitted 112
  - owners must be invited to all meetings 112
- relationship with Administrator 50–51, 98–100
- relationship with committees 126
- terminology: 'Council' vs. 'Board' 87–90
- who should be on your Council? 102–103

council meetings

See meetings (council, committee, & misc.)

cuotas (fees)

See fees

D

deber fiduciario (fiduciary duty)

See duty of care (of administration)

directores (directors) 88

See also Council (Board): councillors (members of Council)

disputes *517–524, 525–536, 537–546*
  between owners
    Council must mediate *522, 525*
    external resolution
      lawyer-led *535*
    four-stage resolution process *525–526*
    internal resolution
      Council-led *526*
      overview of *527*
      step 1 – gather information *527–532*
      step 2 – get specific suggestions *532*
      step 3 – get an agreement *534*
      step 4 – follow-up *534*
    mediation better than court *525*
  complaints *517–524*
    about an owner *520–523*
      are they guilty? *520*
      Council must act on a complaint *520*
      does by-law or rule exist? *520*
      holding a hearing *522*
      notify the violator *521*
      parties must try to resolve themselves *520*
      rules must be applied fairly *520*
    about the administration *517–519*
      abusive or insulting *517*
      reasonable *519*
  dealing with people *537–546*
    administration's perceptions of owners *538–540*
    attitude *537*
    character assassination *541–544*
    owners' perceptions of administration *540–541*
    what are difficult people? *537–538*
    don't wash dirty linen in public *544–545*
  procedures must be in by-laws *432*

dissolution (of condo regime) *549*
  procedures must be in by-laws *432*

dues
  <u>See</u> *fees*

duty of care (of administration) *53, 54, 401*
  common failures of *54*

E

easements *36, 440, 452*
  definition of 'easement' *36*

elections (at assemblies) *303–306, 307–320*
  appointments are not elections *304*
  avoid elections if possible *307–312*
    preventing nominations from the floor *242, 312*
    vote for a list of candidates *303*
  ballots (using) *313–314*
    keeping of *316–317*
    sample ballot *152*
    validation of *315–316*
  condo law and *303*
  extraordinary assembly (at) *304*
  ordinary assembly (at) *304*
  partial voting (avoid) *314*
  policy (adoption of) *303*
  show-of-hands vote
    avoid for candidates *314*
    Chair & Secretary of assembly *290*
  who wins? *317–319*

'El Estado de Jalisco' (official publication) *96*

employees *349–362*
  accountant (may need to hire an) *352, 361*
  cost of employee benefits *360*
  expenses (employment) *352–353*
    aguinaldo (Christmas bonus) *353*
    profit sharing *353*
    seniority bonus *352*
    vacation bonus *352*
  hiring direct employees (avoid) *349*
  other issues to consider *349*
  laws (labour & social security) *350*
  payroll deductions *351–352*
    IMSS (social security) *351*
    income tax *351*
    INFONAVIT (housing fund) *352*
    SAR (retirement fund) *352*
    support payments *352*
  rules (general employment) *353–359*
    day care *358*
    discrimination *357*
    do we need to comply? *361*
    employment certificates *353*
    health & safety *358*
    maternity leave *357*
    minimum age *357*
    overtime pay *354*
    paid holidays *356*
    payment of salary *353*
    tools & materials *357*
    training *357*
    vacation time *356*
    work breaks *354*
    working days *355*
    working hours *354*
  termination & severance pay *359–360*
  types of employment *350*

escritura constitutiva (founding document) *7, 9, 24, 30, 77, 79, 192, 345, 423, 428, 431, 440, 441, 465, 471, 472, 475, 479*
  definition of 'escritura constitutiva' *24*

estatutos (statutes)
  <u>See</u> *statutes*

exclusive-use common property *20, 21*

F

Federal Labour Law *350*

Federal Tax Code *346*

fees *393–408*
  administration must be up-to-date to serve *406*
  Article 1026 is the key *393*
  collected by Administrator *406*
    receipts for *406*
  collecting overdue fees *409–428*
    collection agency (consider a) *418*
    collection policy (using) *411*
      outline of typical policy *411–414*
    don't withhold services or restrict access to property *426–427*
      restricting access to water *427*
    follow-up on promises to pay *417*
    forcing an owner to sell *72, 409*
      an expensive proposition *410*
    keep a file *416*
    make personal contact *415*

Mexican owners (dealing with) *416*
mortgagees (delinquent) *418*
partial payments (applying) *418*
publicising your debtors *424*
reports (on delinquencies) *406*
templates (collection letters) *405, 414*
title holder only is responsible *414–415, 426*
turning over to lawyer (abogado) *419–421*
   judge-led arbitration *420*
   lawsuit may not finish *423*
   lawyer-led mediation *419*
   no more threats – act *421–422*
   what you need to go ahead *422*
confirmation letter (of no fees owed) *404*
  sample confirmation letter *405*
due date for *402*
late interest charge *401–402*
legal requirement to pay *393–395*
owner's statement of account *403*
paid proportionally (fixed fees not allowed) *59, 61, 397–401, 476*
payment basis must be in by-laws *432*
purpose of *395*
  not for use of facilities *396*
reserves are required *397*
sample request for payment *395*
sample statement of account *404*
special assessments *18, 405–406*
  basis of paying *281, 409, 418*
  caused by insufficient reserves *17, 60, 376, 377*

must be charged to prevent a deficit *380, 390, 395, 405, 476*
terminology: 'fees' vs. 'dues' *396*

fiduciary duty (of administration)
See duty of care (of administration)

finances (of condo)
administered by Administrator *70*
bank account *345–348*
  commercial account *345–346*
  property management company account *346–347*
reports *385–390*
  at annual ordinary assembly *388–389*
  monthly report *385–387*
    improvements now included *388*
    sample *387*
  owner's statement of account *403*
  quarterly report *388, 509*
  year-end report
    yearly financial statement *390*
starting fiscal year with a shortfall *390*

Flag Day *454*

FM2 / FM3
See visas

fraccionamiento (fracc) *5, 6, 409, 428*
differences from a condo *11–14*

G

gerente (Manager) *439*

H

Hacienda (Secretaría de) *346, 493*

Index 575

homeowners association
See associations

I

improvements (to common property)
See common property: improvements to

IMSS 350, 351, 358, 367, 493
See also employees

income tax department
See Hacienda (Secretaría de)

income tax number
See RFC (Registro Federal de Contribuyentes)

independence celebrations (month of September) 454

INFONAVIT 352, 367
See also employees

inspector (property inspection) 15, 16, 481, 484

Instituto del Fondo Nacional de la Vivienda para los Trabajadores (Institute of the National Housing Fund for Workers)
See INFONAVIT

Instituto Mexicano del Seguro Social (Social Security Institute)
See IMSS

J

'Jalisco Condo Law in English' (book) 10, 61, 554

Jalisco condo law / legislation
See condo law

junta directiva (board of directors) 87
See also Council (Board)

L

labour law
See employees

law / legislation (condo)
See condo law

legal entity 24, 149
definition of 'legal entity' 8–9
general laws governing 9–10

legislation (governing condos)
See condo law

Ley del Escudo, la Bandera e Himno Nacionales (Law of the Coat of Arms, Flag, and National Anthem) 454

Ley del Seguro Social (Social Security Law) 350
See also employees

Ley Federal de Trabajo (Federal Labour Law) 350
See also employees

Ley Orgánica Municipal (Municipal Bodies Law) 5

libros de actas (minute books) 79, 325

M

Maintenance Manager (or Committee)

See common property: maintenance of

maintenance (of common property)

See common property: maintenance of

maintenance (of condo units)

See unit (condo): maintenance of

mediation

See also disputes

for collection of overdue fees   *419*

meetings (condo owners)

See assemblies (condo owner meetings)

meetings (council, committee, & misc.)   *163–172, 173–174, 175–178*

closed or in-camera meetings & executive sessions not allowed   *112, 165–166*

committee meetings   *173–174*
   advance notice   *173*
   no minimum frequency   *173*
   public meetings (mandatory)   *173*
   quorum   *143, 457*
   sample notice & agenda   *173*

council meetings (board meetings)   *163–172*
   advance notice   *163–164*
   agenda   *166–169*
      sample agenda   *112, 169*
   conflict of interest   *171–172*
   decisions made outside the meeting   *170*
   must be held at least monthly   *99, 164*
   no in-camera or executive sessions   *165*
   public meetings (mandatory)   *163*
   quorum   *169–170, 457*
   sample meeting notice   *112, 164*
   sample reports   *338*
   voting on motions at   *170*

information sessions   *176*

owners must be advised & invited   *112*

terminology: 'assembly' vs. 'meeting'   *149–150*

town hall meetings   *176–177*

working sessions   *175–176*

members of Council (Board)

See Council (Board): councillors (members of Council)

mes de la patria (month of Independence)   *454*

Mexican Constitution

See Constitution (of México)

mexican taxes

See Hacienda (Secretaría de)

Ministerio Público (Public Attorney's Office)   *99*

Ministry of the Treasury

See Hacienda (Secretaría de)

minutes (of assemblies & meetings)

assembly minutes   *191–193, 205, 323–328*
   approved at the assembly   *157, 323*
   contents of   *327*

distribution of *328*
format of (physical) *324–326*
must be in Spanish *324*
registering assembly minutes *57, 158, 190, 191–193, 197, 323–324, 325, 329, 331, 341, 369, 465, 468, 476*
   assembly where Administrator appointed *65*
   assembly where by-laws changed *205*
   assembly where Council elected *91*
   assembly where improvements approved *206*
   assembly where you decide to sue an owner *192, 197, 410*
   definition of 'public registration' *323*
   designation of a representative *158, 190, 205, 293, 305*
   what you need *326–327*
template (assembly minutes) *159, 160, 162, 193, 206, 323, 325*
attachments (all minutes must have) *65, 77, 78, 100, 126, 140, 144, 172, 191, 323, 326, 329, 330, 334, 335, 338, 339, 340, 435, 509*
committee meeting minutes *143, 174, 341–342*
   distribution of *341*
   format of (physical) *341*
   no registration needed *341*
   sample minutes *341*
council meeting minutes (board meetings) *172, 329–340*
   contents of *331–332*
   distribution of *340*
   format of (physical) *329–331*
   misc. practices *338–340*
   no registration needed *329*
   sample minutes *172, 338*
   typical outline *332–338*

examine minutes before buying *19*

Municipal Bodies Law (Ley Orgánica Municipal) *5*

N

Napoleonic Code *3*

National Water Commission
   See CONAGUA

notario (civil law notary) *24, 57, 58, 65, 73, 91, 158, 159, 160, 161, 187, 190, 191, 192, 193, 205, 323, 325, 326, 327, 330, 331, 369, 404, 418, 428, 454, 458, 469, 473*
   definition of 'notario' *24*

O

open and transparent administration *111–118*

open bidding process *113*

Order of the Day (orden del día)
   See also assemblies (condo owner meetings): order of the day
   definition of 'order of the day' *154*
   terminology: 'Order of the Day' vs. 'Agenda' *153–154*

owners association
   See associations

owners meetings
   See assemblies (condo owner meetings)

owners (of condo units)
   definition of 'owner' *35*

must be title holder of the unit   *35, 270, 285, 92, 426*
obligations of   *41-46*
  comply with condo law & by-laws   *41*
  hold an annual assembly (AGM)   *41*
  pay condo fees   *41*
  restricted activities   *42-43*
rights of   *35-40*
  equal & fair treatment   *38*
  owners' rights must be in by-laws   *432*
  participation in administration   *37*
  quiet enjoyment   *36*
sample FAQ for new owners   *512*

P

papelería (stationery store)   *326*

penalties & sanctions

See by-laws: penalties & sanctions

power of attorney (poder)   *99*

See also proxies

from a trust holder   *35, 286, 415*
granted at an assembly to Administrator & President   *60, 67, 69, 93, 106, 156-157, 190, 308, 309, 345*

'Practical Guide to Buying Property in México' (book)   *492, 491, 10*

President of Condo (doesn't exist)   *105*

private unit

See unit (condo)

proportional ownership (of common property)

See common property: co-ownership of

protocolise   *57, 65, 91, 158-159, 190, 191, 192, 193, 197, 205, 293, 305, 323, 324, 325, 326, 327, 329, 341, 410, 411, 436, 465, 468, 476*
definition of 'protocolise'   *159, 323*

proxies   *261-264, 265-268, 269-274, 275-278*
accept by email & fax   *272*
adopting use of   *268, 273*
assemblies (use at)
  extraordinary assembly   *265-266*
  ordinary assembly   *266-268*
    quorum   *276, 283-284*
  validating proxies   *275-276*
  vote by proxy (recording of)   *276*
changing   *272, 276*
condo law and   *261*
definition of 'proxy'   *261*
destruction of proxy forms   *277*
disadvantages of   *262*
  uninformed voting   *262-263*
  voting blocks   *262*
general vs. limited   *271-272*
  avoid general proxies   *275*
must be from title holder of unit   *270, 286*
Robert's Rules and   *263-264*
submitted to an authority   *271*
template (proxy form)   *268, 270*

Public Attorney's Office   *99*

Public Registry of Property   *65, 91, 158, 192, 193, 286, 471*

R

records (official condo records) *77–80*
  computer records vs. bound record books *78*
  kept (how long) *79*
  maintained by Administrator *77*
  minutes must have attachments *78*
  optional records *77*
  required records *77*

régimen del condominio
  See condominium: regime (legal entity)

registration (public)
  See protocolise

Registro Federal de Contribuyentes (RFC) *346*

Registro Público de la Propiedad (Public Registry of Property) *65, 91, 158, 192, 286*

reglamentos
  See by-laws

repairs (to common property)
  See common property: repairs to

reserves
  See budget (operating): reserves

reunión (meeting) *439, 440*

RFC (Registro Federal de Contribuyentes) *346*

Robert's Rules
  See rules of order: Robert's Rules

rules of construction (architectural standards) *98, 449–452*

rules of order *152, 161, 162, 172, 175, 188, 201, 209–216, 217–240, 241–246, 247–248, 250, 252, 256, 257, 262, 263, 264, 267, 291, 312, 339, 340, 431, 433, 457*
  adopting an authority *215*
    recommended changes to *241*
      excluded motions *242–244*
  applied to a condo *212–213, 215*
  assemblies (for) *241–246*
    dealing with secondary motions *245*
    discussion on motions *245*
    preventing nominations from the floor *244, 312*
    recommended changes *241*
      excluded motions *242–244*
    time limiting speakers *245*
  chairing a meeting or assembly *105, 106, 142, 160–161, 162, 187, 188, 191, 200, 201, 205, 218, 219, 220, 221, 222, 223, 224, 225, 226, 227, 228, 229, 230, 231, 232, 233, 234, 235, 236, 237, 238, 239, 240, 243, 245, 248, 249–258, 282, 283, 290, 292, 293, 294, 304, 312, 327, 333, 338, 340*
    appealing the Chair's rulings *239–240*
    Chair of the assembly *160*
    effective chairing *254–257*
    goal of the Chair *249*
    handling problem speakers *222*
    skills needed *250–254*
    things to avoid *254*
    voting rights of the Chair *223*

communicating rules to owners 240
council & committee meetings (for) 247–248
  abstaining from voting 248
deliberative assembly (defined) 209
explained 217–240
motions and resolutions 57, 58, 78, 94, 108, 140, 143, 150, 155, 160, 170, 171, 172, 182, 186, 188, 189, 190, 197, 198, 199, 201, 204, 205, 211, 212, 218, 219, 219–220, 220, 221, 222, 223, 224, 225, 226, 227, 228, 229, 230, 231, 232, 233, 235, 237, 238, 239, 242, 243, 244, 245, 246, 247, 252, 263, 266, 267, 275, 276, 282, 283, 284, 285, 289, 290, 291, 292, 293, 294, 295, 296, 297, 298, 299, 303, 304, 313, 327, 333, 338, 339, 382, 435, 436, 549
  amending a motion 222–223
  appealing rulings made by the Chair 239–240
  debating a motion (discussion) 220–221
    discussion before making a motion 220
  difference between 'motion' & 'resolution' 218
  mover can't oppose own motion 221
  overview 218–219
  passing resolutions by general consent 224, 292–294
  secondary motions 160, 224–226, 291, 327
    at an assembly 245
    incidental motions 233–239
    privileged motions 226–228
    subsidiary motions 228–233

voting on a motion
  See voting (at an assembly)
voting rights of the Chair 223
wording of motions 219–220
parliamentary procedure (defined) 210
  basics of 211–212
recommendations 240
reference
  incidental motions
    Consideration by Paragraph or Seriatim 235
    Division of the Assembly 236
    Motions Relating to Methods of Voting 236
    Motions Relating to Nominations 236
    Objection to the Consideration of a Question 235
    Parliamentary Inquiry 237
    Point of Information 237
    Point of Order 233
    Request for Any Other Privilege 238
    Request for Permission to Withdraw or Modify a Motion 237
    Request to Read Papers 238
    Suspend the Rules 234
  privileged motions
    Adjourn 226
    Call for the Orders of the Day 228
    Fix the Time to Which to Adjourn 226
    Raise a Question of Privilege 227
    Recess 227
  subsidiary motions
    Amend 231
    Commit or Refer 231
    Lay on the Table 228
    Limit or Extend Limits of Debate 230
    Postpone Indefinitely 232

Index 581

Postpone to a Certain Time 230
Previous Question or Call for the Question 229
summary of rules 240
Robert's Rules 108, 158, 214, 215, 217, 218, 222, 223, 225, 237, 240, 241, 247, 263, 264, 273, 313, 332
 adopting use of 215
 citation conventions (in this book) 218
 proxies (not allowed) 263
 recommended version of 214
 why needed? 209
 only a means to an end 217

S

salitre
 See transfer from the developer: construction problems: salitre

sanctions & penalties
 See by-laws: penalties & sanctions

SAR 352, 367
 See also employees

Secretaría de Trabajo y Previsión Social (Secretary of Labour and Social Welfare)
 See STPS

Septic systems
 See transfer from the developer: construction problems: septic systems

servidumbre (easement)
 See easements

Sistema de Ahorro para el Retiro (System of Savings for Retirement)
 See SAR

Social Security Institute (Instituto Mexicano del Seguro Social) 350
 See also employees

Social Security Law (Ley del Seguro Social) 350
 See also employees

Spanish language
 assembly call notice must be in 151
 assembly minutes must be in 324
 by-laws must be in 39, 438
 other documents provided in 115

state condo law / legislation
 See condo law

statutes 6, 7, 9, 13, 14, 440
 fraccs (for) 13, 14
 not used for condos 440
 See by-laws

STPS 357
 See also employees

T

tax department
 See Hacienda (Secretaría de)

tejas (clay roof tiles) 490

terminology issues
 'assembly' vs. 'meeting' 149–150

by-law terms must agree with condo law *439*
'Council' vs. 'Board' *87–90*
'fees' vs. 'dues' *396*
'order of the day' vs. 'agenda' *153*

tesorero (Treasurer) *439*
not used in a condo *106–107*

tinaco (roof-top water tank) *29*

transfer from the developer *465–470, 471–500*
accounting (may be a lack of) *477–478*
construction problems *480*
drainage problems *486*
gated community perimeter wall *481*
inspect buildings & structures *481*
mould *487*
salitre *482–485*
dealing with *485–486*
in building walls *483*
in perimeter wall *485*
on ceilings *484*
septic systems *491–492*
termites *488–491*
wood rot *487*
definition of 'transfer' *465–466*
developers – law vs. reality *465*
documents (important to get)
escritura constitutiva *471–473*
minimum condo records *475–478*
assembly & council minutes *475*
by-laws *479*
financial statements *476*
inventory of assets *478*
plans & drawings *474*
first owner-administration *500*
getting ready for *468–469*
goal is zero-sum transfer *492*
reserves (make sure they exist) *499*
services (common property) *492–495*
general maintenance staff *494*
pool maintenance *494*
property management company *494*
security guards *493*
transition team
definition of 'transition team' *469–470*
meetings with developer *470*
utilities must be paid up *495–499*
electricity *496*
gas *499*
misc. outside utilities *499*
telephone *495*
water *496*
when does transfer take place? *466–468*

transparency of administration *111–118*

Treasurer (not used in condo) *106–107, 439*

U

unidad privativa (private unit)
See unit (condo)

unit (condo)
changes & renovations to *43, 449*
co-ownership of common property included in title *281, 426*
definition of 'private unit' *441*
forced sale of *197, 291, 409, 420, 422, 443*
maintenance of *42*
one vote per *285, 298, 314*
sale of *404*

Index   **583**

understand what you own   *19–21*

urgent repairs (to common property)
See *common property: repairs to*

visas
  inmigrante visa (formerly FM2)   *326, 345, 423*
  no inmigrante rentista visa (formerly FM3)   *326, 345, 423*

Vista del Basurero   *56, 103, 183, 186, 290, 296, 354, 400, 496*

voting (at an assembly)   *281–300*
  absentee votes (after an extraordinary assembly)   *295–298*
    sample request   *199, 298*
  get support BEFORE your assembly   *299*
    sample request for input   *203, 299*
  ilegal voting   *287*
  one vote per unit   *285*
    registration of voters   *287–289*
      sample registration sheet   *289*
    passing a resolution   *223, 289–290*
      items having no motion or vote   *292*
      items that always need a motion   *294–295*
      motions that can be passed by general consent   *292–294*
      proportional voting must be used for resolutions (by condo rights)   *281–282*
        exceptions to proportional voting   *290–291*
      roll-call voting   *284–285*
  rights of the Chair   *223*

scrutineers   *187, 200, 282–283*
  sample scrutineer's instructions   *284*
spreadsheet for voting (using a)
  sample spreadsheet & scrutineers' instructions   *284*
title holder only can vote   *285*
  sample voting certificate   *287*

web site   *511–512*

www.ingramcontent.com/pod-product-compliance
Lightning Source LLC
Chambersburg PA
CBHW071230300426
44116CB00008B/982